Japan's giant corporations are household names and dominate our views of Japan and the Japanese economy. In fact, Japan ranks alongside Italy as having the highest proportion of small firms – and employment in them – amongst the OECD countries. These small firms have either been ignored, or they have been treated as appendages of large firms.

This book paints a balanced picture based on a unique and statistically rich survey. It looks at small firms in Japan's leading machine industries, their relations with each other as well as with large firms, and their internal management, employment, and technology dynamics.

Paradoxically, in contrast to the 'resurgence' of small firms in other industrialised countries, their number and employment share in Japan are currently in decline. This book explains the reasons why, and challenges established views of the Japanese economy, society, and political economy.

The research is focused on the Ota district of south Tokyo, and is compared with the agglomeration of small firms in Birmingham in the UK. The information is mainly drawn from interviews with factory owners and workers, policy makers, cooperative associations, and financial institutions. This book should appeal to scholars spanning different disciplines such as economics, business, industrial relations, East Asian studies, as well as the broader public.

Small firms in the Japanese economy

Small firms in the Japanese economy

D.H. WHITTAKER

CAMBRIDGE
UNIVERSITY PRESS

Published by the Press Syndicate of the University of Cambridge
The Pitt Building, Trumpington Street, Cambridge CB2 1RP
40 West 20th Street, New York, NY 10011-4211, USA
10 Stamford Road, Oakleigh, Melbourne 3166, Australia

First published 1997

Printed in Great Britain at the University Press, Cambridge

A catalogue record for this book is available from the British Library

Library of Congress cataloguing in publication data
Whittaker, D. H. (D. Hugh)
    Small firms in the Japanese economy / D. H. Whittaker.
        p.   cm.
    Includes bibliographical references and index.
    ISBN 0–521–58152–4 (hardback)
    1. Small business–Japan–Tokyo Metropolitan Area–Cross-cultural
studies. 2. Small business–England–Birmingham–Cross-cultural
studies. 3. Machinery industry–Japan–Tokyo Metropolitan Area–
Cross-cultural studies. 4. Machinery industry–England–Birmingham–
Cross-cultural studies. I. Title.
HD2346.J32T69   1997
338.6′42′0952135–dc20   96–26541
                                                                CIP

ISBN 0 521 58152 4 hardback

SE

To the small factory owners in Japan and Britain about whom this book is written, and my father, for many years a small factory owner, too.

Contents

Figures

x

Tables

Acknowledgements

It is impossible to list all the individuals who have contributed ideas and information to this book. I am extremely grateful to all the small factory owners and workers in Japan and Britain who allowed me to study them, to those in support organisations and government agencies who freely shared their knowledge, and to all the researchers who knowingly or unknowingly provided helpful insights. Most unfortunately will remain nameless, but I would especially like to thank Ronald Dore for his many valuable comments throughout the duration of this project, and Takeshi Inagami for his encouragement and insights. I also owe a special debt to Masahiro Ogawa of the Tokyo Metropolitan Management Consultant Office, and Hiromi Ito and colleagues of the Industry Promotion Section of the Ota Ward Office for their help in facilitating this research and their congenial company on many factory visits. Many thanks, too, to Tony Bradley at the Birmingham Chamber of Commerce, Alan Hughes and other researchers at the SBRC, Cambridge University, and Mari Sako at LSE in the UK; and (in alphabetical order) Masaaki Ito, whose help I particularly appreciated, Naoyuki Kameyama, Tadao Kiyonari, Tomohiro Koseki, Yasuo Kuwahara, Ichiyo Miura, Shigeo Momose, Toshihiro Nishiguchi, Koichi Sakamoto, Kuniyuki Shoya, Tetsuo Sonoda, Atsuhiko Takeuchi, Shin'ichi Ukai and Yukio Watanabe in Japan. Shinzo Hanabusa kindly provided the photograph for the cover. I might say that the subject is not just a veteran craftsman but an accomplished painter as well.

Fellowships from the Japan Foundation and the Leverhulme Trust funded significant parts of the research, and are gratefully acknowledged, as is a travel grant from Cambridge University. Thanks, too, to CUP and especially Patrick McCartan and (Anne Rix) for making publication of this book possible, and finally, Toshie, Toby and Nina for all their patience and understanding.

1   Introduction

Japan's giant firms are household names. Toyota and Nissan, Hitachi and
Toshiba, Canon and Nikon are known in all corners of the globe. An enormous literature has been produced to explain why, ranging from Japan Inc.
and industrial policy, corporate finance and long-termism, to production
technology and just-in-time, employment and industrial relations practices,
and of course culture. By contrast, very little is known about the small firms
which make up the backbone of the Japanese economy, which employ the
vast majority of workers and which are every bit as representative of
modern Japan as the giant corporations. In fact, Japan ranks alongside
Italy as having the highest proportion of small firms – and employees in
them – amongst OECD countries. It provides a distinct contrast to the UK,
especially in manufacturing, despite the latter's small firm 'resurgence'.[1]

Japan's giant firms also colour our perceptions of its small firms. What
little is known about them is in their role as subcontractors. Yet there is
much more to Japan than Toyota and Toyota-*ism*. Over 40 per cent of manufacturing SMEs (small- and medium-sized enterprises) do not subcontract at all, and some subcontractors have other income sources as well.
Even dedicated subcontractors are not simply large firm appendages. This
bias, on top of the knowledge gap, has unfortunately resulted in Japan's
small firms remaining peripheral to the new competition and small firm
resurgence debates elsewhere (except, as a particular case, within subcontracting networks).

Within Japan there has been a very lively debate about the role of small
firms, in part stimulated by the resurgence debates abroad, in part by

---

[1] Direct comparison is difficult since statistics are collected differently. Census of production
figures suggest that the proportion of British workers in manufacturing units of less than
100 employees doubled between 1975 and 1990 to over 30 per cent, but this was still only
half the Japanese figure. Conversely, twice as many people were employed in units of 1,000+
employees. The actual gap may be smaller, but is still significant. Cf. Sengenberger *et al.*
(1990); Storey (1994).

1

domestic economic circumstances. Large firms have been busy moving production abroad and restructuring. Hopes that they can rejuvenate the Japanese economy have steadily faded, but can SMEs take up the mantle in their place? One school claims they can, or will eventually, and in the process Japan will experience a 'paradigm shift' towards entrepreneurial SME activity similar to that experienced by other industrialised countries. A more pessimistic school points to rising small firm closures and declining startups, deep-rooted barriers to unleashing new entrepreneurial energy, and predicts 'hollowing out' rather than a paradigm shift. Both schools would agree that Japan is turning a new page in its economic history, and that the role of small firms is undergoing significant change.

This book explores the changing role of small firms in the Japanese economy, the controversies surrounding them, and ultimately Japan's status as a particular – or peculiar – case. With the exception of the final chapter, it focuses on small firms in the machine industries, which have been the powerhouses of the Japanese economy in recent decades. Hopefully it will go some way towards filling the knowledge gap, rectifying the large firm bias (which applies to the way small firms are viewed as well) and adding a Japanese perspective to the small firm resurgence debates of Western countries.

Another Japan

The world of small firms in Japan is a fascinating one. In the *machi koba*, or small factories packed into back alleys and narrow streets in the metropolitan centres, you will find antique machines and tools cluttering one side of a workshop, and gleaming laser cutters and machining centres on the other. The figures bent over them may sport caps and overalls from other companies. Some are spontaneous and outspoken in their views, others are more withdrawn, but they are hardly stereotypical 'company men', and their informality is a refreshing contrast to the order and predictability within the large corporation.[2]

Indeed, the rise of the large corporation and their 'company men' represents only one branch in the evolution of Japan's industrial culture. The identification of workers with their craft rather than company and the ambition of workers to start their own business, evident and documented at the beginning of the century, persisted long afterwards in small firms. As Florence once said of small firm owners: 'They prefer power over their own little works to having a small share, with possibly very little power, in a large

---

[2] It is a world with which British small firm owners can readily identify, often to their surprise, judging from the comments of returning delegations.

Table 1.1 *Small establishment contribution to the Japanese economy, 1983, 1993 (manufacturing, %)*

	1983				1993			
Est. size	Est. size	Employees	Output	Value added	Est. size	Employees	Output	Value added
4–9	58.7	14.6	5.5	7.9	55.4	12.6	4.8	6.8
10–19	19.5	11.2	6.2	7.5	19.8	10.4	5.6	6.8
20–99	18.6	29.9	22.4	23.2	20.9	30.8	22.3	23.9
100–299	2.4	16.5	17.8	17.4	2.9	18.0	19.0	19.3
300–999	0.7	13.7	22.7	19.7	0.8	14.6	22.1	20.9
1000+	0.1	14.0	25.5	24.2	0.2	13.6	26.2	22.4

Notes:
Est. size = establishment size by number of employees
N = 446,942 (1983) and 413,563 (1993)
Figures do not necessarily add up to 100 because of rounding.
Source: Chusho kigyo cho (ed.) (1992a, 1995a), statistical appendices; orig. *Kogyo tokei hyo* (Census of Manufactures).

amalgamation. . . . [T]he most important reason for their wishing to cling to their own little businesses is the feudal idea of handing it on to their family.'[3] This 'feudalism' may have disappeared in Birmingham (along with many small firms), to which he was referring, but it has persisted in Japan and is one reason for the continued high proportion of small firms, despite expectations that they would disappear as Japan modernised.

The world of small firms is not simply different and fascinating, but, and this is worth stressing, it is every bit as representative of modern Japan as that of large firms. Almost three quarters of Japanese employees work in SMEs (defined in manufacturing as having less than 300 employees or capitalised at less than ¥100 million) and only a quarter in large firms. More are employed in establishments with less than ten employees than those with over 1,000 (table 1.1, table 2.2)! Small firms are crucial to the Japanese economy, and always have been. Revenue from their exports played a crucial role in funding early industrialisation and reconstruction after World War II. They have provided employment for the majority of the labour force, easing the social transition as Japan industrialised and enabling an effective mix of capital and labour resources. They still supply a significant share of the value added in Toyota and Nissan, Hitachi and

[3] Cited in Hannah (1983, 129).

Toshiba, Canon and Nikon products. And they are critical for Japan's economic future.

Yet they have been ignored. The debates on industrialisation, on Japanese capitalism and management, about whether Japanese firms are quasi employee-controlled, under the dual control of financial institutions and employees, and so on, have largely referred to the minority of giant firms. Where they have not been ignored, they have received a 'bad press'. They threatened to delay Japan's modernisation. While large firms made rapid technological progress, small firms inhabited stagnant backwaters, engaged in atomistic competition and eked out a precarious existence with sweated labour. Their machinery was seen as primitive or pathetic, not clever improvisation in the face of limited resources. Long hours of toil were evidence of backwardness and exploitation, not efforts to build up skills and financial resources to establish a viable business.

Views of small firms in Japan have undergone pronounced change in recent years, but subtle biases persist. They still tend to get lumped into a uniform box labelled 'SME, subcontractor'. In the 1980s subcontracting relations came to be seen as economically rational, not exploitative, but if a subcontracting relationship was severed, it was attributed to the subcontractor being unable to keep up with the large customer's requirements, not because of a decision to resist new cost cutting pressures, or to take the plunge and launch its own product. They are said to have improved their position, after all, through the transfer of technology from 'parent' firms rather than through their own efforts.

Such views are reinforced by the way small firms are approached, which is often through a large firm they subcontract for. As a result, we get a picture of relations focused on the large firm, and how the subcontractor fits into this, but a hazier view of the web of relations focused on the SME subcontractor, and its development strategies. Moreover, the subcontractor is frequently a first tier, medium-sized company. Below this stratum lies a lumpen mass: 'The bottom of the supplier pyramid is made up of small sweatshops which are ready to submit to outside pressures and accept long-term risks and cutbacks to existing firm goals. Their "passive pliability" is very different from the "active versatility" for which small firms are commonly celebrated.'[4] Even within the new competition, flexible specialisation, post-Fordism . . . literature, which hails the new role of small firms in industrialised countries, Japan's leading actors have been large assembler firms and first tier suppliers their supporting cast.[5]

---

[4] Grabher (1993, 18).
[5] Even for Best, for instance, the entrepreneurial firm in Japan is primarily the large firm. He does note in passing (1990, 163) that many SMEs 'have responded to the pressures from the parent companies and are pursuing product-led strategies in ways that can ultimately increase their independence', but does not pursue the point.

My point is not to criticise subcontracting studies *per se*; some are excellent and have extended our knowledge of Japan's small firms.[6] But small firms also need to be studied in and of themselves, explicitly looking at the views and motivations of the people who own and work in them and how interfirm relations work from their perspective. We might then find less passive sweat and more active versatility. This is not an invitation to engage in small firm romanticism, but to work towards a balanced view of the Japanese economy which includes small firms, and a balanced view of small firms themselves.

Within the small firm world there is a tremendous diversity, according to size, sector, business activities, and management. This makes it difficult to develop an alternative model to those advanced for large firms. A widely cited *management typology* is that of Kiyonari, who sees four types of small business: enterprise-type businesses, enterprise-type family businesses, livelihood family businesses (in which profits and wages are not distinguished and separate accounting books are not kept), and side businesses or house-based pieceworking. He estimated that the first two types accounted for less than a third of all small businesses in the late 1960s, but the proportion progressively rose to over half during the next two decades.[7]

The rising proportion, Kiyonari suggested, was the result of twin dynamics: the Darwinian replacement of stagnating firms with more dynamic ones, which was happening at a brisk pace, and upgrading within a portion of existing firms as a result of innovative management. He and others criticised dual structuralists for their failure to recognise these dynamics. High startup rates relative to closures did not perpetuate Japan's dual structure – disguising unemployment, maintaining low wages, and hindering resource accumulation and modernisation – but led to its dissolution, was their argument, based on surveys which showed startups being founded for positive reasons, with relatively high levels of remuneration, and responsive to new market opportunities. Likewise, wage differentials between small and large firm blue-collar workers did not necessarily indicate misery and exploitation; viewed dynamically, these workers had a good chance of becoming white-collar workers or independent, where their lifetime wages might be every bit as good if not better than their large firm cousins (even if their average hourly incomes were still less).[8]

These assertions of course provoked a vigorous debate, but they rightly point to the need for a dynamic rather than a static, snapshot view of small firms. The dynamics they portray, too, are very different from those used to

---

[6] See, for instance, Smitka (1991); Sako (1992); and Nishiguchi (1994).

[7] Kiyonari (1972, 1990a, 1990b).

[8] Koike (1981), was the most vigorous exponent of this thesis, which has become less persuasive as startup rates have declined, although diminished prospects for startups may contribute to labour shortages in SMEs.

explain the success of Japan's large corporations, such as the 'three pillars' of lifetime employment, *nenko* (seniority plus merit), wages and promotion, and enterprise unions, with a fourth pillar – social norms within the enterprise – sometimes added as well.[9] They are, in essence, 'centrifugal' rather than 'centripetal'. Small firm owners – and many of their workers – have traditionally been motivated by the desire to be their own boss. They have gone to great lengths to build and maintain their little businesses or 'castles', no matter how small, and are very reluctant to abandon them. The expression *ikkoku ichijo no aruji* neatly sums up this proclivity (and is similar if not as exclusionary as the adage cited by Marshall: 'An Englishman's home is his castle').[10]

Industrial communities and districts

The drive to be 'lord of a castle' is essentially individualistic, but it is nurtured in industrial communities or districts.[11] As Marshall wrote: 'The strong individuality of the British race may find its highest development under the guidance of the spirit of constructive cooperation.' This was most fully developed, he argued, in industrial districts: 'The broadest, and in some respects most efficient forms of constructive cooperation are seen in a great industrial district where numerous branches of industry have been welded together almost automatically into an organic whole.'[12] Such industrial districts enable the proliferation of small, specialised firms which can make use of economies of scale external to them, with the result that average firm sizes are smaller in industrial districts than outside them.[13] Like Florence, Marshall would find more evidence of this in the Japanese than in the British economy today.

Marshall believed that high social standards and altruism on the part of individuals improved the environment, with beneficial consequences.[14] High social standards and altruism are similar to Dore's concept of goodwill, with which he explored interfirm relations in Japan. As he notes, neoclassicists and transaction cost analysts have considerable difficulty with this concept in its common meaning, but it was well understood 'back in

---

[9] The fourth pillar comes from OECD (1977).   [10] Marshall (1923, 583).

[11] 'Community' does not imply strong self-governing or coordinating institutions, but at least, widely shared norms and common interests.   [12] Marshall (1923, 577, 599).

[13] Florence (1948). According to Florence: 'The localisation of a great number of medium-sized or small firms, each specialising in some single process or service and depending on a general background of metal and services is an alternative to a few larger firms integrating those processes and services.' In fact, in some respects it is superior (pp. 59, 79). The best example, he suggests, is the machine industries of Birmingham. This book is curiously overlooked by industrial district researchers.

[14] Marshall (1947); Wilkinson and You (1992).

the old Marshallian days when economists took their concepts from everyday life rather than trying to take everyday life from their concepts'.[15]

Such altruism or goodwill may also reduce firm sizes, as the following everyday examples suggest. Owners may agree to support employees wishing to start out on their own on the understanding that they will not poach customers or engage in direct competition. They may channel orders to them (possibly taking a percentage in the process), with the expectation that their former employees will repay their favours (possibly with interest) by helping out with rush or overflow orders. Normally this expectation, which is seldom contractual, is met. Without such assistance, which can come from other sources besides employers, the number of startups in Japan would undoubtedly have been lower. As Sako's study suggests, it contrasts with common attitudes in Britain.[16] Second, firms are more likely to subcontract work out if they can be sure it will be done competently and on the basis of goodwill. A number of small firms in Birmingham cited problems in both respects as reasons why they do not subcontract out work. This reduces the opportunities for more small firms.[17]

Small firms in Japan are economically and socially 'embedded', to use Polanyi's popularised expression. In the case of Japan, this is commonly taken to mean embedded in subcontracting networks headed by large firms. In a neat dichotomy, Italy provides the industrial districts and Japan provides the subcontracting. Yet Japan has a large number of small firm industrial districts, some of them unmatched in scale by any other industrialised country, Italy included. These industrial districts figure prominently in this book for the following reasons.

The first is methodological: an alternative to approaching small firms through subcontracting relations is to look at them in the context of industrial districts. The result will be a more holistic and balanced view, which includes relations with other small firms as well as subcontracting. The second has just been noted. The drive to be 'lord of a castle' is nurtured in the broader context of such industrial districts, and small firms are embedded in them. They cannot be understood in isolation from this environment. Third, a voluminous literature has been generated on industrial districts in recent years, but with very little Japanese input. An exception is

---

[15] Dore (1987, 170); Dore and Whittaker (1994).

[16] Sako (1992, 215). See also chapters 7 and 10 in this book.

[17] Dore (1987, 1790); Sako (1992, esp. pp. 37–40). In transaction cost economics firm size is determined at the point in which internal transaction or governance plus production costs equals the cost of procurement in the market place. If the propensity to act opportunistically (or altruistically, if you take a different view of human disposition) differs, so will firm size. Williamson (1985, 122) concedes that 'the hazards of trading are less severe in Japan than the US because of the cultural and institutional checks on opportunism', but sheds little light on these externally imposed checks.

Sakaki, from Friedman's study, but this district is very small by Japanese standards, and there is no way of judging from his account how representative it is, or how it fits into Japan's broader industrial structure. For these reasons, perhaps, Sakaki tends to be referred to only in passing and with caution.[18]

Various types of industrial district exist within Japan. There are several hundred *sanchi*, or clusters of small firms making a particular consumer product, ranging from traditional foods, crafts, or cloth, to furniture, cutlery, and sophisticated spectacle frames.[19] Machine industry districts range from the so-called 'company castle towns' (*kigyo joka machi*), dominated by large assemblers such as Toyota and Hitachi, to medium-sized districts with comparatively self-contained, medium-sized manufacturers, and finally the vast concentrations of small factories in the metropolitan centres.

The book concentrates on the last type, which has been critical to Japan's machine industries and which is closest to the Marshallian concept (closer, perhaps, than some 'Marshallian' districts in the Third Italy in that district-wide collective, institutionalised cooperation and standard setting plays a more minor role).[20] Large firms used to be prominent in these districts, but they relocated their production factories in the hinterland, leaving behind purchasing departments and R&D facilities, as well as great numbers of small factories – *machi koba* – which began to forge a new industrial structure. Far from entering into decline, a combination of competition and cooperation, *sessa takuma* (friendly rivalry) and *nakama torihiki* (confrere trading) gave some of these districts tremendous vitality. Small product makers emerged, making use of the diverse subcontractor base, and new startups made use of external economies and niche opportunities, contributing to the extremely fine division of labour.

Although it is not my intention to defend or rebut the flexible specialisation thesis (or competing variants), Japan's industrial districts can inform such debates. A particular strength is in detailed surveys – of interfirm trading, for instance – which lend quantitative support to qualitative argument. This is often conspicuous by its absence in the wider debates. Proponents of flexible specialisation will find support for a very *liberal* interpretation of their ideas; critics will probably find support as well.[21]

---

[18] Friedman (1988).   [19] See Dore (1986), for a discussion of textile *sanchi*.

[20] Wilkinson and You (1992), discuss the difference between Marshall's concept of industrial districts and modern 'Marshallian' industrial districts.

[21] By liberal I mean shorn of evolutionary determinism, utopianism, a prescriptive orthodoxy, and a recognition that industrial districts are often part of wider production structures. In their responses to criticisms by Amin and Robbins, Piore and Sabel appear to advocate such a liberal interpretation (Pyke *et al.* (eds.) 1992).

Before leaving the subject, a further comment on independence, dependence, and interdependence is probably in order. Small subcontractors are sometimes disparagingly referred to as 'quasi firms' because of their high degree of dependence on one or two customers. Yet the independence owners gain when starting out on their own (*dokuritsu kaigyo*) is not meaningless. First, though this may be a matter of degree, they have become their own boss, able to plan and adjust their own levels of earnings, and take on more work or employees if necessary. Second, they may now write 'company president' on their name card to indicate their new status. Third, initial dependence may be the first step towards greater substantial independence, through slowly diversifying order sources, accumulating resources, and ultimately launching a product. Many flourishing companies have grown from such humble beginnings. This illustrates not only the importance of a dynamic view of small firms, but also of taking into account the motivations and perceptions of the people involved.[22]

An important dynamic in the maintenance of large numbers of small firms in Japan has been the (individualistic) desire to be 'lord of a castle', no matter how small, but this is underpinned in many cases by dependence and interdependence in an industrial community or district. The culture of these communities or districts is very different from that of large firm 'corporate communities'.

Economy in transition

The Japanese economy is in a state of transition, which is thrusting small firms into the limelight as never before. Large firms have been busy shifting production abroad and making their competitive presence felt globally, but they have begun restructuring within Japan. There is a growing belief, partly a product of the prolonged recession, that their contribution to domestic economic growth and recovery will decline. Can small firms step in and fill the void, or will they be the principal victims of the transition?

Optimists predict a new dawn. They point to small firms' growing technological and managerial capabilities in the 1980s, market changes in their favour and the fact that dynamic small firms and OTC (Over the Counter)-listed companies rebounded much more quickly than large firms after the burst of the 'bubble' in 1991. They also point to changes in government policy which provide a much more supportive environment for such

---

[22] Aoki recognises this. His 'quasi integration' refers to the dual characteristics of integration *and* autonomy (1988, 214). Cf. also Penrose and her study of small firms in the 'real world' (1959, 1–14).

firms, which have piqued established business leaders.[23] They concede that small firms which are unable to adapt to new conditions will fall by the wayside but that others will blossom in the new age, and they cite lists of examples to prove their point.

Pessimists have no shortage of material to work with. The reality facing many small firms is unprecedented tribulation. Large firms are placing fewer orders, on worse terms, and competition from abroad has become unbearable at current exchange rates. Closures have increased, while start-ups have decreased, undermining the first of Kiyonari's dynamics. In many sectors of the economy, including manufacturing, startups have dropped below closures, and, if the rising proportion of new firms started by existing companies is taken into account, the decline in 'independent' startups has been precipitous.[24]

Optimists predict that greater diversity and individuation if not individualism in Japanese society, combined with large firms restructuring and improved support structures, will lead to the sprouting of innovative new firms in tune with the times. The 'reserve army' of would-be founders stands at over a million, almost half of whom have made some preparations to become independent.[25] Pessimists, on the contrary, argue that social change has worked against small firms. It is not just a sharp rise in costs and fewer opportunities in a mature economy that has depressed startup rates, but increasing affluence which has undermined the 'hungry spirit' and raised the reserve wage needed to endure the privations of life in a small firm. In other words, 'stability-oriented social consciousness, as represented by progression through a single firm rather than founding a firm and developing it, has been one factor in stagnating startup activity'.[26]

Schools have become extremely refined as sorting mechanisms. In earlier decades people left school early for a variety of reasons, including family hardship, and went to work in small firms before finally establishing their own companies. Nowadays the academically able are likely to go on to further education, aiming as high up the finely graded hierarchy of colleges and universities as possible, from which they will tend to seek jobs in large companies, equally graded in terms of desirability. (Children of small firm owners are an exception, but where they have seen their parents struggling day and night at the expense of family life, the attractions of being their own boss and taking over the family business may not be enough to make even

---

[23] H. Okuda, president of Toyota, claimed: 'The government felt that if you drove up the yen high enough to destroy the car and electronics industries, it would be better for the economy because it would encourage the growth of new industries' (interview in *Financial Times,* 4 October 1995).

[24] Peoples' Finance Corporation (1994); Kokumin kin'yu koko (1992, 1995).

[25] Kamata (1995, 4).   [26] Kamata (1995, 4).

them deviate from this path.) Unless they are recognised innovators, small firms find it very difficult to recruit good young workers, even in a recession and with rising unemployment. The average age of workers is thus rising more rapidly than in the overall population. It is especially the case in manufacturing, which suffers from an image problem. Many small firm owners themselves are aging, and, where they have no successor, their business will eventually close.

The world of small firms is in a state of transition, as well as the Japanese economy. One facet of this transition is generational changeover. Postwar founders, many of them migrants from the countryside or children of such migrants, with limited formal education and with blue-collar backgrounds, are retiring, and successors or new founders, born and raised in cities, with tertiary education and white- or grey-collar backgrounds, are taking their place. This will probably accelerate the evolutionary trend from livelihood business towards enterprise-type business, but will it also weaken the businesses, as appeared to happen in Britain where children or grandchildren of Victorian founders felt less compelled to carry on the family business and in some cases sold it?[27] Japanese banks appear to think so, judging from the small firm M&A desks they have set up, although they do not appear to be very busy.

Japan has always had a high proportion of small firms, but this proportion has been declining, while other countries which experienced declines have seen a resurgence in recent years.[28] Is Japan an anomalous case, or can it be reconciled with the apparent general trend? Such issues will be addressed in this study.

Focus and structure of the book

The book focuses on the machine industries (metal products, machinery and equipment, transportation equipment, electrical machinery, and precision equipment), a critical sector of the economy which has been at the forefront of Japanese manufacturing for the past two decades, and which today account for about 40 per cent of its output and three quarters of its exports. Historically these industries were concentrated in a small number of regions, notably Keihin (Tokyo-Yokohama/Kanagawa), Hanshin (Osaka-Kobe/Hyogo), and Chukyo (especially Nagoya/Aichi). Particular attention will be paid to the Keihin Belt and, within it, the district in and around Tokyo's Ota Ward, about which has been written:

[27] Cf. Marshall (1923, 579).
[28] Cf. Acs and Audretsch (eds.) (1993) and Sengenberger, Loveman, and Piore (eds.) (1990). Koshiro's chapter on Japan in the latter gives equivocal support to the resurgence thesis, but is based on evidence up to the early 1980s. Storey (1994), has questioned whether in fact there is a generalised 'U'-shaped decline and rise pattern.

If a single atomic bomb were dropped on the industrial district stretching from Meguro to Kawasaki centring on Ota, what do you think would happen? The whole of Japanese industry would be wiped out in an instant.[29]

The claim is remarkable given that 80 per cent of the factories in Ota have fewer than ten employees and 95 per cent have fewer than 30. We will be looking at a concentration of factories which is important for the Japanese economy, and of considerable interest as an industrial district. Moreover, the restructuring that occurred in the 1960s and 1970s foreshadowed the restructuring that other districts have subsequently been forced into, as the giants moved production facilities further afield within Japan and eventually overseas. Thus it also provides an ideal vantage point for looking at the prospects for small machine industry firms in industrial restructuring. These prospects are not all rosy; the number of factories in Ota declined from around 9,000 in 1983 to 7,000 a decade later, and by 1995 were estimated unofficially at nearer 6,000. The fear that more quiet forces may ultimately have the same effect as an atomic bomb are the fears of the 'hollowing out' of Japanese industry.

A comparative view is given in a sketch of industrial districts in Ota City (Gunma Prefecture, not to be confused with Tokyo's Ota Ward), Ueda City (Nagano Prefecture), and from some references to Osaka. An international comparison is provided by Birmingham, which has likewise been pivotal to the machine industries in Britain. The two districts share many similarities, but have experienced divergent fates. Is this because of different characteristics of their small firms and industrial districts, or do we see in Birmingham a portent for south Tokyo's future?

In common usage, small- and medium-sized enterprises (SMEs) in Japan get lumped together, with the upper cut off point being 300 employees or ¥100 million in capital in manufacturing according to government statistics and policies. This is problematic, both for policy and for this study, since firms with 299 employees are vastly different from those with one or two. Here 'small firms' will be used in a way that reflects the structure of Ota's industry, where most firms have fewer than 20 employees and are owner-managed or family businesses. Firms with 70–80 employees may be considered middle sized. It will be clear from the context whether I am referring to 'small firms' in this restricted sense, or the common, wider SME usage. Some specialists avoid using the word 'firm' altogether when referring to the self-employed or businesses employing only family labour. Here 'firm' simply means a business registered either as a private or incorporated company for tax and legal purposes. Many statistics are collected on an

---

[29] H. Karatsu, a former research director of Osaka-based industrial giant Matsushita (hence by no means a propagandist for the district; cited in Koyo joho senta (1991, 7)).

establishment rather than on a company basis, but, as most small firms operate only one establishment, they are a reasonable approximation.[30]

Information comes from interviews with factory owners and workers, support organisations, policy makers and implementers at various levels, financial institutions, trade unions, purchasing managers in large firms, and so on, carried out between 1989 and 1995. Twenty factories and cooperative associations were studied at least twice during this time, at the height of the 'bubble' boom and the trough of recession, and a number of other factories were visited once. A second and complementary source is various large-scale, detailed surveys, which are really quite exceptional in the quantitative information they provide. These plus various reports, articles, books, and discussions with researchers form the basis of the observations in this book.

Chapter 2 gives a historical overview of small firms in Japan's economic development and the debates surrounding them. Their critical role in the Meiji period (1868–1912) is widely acknowledged, but after World War I, and with the emergence of the 'dual structure', their existence became more problematic. Large firm–smaller firm subcontracting relations emerged, which gradually became systematised, but were considered a negative feature of Japan's peculiar capitalist development. From the 1960s the pendulum began to swing in the other direction. The exploitative dual structure orthodoxy was questioned and small firm diversity recognised. A new orthodoxy has emerged and, with this, a retrospective reinterpretation of the role of small firms in Japan's economic development. This has implications for lessons which may be gained from Japan's economic development and for the debates about small firms in developing economies today.

The next chapter adds a geographical dimension to this picture. Before World War II the machine industries were concentrated in the main urban centres. Dispersion occurred during and after the war and reached further and further out into provincial Japan, but key functions are still retained in the urban centres today, along with large concentrations of small factories. A serious study of machine industry districts must take these locational characteristics into account. We shall see how Ota City and Ueda City fit into this broader picture, and their prospects as industry spreads offshore. There are implications here for the debates about how self contained industrial districts are and whether they should be studied as such.

Chapter 4 introduces the industrial district in and around Ota Ward in south Tokyo. Orders for technically advanced, prototype, and industrial machinery-related work flow into the district and, through medium-sized

---

[30] Some small firms operate multiple establishments, but then, some owners also register more than one company, including 'paper companies' at a single premises.

firms, filter downwards and outwards to a vast array of specialised and semi-specialised factories and workshops. An exemplary Marshallian industrial district, it has been dubbed a 'spatial FMS' (flexible manufacturing system). Flexibility, specialisation, and cooperation may be necessary conditions for such industrial districts, but they do not ensure their survival. Ota's industrialists fear for its future as a result of encroaching housing, high land prices, worker shortages, succession problems – not to mention pressures from large firms and, increasingly, intensified competition between districts.

These three chapters give a broad overview. The following four chapters explore interfirm and intrafirm issues in some depth, based mainly on small firms in Ota Ward. Chapter 5 looks at subcontracting, not between large assemblers and large- or medium-sized suppliers ('suppliers' being the preferred word these days) but with small firm subcontractors. Long-term relations, informality, and mutuality have a somewhat different nuance in this context. Growing technological resources of subcontractors do not mean a relational equality, as some suggested in the 1980s. This has become particularly evident in the post 'bubble' recession, in which orders have been reduced and cost-cutting pressures are intense, wreaking havoc even in hitherto 'recession-proof' industries such as dies and moulds, strongly represented in south Tokyo. Small subcontractors as a result have been trying to reduce their reliance on mass production networks and to link into 'skill concentration' networks.

Contrary to popular perceptions, relations between small firms are not singularly competitive. Complementing the discussion of subcontracting, chapter 6 looks at 'horizontal' interfirm relations, ranging from farming out work and trading among friends (*nakama mawashi, nakama torihiki*) to friendly rivalry (*sessa takuma*) and information sharing. Much of this is informal, but it also takes place in cooperative and industry associations, which number around 45,000 in Japan. Examples are given from the die and mould industry. Horizontal relations are complementary, but may also be developed as an alternative, to subcontracting. Some see strengthening horizontal links as a way forward for small firms, but others fear that the horizontal cooperative spirit is in decline.

Chapters 7 and 8 look at *intrafirm* characteristics, starting with the drive of founders to be their own boss or lord of their own castle. In many cases their castle is their home, for they live above their factory. Life and work are not clearly separated, and a life's work is not easily parted with. They may not be thrusting, high-risk, high-return takers, but there is plenty of evidence of active versatility in their craft-based entrepreneurship. Far from being the conservative force with which Florence associated it, the 'feudal' idea of handing on a going concern has been a source of innovativeness; the introduction of mechatronic equipment like CNC machines, not to mention an own product, is more closely linked to the presence of a successor than to subcontracting status. Succession, indeed, is a critical issue, the more so given the sharp decline in startups.

Stereotypes colour our image of employment in small firms in Japan. Core employees in large firms have benefited from job security through 'Japanese style employment', while employees in small firms are viewed *en masse* as a peripheral workforce, subject to exploitative conditions and layoffs. The reality is more complex. Factory owners in south Tokyo have to rely on skilled workers and adopt a variety of strategies to recruit and retain them. Some of their older craftsmen have remarkable lengths of continuous employment, but they too are reaching retirement age, and owners have had great difficulties in attracting the new generation to take their place.[31] Technology can only partially fill the resulting skills gap. Chapters 7 and 8 show how internal dynamics are important for shaping the policies and activities of small firms.

Government policy and its effects on small firms are the subject of chapter 9, with a particular focus on SME policy. Although small firms were traditionally seen as a problem which threatened to delay Japan's modernisation, the problem had to be addressed, and over the years an extensive range of policy measures was has been devised. Government financing accounts for only 8–9 per cent of all SME loans, but its significance is much greater than this. Yet government policy cannot be considered a primary reason for the large number of small firms in Japan. In the machine industries, especially, it has only supported private initiative, and, as far as small firm owners in Ota are concerned, they have had to face significant policy-derived obstacles. This chapter provides a different perspective to the markets versus 'revisionist' debates over Japan's political economy.

Chapter 10 brings south Tokyo's small firms into sharper relief through a comparative view of industry in Birmingham. The two districts share much in common, but Birmingham's once large concentration of small firms declined progressively over several decades, through closure or M&A. Reasons advanced for this decline include waning 'feudal' drive, a lack of innovative competitiveness, failure of alternative forms of interfirm cooperation, financing problems, and policy and macroeconomic instability. Various views, including those of small firm owners themselves, will be considered. In recent years an unprecedented support structure has been put into place to prevent Britain's industrial heartland from becoming a wasteland. Can de-industrialisation be reversed? Are there lessons here for south Tokyo?

---

[31] Masculine forms reflect the situation in the factories studied rather than a personal bias.

Will Ota follow the same path as Birmingham? The final chapter begins by looking at Ota's response to declining factory numbers and fears about its long-term future. Micro-firms in particular will continue to decline, but will Ota be able to maintain a 'manufacturing minimum' needed to maintain its vitality? The prospects for Ota are in some respects a portent for small firm manufacturing in Japan. The scope is then extended beyond Ota and the machine industries to prospects for a small firm resurgence in Japan. Interest here is focused on whether the current 'venture boom' will end in bust, as on previous occasions, or whether it marks the beginning of a fundamental shift away from large corporations towards entrepreneurial smaller firms. Those who foresee such a 'paradigm shift' are apt to underrate the vitality of small firms under the old paradigm, which ironically is waning with the retirement of the 'miracle' generation.

2   Small firms and Japan's small firm 'problem'

Japan's transition from a feudal, inward looking nation to a highly industrialised, global economic power in little more than a century has inspired a profusion of books and articles. The initially small but rapidly expanding large firm 'modern' sector of the economy has attracted most attention, although the vital role of the small-scale 'traditional' and 'hybrid' sectors prior to World War I is well recognised. Thereafter small firms become the problematic half of a 'dual structure', associated with lingering feudalism or late development and threatening to delay Japan's modernisation. As Japan successfully modernised, however, it was expected that they would disappear.

Japan's social transformation has been treated in similar fashion. Samuel Smiles' *Self Help*, published in Japanese in 1871, was so widely read that it was dubbed a bible for former samurai. Yet its message was steadily modified as employment problems for the aspiring educated elite mounted and deferential cultivation of human relations rather than individual achievement became the key for advancement in large firms and bureaucracies. Thus was born the 'salaryman', whose further rise after World War II was graphically documented by Vogel.[1]

Small firms did not simply survive Japan's transition, they were an integral part of it. They represent a different path of development, closer to the ideals espoused in *Self Help*, although no doubt few owners had ever read the book. They were not 'salarymen'. They persisted in spite of harsh conditions and, as Marxist scholars remind us, exploitation first from merchant capital and then industrial capital. In recent years, their contribution, and their improvisation and innovativeness in spite of limited means, is beginning to be seen in a more positive light.

---

[1] Kinmonth (1981); Vogel (1963). Kinmonth, interestingly, concludes his study with the remark: 'Until proven otherwise, it is perhaps best to conclude that Japan grew *in spite of* and not because of its elites. Those who stayed out of the competition (or who were kept out) deserve more credit than they usually receive' (p. 349).

17

The retrospective reevaluation is linked to a changing view which sees small firms as progressive in the main, adaptable and creative, indeed a barometer of economic vitality. This view in part reflects changes in the position of small firms themselves, Japan's changing position in the world economy, revised models of modernity, and new approaches to the study of small firms. It is ironic, however, that it coincides with unprecedented tribulations for many small firms and perhaps a dilution of their distinctive culture.

This chapter traces the historical development of small firms following the Meiji Restoration in 1868 and the controversies surrounding them (the two are very difficult to disentangle). It looks at production organisation and the growth of subcontracting, both before and following World War II. It then considers challenges to dual structure orthodoxy, the emergence of what may be considered a new orthodoxy and its relation to the improved position and independence of small firms.

Small firms in Meiji Japan

The Meiji Restoration in 1868 brought to power a new government committed to creating a 'rich country with a strong army' through rapid industrialisation. It sought to achieve this through importing Western technology and institutions where necessary, yet maintaining the 'traditional' Japanese spirit. The Restoration provides a convenient place to start, but its decisiveness for Japan's economic development is open to question. Some see a basic continuity in the economic upswing from the preceding decades right through the Meiji period, based on developments in small-scale industry and agriculture. Parallels have been drawn with 'proto-industrialisation' in preindustrial Europe.[2]

By the early 1880s less than 1 per cent of the working population were engaged in modern private enterprise (factories using inanimate power and foreign-inspired or purchased technology). In the following three decades employment in the modern sector increased four times as opposed to 60 per cent for traditional non-agricultural occupations, but it was from a very low base, and the modern sector accounted for less than a third of the total growth during this time. Agriculture continued to provide the bulk of employment, as well as valuable export and tax revenues. Japan's industrial and military power was growing (reflected in and spurred on by wars against China, 1894–5 and Russia, 1904–5), but at the end of the Meiji period in 1912, around three quarters of gross domestic expenditure was still accounted for by personal consumption.[3]

[2] E.g., O. Saito, cited in Francks (1992, 84).
[3] Crawcour (1988, 404–6); also Ohkawa and Rosovsky (1973, 12–18).

Crucially, the persistence of traditional consumption patterns encouraged the development of small-scale industry, which was technically superior in addressing local and individual preferences and was organised in discrete handicraft stages appropriate to small producing units and cottage industry.[4] Small-scale industry also flourished beyond the traditional personal consumption sector, however. About half of Japan's key early export – raw silk – was produced by hand reelers until the 1890s, and hand-reeled output did not drop significantly until the 1920s. Traditional handicraft goods like lacquer ware were also important early exports. In addition, traditional production methods were applied to new goods, which were then exported.

In some cases small-scale industry replaced large-scale, capital-intensive production as skills diffused and cheap alternatives to expensive machines were devised. Shell buttons were initially produced with whetstones, files, and knives in the 1870s. Innovations in these methods enabled small producers to compete with new integrated factories, notably that of a German merchant Winkler, established in 1890 with some 200 imported machine tools (most of which were soon abandoned). Average factory sizes in this industry plummeted from more than 60 workers in the 1890s to a mere seven by the end of Meiji as workers set up on their own and competed successfully. Their advantage lay partly in low-cost labour and long working hours, but skilled hands and cumulative innovations (including cheap substitutes of Winkler's abandoned machinery) raised productivity enormously.[5]

Small-scale brush producers, too, survived the challenge of integrated factories, beginning with the forerunner of Teikoku Brush, imported complete from the US by an Osaka banker in 1888. Moulding, polishing, and boring could be done more efficiently on machines, but workers becoming independent were able to take advantage of the growing number of power-lending plants which sold surplus power capacity. The technical problem of planting bristles which so frustrated small producers was allegedly solved when a craftsman slipped into Teikoku Brush, observed the planting machinery, and devised a simple wooden substitute which, with two or three extra hours of work a day, could produce a comparable output. Many of the early large brush factories had disappeared by World War I.[6]

---

[4] Cf. Reubens (1947, 583).   [5] Takeuchi (1991).

[6] Ibid. Takeuchi suggests that early factories suffered from excessive capital intensity, volatility in export markets, lack of effort in developing domestic markets, and a lack of commitment to production improvement by merchant owners. A second generation of factories which appeared in the interwar years under more committed ownership, which developed domestic markets, was more successful.

Small-scale industry also thrived in the emerging engineering sector. In some cases production was carried out by modified traditional methods. Narrow looms, for instance, were produced mostly by small-scale producers. Innovations in narrow loom manufacture, and then the quantum leap to broad-width looms which required more sophisticated metal frames, launched the famous businesses of Toyota and Suzuki. This route was exceptional, however. More commonly, traditional craftsmen, such as blacksmiths or members of other classes with an interest in machines, either worked in government factories or early factories stocked with imported technology before setting up on their own, or they undertook repair work on imported equipment and gradually moved into manufacture. Tanaka Hisashige, a mechanical device maker from Saga who came to Tokyo and established a repair shop which eventually grew into Toshiba, was archetypal.

Machine tool maker Ikegai Shotaro, one of the many craftsmen who worked for Tanaka before setting up on his own, also exemplifies this pattern of technological diffusion amongst early pioneers. After subcontracting for Tanaka and making machine parts, he received small arms orders for the Sino-Japanese War. He was able to import two new lathes for these, manufacture a small steam engine as his prime mover, and, subsequently, import a milling machine to cut gears, another technical weak point of small machine manufacturers. Ikegai then went on to develop various types of engines as well as machine tools, receiving advice from Charles Francis (who also advised Toyoda Sakichi) and procurement orders from the government.[7]

In the bicycle industry, another springboard for small manufacturers, Miyata Eisuke worked in an arsenal before repairing bicycles and manufacturing them himself. His son had worked in Tanaka's factory. Technology also diffused through small manufacturers consulting each other over technical problems. When Miyata had trouble making small bolts, he sought advice from the founder of Yoshikawa Manufacturing, a former employee of Seiko, and purchased the necessary machinery from Seiko. Yoshikawa in turn consulted Miyata over machine tools and finishing.[8]

By the 1920s, with more and more entrants, a tiered market structure had emerged in the machine industries. The top tier was dominated by imported machine tools, whose customers were government and major private manufacturers. In the second tier manufacturers like Ikegai vied with imported machine tools. Their customers overlapped with those of the top tier, but included middle-sized factories as well. In the third tier, to which

---

[7] Nakaoka (1994).   [8] Takeuchi (1991, 130–1).

most small businesses belonged, domestic machines were produced with domestic machinery. In this tier were many parts and non-integrated producers, as well as repair shops, whose limited resources were supplemented by other small-scale producers. The products were of inferior quality to the tiers above, but, critically, they were affordable to other small manufacturers, and of a technical level they could service and adapt to their own needs. Growth of small businesses in this sector, therefore, facilitated the growth of yet more small businesses. Many disappeared, but some grew into major companies.[9]

The following example shows the fluidity of this world. Aida Yokei started as an apprentice in a small press factory in 1901 at the age of 12, and became an independent machine maker at the age of 23. His business folded when a major order fell through, and, after doing various jobs to pay off his debts, he finally managed to establish a company which today is one of Japan's leading press, robot, and production line manufacturers (Aida Engineering).[10] Others were not so lucky. Increasing competition between the growing number of small workshops and factories, producers in other low-cost Asian countries, and from adaptable larger factories within Japan, resulted in a deterioration in conditions in the small-scale industry sector in the 1910s.

This deterioration was debated at the famous Social Policy Association's conference in 1917.[11] As the name suggests, the views of German social policy economists like Schmoller and Sombart were influential in Japan at this time. Fears about the displacement of small-scale by large-scale producers actually surfaced in the early 1880s, when the government's deflationary policies brought severe hardship to traditional industry. Maeda Masana, of the Ministry of Agriculture and Commerce, criticised these policies, arguing that traditional industry should be nurtured, not sacrificed. During the 1910s in Japan, however, employment in small-scale industry was *increasing*, not decreasing. Merchants were roundly criticised for their role in creating and benefiting from the harsh conditions, which overshadowed their more positive roles of coordination, technology diffusion, and marketing. The pressure they applied on small producers was seen to keep them in a vicious cycle of low wages and low capital accumulation.

World War I and the interwar years

Modern large-scale industry probably entered the 'takeoff' stage of self-sustaining development during World War I, when the interruption of

[9] Minami and Kiyokawa (1987), cited in Nakaoka (1994).
[10] Iwauchi (1989, 256–7). The founder of Mazda, too, started out as an 'apprentice' and allegedly changed jobs 20 times before opening his factory; Takeuchi (1991, 9).
[11] Shakai seisaku gakkai (ed.) (1918).

Western imports to Japan and exports to Asia provided a golden opportunity for fledgling industries to establish themselves. Manufacturing output increased by almost 75 per cent between 1914 and 1919, with substantial productivity gains through investment in capital equipment. All was not rosy for employers, however, who in addition to a growing labour movement, had to confront high levels of labour turnover, commonly 75 per cent or more per year. Their response in the following years was a mixture of confrontation, cooptation, and personnel management reforms designed to tie core workers closer to their companies, ultimately evolving into 'Japanese-style' employment.[12] Scientific management principles permeated large factories and production methods were rationalised. These reforms corresponded with the growing professionalisation of management, especially in *zaibatsu* companies, which were becoming more prominent through growth and amalgamation.

The post World War I years were difficult, not only for small-scale industry, but for factories which had grown rapidly during the war to medium size. Business failures and layoffs increased the number of small-scale operators and this in turn intensified competition and contributed to deteriorating conditions. Small firms were scorned for the shoddy quality of their goods, their lack of horsepower, and their primitive machinery. One commentator described small-scale manufacturing in this period as a 'premodern sweatshop system used for modern purposes', but he also showed another side to this. Primitive machinery made good economic sense given the availability of cheap labour and irregularity of orders. This irregularity, and cost-cutting pressures, also encouraged owners to hoard work and cut corners. Furthermore, before World War I the use of motive power was largely restricted to factories of 30 or more workers. During the war it was adopted by factories with 15–29 workers, and after the war rapidly by small factories with 5–14 workers. In 1909 a mere 14.4 per cent of the last category employed a power source, by 1920 the figure had risen to 55 per cent.[13] The rapid diffusion of electricity not only enabled small firms to persist, but it was also indicative of their receptiveness to change.

One pillar of the 'sweatshop system' (which contributed to the growing wage differentials between large and small firms) was the widespread use of young 'apprentices', aged between 13 and 16, the children of friends or relatives from the countryside. Skills these apprentices acquired were often rudimentary and had to be rounded off in other factories. At least some, however, like Aida Yokei, did acquire advanced skills, earned higher wages, and managed to start their own factories. A later example was Honda Soichiro, founder of Honda Motor Company. Training in small factories

[12] See, for instance, Gordon (1985).   [13] Komiyama (1941, 13–14, 80, 93–6).

might have been hampered by limited and inferior equipment, but then part of the craft pride of the small factory worker has traditionally been in how to compensate for mechanical deficiencies with manual skills and ingenuity.[14]

For Komiyama and others, small urban workshops or factories – *machi koba* – were by definition unstable (*fudoteki*), characterised by irregular work supply, high labour turnover, and high birth and death rates, and were for the most part premodern. On the other hand, some have seen 'real' *machi koba* as built by people with a passion for machines and technology, who worked hard and attempted to apply new methods rare even in large factories.[15] A romantic view, no doubt, but this has also been a source of pride on which *machi koba* owners draw. Most observers would concede a great variety amongst *machi koba*, even in this period.

Small factories gained in both establishment and employment share during the 1920s, as table 2.1 shows. Large factories also gained, while medium-sized factories lost ground, as mentioned above. Table 2.1 covers only establishments with five or more workers, which was considered the bottom limit for modern factory production. If workshops with less than five workers are included, the small-scale nature of much of manufacturing industry becomes even more apparent. Calculated by subtracting workers in the factory statistics from those registered similarly in the National Census, first carried out in 1920, they appear to have employed up to half the entire workforce. According to other calculations, they also produced a quarter or more of Japan's industrial output in the early 1930s.[16]

The 1930s was marked by a great upsurge in engineering output, including armament production. By mid-decade more workers were employed in the metal/machine industries than in textiles, and the share of heavy industry, engineering, and chemicals (including rayon and artificial fibres) in manufacturing output increased from 35 per cent in 1930 to almost 60 per cent in 1940. Large new concerns such as Nissan joined established *zaibatsu* conglomerates as powerhouses of economic growth. Employment in factories with more than 1,000 workers climbed from 18 per cent to 26 per cent of the total. While the size bands between 50 workers and 999 all shrunk, however, employment in factories of 5 to 49 workers actually increased from 35 to 38 per cent. Rapid growth in the machine industries provided new opportunities for workers to become independent, starting out by doing repair work or subcontracting. Tasugi called the mid 1930s the 'golden age' of machine industry SMEs. If micro-workshops are consid-

---

[14] Cf. Tasugi (1941, 209).

[15] E.g., Mori (1981), also Odaka *et al.*'s classic study of casting in Kawaguchi, where owners were more interested in technology than money (Odaka (ed.) (1956).

[16] Lockwood (1954, 203); Reubens (1947).

Table 2.1 *Factory and employment distribution by factory size, 1920, 1930*

Size (no. of workers)	All manufacturing			Machines		
	Factories	Employees	Output	Factories	Employees	Output
1920						
5–29	83.0	26.5	na	85.1	21.3	na
30–99	12.4	19.3	na	10.4	13.1	na
100–499	3.8	22.2	na	3.4	16.8	na
500+	0.8	31.9	na	1.0	48.8	na
total	100	100		100	100	
	(45,806)	(1,486,442)		(6,245)	(248,404)	
1930						
5–29	85.2	28.6	22.4	87.3	25.3	13.3
30–99	10.6	19.9	19.9	9.0	14.7	13.2
100–199	2.2	11.4	11.8	1.9	8.8	8.5
200+	2.0	40.1	45.9	1.8	51.2	65.0
total	100	100	100	100	100	100
	(62,234)	(1,683,563)	(¥5,955m.)	(5,604)	(168,338)	(¥694m.)

Note:
Machine industry figures for 1920 and 1930 are not directly comparable due to changes in inclusion. Broadly the industries covered are machines, tools, ships, vehicles and metal products. Non-direct (supervisory, technical and clerical) employees are excluded from all figures.
Sources: Noshomusho/Shokosho (ed.), *Kojo tokei* (1920, tables 1–3) (1930, pp. 1–26).

ered, Yamanaka's characterisation of Japan's 'bipolarised' industrial structure is evident.[17]

Why did small firms persist, giving Japan this characteristic industrial structure? Arisawa (later inspiration of the 'dual structure' Economic White Paper) attributed it to three factors: the diffusion of electricity, which offered small firms an affordable power source early on in Japan's industrialisation, the development of a division of labour based on specialisation, and a plentiful supply of cheap labour. Of these, he stressed the third: the small-scale industry 'problem' was in essence a labour or demographic problem. This view was criticised by Minoguchi for its apples and lemons comparison of large and small firm workers and by Komiyama for not care-

[17] Reubens (1947); Tasugi (1941, 400); Yamanaka (ed.) (1944). In some cases, such as the electric lamp industry, small firms again made strong inroads into markets previously the preserve of large firms.

fully analysing the productive division of labour.[18] It is this we shall now look at.

Production organisation and the growth of subcontracting

Small-scale production in the Meiji period was frequently organised by *tonya* factor-merchants, who provided materials and orders to cottages or workshops, collected the produce, took it on to the next stage, and marketed the final product. The system evolved as the production process became more complicated, and small producers began to act as intermediate coordinators. This enabled a more complex, layered division of labour, and reduced capital demands on the *tonya*.[19] At the same time, the *tonya* became reluctant to provide advance or relief payments, and their piece rates were often cut-throat. They were condemned as parasitic.

To some extent the *tonya* system was compatible with factory production. Under the 'new *tonya* system' which spread during World War I, the merchant or agent still provided the materials and collected the finished article, but the producer now rented a workshop, had a power source and machines, and employees of his own. It was not unusual for him to subcontract out work. (Merchants also set up their own factories, especially after attempts to exclude them from industry associations in the mid 1920s. They retained key processes in their own factories and coordinated others as *tonya*. In this way they came to dominate many of the associations.) From the viewpoint of efficiency, however, the new *tonya* system had its limitations. At a time of rapid technological change, innovation, and rationalisation, the profit orientation and price cutting behaviour of the merchants prevented capital accumulation of those coordinated by them, and they paid insufficient attention to production technology and process improvements. They proved less able to control and coordinate the increasingly complex production processes than did a new generation of technically oriented factory managers, both inside and outside their factories.[20] *Tonya* also faced concerted efforts on the part of some producers to market their own products, a famous example being Matsushita Konosuke (founder of National/Panasonic), who bought back his distribution rights for an exorbitant price.

It is difficult to know the extent to which small firms traded with each other or organised production amongst themselves directly. The stereotypical picture is of atomistic competition between small firms controlled by the *tonya*, but anecdotal evidence suggests a more complex picture, with

---

[18] Arisawa (1937); Minoguchi (1936); Komiyama (1941); Takizawa (1985, 11–12).
[19] Takeuchi (1991, 169–77).   [20] Tasugi (1941, 133–5).

confrere trading and mutual aid playing a significant role. One of the few prewar subcontracting surveys, carried out by the Ministry of Commerce and Industry in 1934, showed that almost 13 per cent of the production of machine industry factories with over 30 workers was subcontracted out, and a further 12 per cent went to purchased components. The smaller the factory the higher the proportion, and we can suppose that it was even higher for factories with fewer than 30 workers.[21]

Many large factories, by contrast, had followed a basic policy of self-sufficiency during the 1920s, although they did place overflow orders, both directly and through merchants, with medium-sized producers who made products themselves, as well as taking on subcontracting work. From the late 1920s, large firms began to use subcontracting more extensively. It is tempting to see this shift as a result of the emerging dual labour market; subcontracting would enhance employment stability and conditions in the large firms, and they could get rough work done more cheaply outside. This might have been a factor, but not the primary one. Large factories did not subcontract directly to small workshops, where cost savings would have been highest, but to the next tier down on the size ladder, where cost savings were less, but quality was more easily assured. And the subcontracting pattern was already established in smaller factories, some of which had grown into larger factories.

The crucial impetus for the switch by large firms was probably an attempt to improve capital efficiency by subcontracting out work which required underutilised plant and equipment, or rough work. The switch was accelerated by the rapid expansion of industrial output in the 1930s, and the sharp rise in military orders. Industrial leaders did not expect the boom to continue indefinitely, and did not want to be caught with enormous surplus capacity when it ended.[22] By the mid to late 1930s, they were subcontracting out significantly more work, and smaller factories were increasingly organised to do it.

A functional division of labour by size of factory had emerged which correlated with the sophistication of machinery. Medium-sized factories of around 70–80 workers, with 30–50 reasonable quality machine tools, took in work which they machined and finished in addition to making their own products. Smaller factories with around 30 workers and about ten inferior machine tools got machining but not finishing work, often from medium-sized factories. There was a further tier of small factories below this.[23] Surveys in Tokyo in 1936–7 suggest that up to 20 per cent of small machine industry factories had become dedicated to a single 'parent' factory. In the

[21] The survey covered 571 factories with 30 or more workers. Hondai (1992, 44–5); Komiyama (1941, 44–5).   [22] Cf. Hondai (1992).   [23] Tasugi (1941, 193–203).

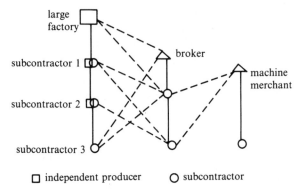

Figure 2.1 Structure of subcontracting relationships, 1930s
Source: Komiyama (1941, 54).

words of Komiyama (whose representation of the relationships is shown in figure 2.1): 'The smaller the factory size, the more pure subcontractors there are. They get by from day to day with this and that bit of sub-contracting, and the owners are practically labourers. These small work-shops have little chance to approach large factories, and get work from their primary subcontractors or equivalent brokers. . . . What is particularly noteworthy is the extremely high "mediation fee" the latter charge for doing this.'[24]

Thus there appeared to have been a shift in small-scale industry from domination by merchant/commercial capital to domination by industrial capital. Fujita argued that there was little difference between the two. Subcontracting was primarily a means by large companies of avoiding fixed capital costs and dealing with labour directly, a means of dividing and exploiting labour. Subcontractors were simply an intermediate structure between labour and capital, and their technical levels would not be raised until they were free from this structure of domination. Komiyama, on the other hand, maintained that there was a fundamental difference, and that subcontracting offered the possibility of technical advancement and ulti-mately independence. Fujita was right in the sense that the distinction between merchants and industrialists was far from clearcut and the latter did not simply replace the former, but from today's vantage point Komiyama was the more prescient.[25]

Subcontracting offered industrialists the prospect of capital efficiency as

---

[24] Komiyama (1941, 56).
[25] Komiyama (1941); Fujita (ed.) (1943); Fujita (1965). The fact that Fujita looked more closely at Osaka and Komiyama at Tokyo may have influenced their views.

well as a buffer against fluctuations, but it raised new problems of quality assurance and interfirm coordination. They bemoaned the quality of work done in smaller factories. Some made concerted efforts to change the situation. At Okuma Tekko, according to a senior director in 1937:

Since beginning our guidance in 1932, we now have over 60 subcontractors, over half of which machine parts and are dedicated to our work. They have been encouraged to specialise their equipment, selling off some and buying in more where necessary. They are given financial assistance to buy Okuma machine tools. All raw materials are supplied by Okuma, and they are loaned tools and gauges at first, or encouraged to buy on instalment, gradually building up their own stock. Unit prices are determined by our company, not by asking for estimates. Since stable working conditions are necessary, the standard rate is 2–3 times the wage cost of an Okuma worker, which will ensure that around 40 per cent goes to workers' wages. (This amounts to Okuma setting the wages of the subcontractor workers.) Since it is difficult for subcontractors to recruit craftsmen, Okuma mediates, and sends in workers where necessary. Technical guidance for core workers is carried out, and our craftsmen are sent to the factories for up to a month. The subcontractors lose management and technical independence; since they are integrated into the production system, their withdrawal would cause disruption.[26]

The government, too, became very concerned about the 'anarchic' state of subcontracting relations, and quality and coordination problems, as they threatened to compromise Japan's war effort after 1937. In provincial towns, where there were few large engineering factories, associations of smaller factories (*tosei kumiai*) were formed to raise standards and coordinate production for military orders. In the major cities, small factories were much more numerous, diverse, and difficult to organise, and large factories already had vested interests in the organisation of their subcontractors. (To the idea of small factories – including his subcontractors – organising to receive military orders directly, an executive of Tokyo Precision Instruments threatened: 'It would destroy our parent–child relationship and we would not be able to look after them in a downturn.'[27]) Here orders and materials were channelled through designated factories (*shitei kojo*), from whom smaller factories were obliged to subcontract. This consolidated the foundations for systematic subcontracting. At the same time, from the perspective of small factories, wartime controls were never complete, and technical upgrading was not simply a product of guidance from 'parent' factories.[28]

---

[26] Summarised from Komiyama (1941, 109–11). Nishiguchi (1994), describes these developments, citing the case of Toyota.   [27] Komiyama (1941, 131).

[28] Mori (1981, 253–76).

Postwar reconstruction and the growth of keiretsu

At the end of the war Japan's productive capacity lay in ruins, at just 30 per cent of the peak prewar level. Per capita GNP was half the prewar level, which was not regained until 1953. The number of small firms had dropped towards the end of the war as government controls, material shortages, and conscription took their toll. In the early postwar turmoil, however, small firms catering for daily needs mushroomed. In a repeat of the Meiji pattern, too, small labour-intensive firms began to generate valuable export revenue. Their products included textiles and a range of goods from plates and cigarette lighters, to footwear and Christmas tree decorations. The SME share of exports exceeded 50 per cent until 1963.[29]

In the machine industries, former craftsmen and small firm owners took full advantage of the 'new age' and laid the foundations of some of today's major companies – Sony and Honda are the most famous examples. Some started out amidst the rubble of war by repairing machines, reconditioning good machine tools for themselves (or buying them in the sales from military factories in the early 1950s), and in some cases importing new technology, establishing themselves in strategic areas which later expanded rapidly with Japan's recovery. Aida Engineering, mentioned earlier, Hosokawa Micron, and Makino Milling Machines are good examples.

For many small firms, however, this flowering was brief. The initial zeal of the occupation authorities for demilitarising and democratising Japan, which included dismantling the *zaibatsu* and antimonopoly measures, gave way to other priorities. Government intervention in favour of selected strategic industries resumed; the 1947 'priority production plan' in particular channelled scarce resources to the large-scale coal (energy) and iron and steel (industry staples) industries. A survey by the newly formed SME Agency in 1948 showed that over 70 per cent of SMEs were having difficulties in securing funds. Deflationary policies of 1949 put a clamp on government expenditure, drastically reduced consumer demand, and led to large firms simultaneously halting orders and delaying payment for goods received. The outbreak of the Korean War in 1950, which breathed life into Japanese industry and helped it towards its post-war 'takeoff', failed to provide relief for most small firms. Six months into the war, only one in ten SMEs had received special procurement orders, and only a third had seen order books pick up with increasing economic activity.[30]

The small firm sector nonetheless absorbed excess labour in this period – over half of all workers worked in establishments with less than 30

---

[29] Chusho kigyo kenkyujo (1987, 506).
[30] SME Agency survey, cited in Nakamura *et al.* (1981, 35–55). Cf. Yamanaka (ed.) (1948; 1950).

employees – and small firm owners competed fiercely for limited orders. Wage differentials between large and small firms widened. Workers in establishments with 30–99 employees earned 67.3 per cent of those in establishments with 500+ employees in 1950, but only 58.8 per cent in 1955.[31] The 1956 Economic White Paper declared the end of the postwar period, while that of the following year lamented the problems of Japan's dual structure. Large companies were seen to be fast approaching world standards but SMEs were seen to be languishing in a backward, pre-modern state eking out an existence on the basis of low wages. To policy makers, 'too many, too small' SMEs threatened to delay Japan's modernisation.

Once again, the dual structure was not just a dual economy. As large firms began to recover and then move towards mass production, to stabilise labour relations and reorganise their own production, they not only established new (or old) subcontracting links, but began to organise tightly knit groups of subcontractors, or *keiretsu*, which became the focus of intense debate. Most agreed on two points; the technical standards of subcontractors were very backward and subcontractors were exploited by their 'parent' companies.[32] 'Monopoly capital' was rebuilding itself on the basis of cheap wages in dependent firms, using them as buffers, delaying payments (promissory notes of six months or even more were common), and so on. Fierce competition between small firms forced them into relationships on disadvantageous terms, and even would-be independents found themselves the dubious beneficiaries of 'capital participation' by large assembler-manufacturers.

As mass production got under way in the late 1950s and early 1960s, however, large manufacturers faced new priorities. They needed specialist parts makers and process subcontractors who could produce in much greater volume than before, but to higher specifications, with improved productivity and lower costs, in order to enhance the competitiveness of their products. Rapid quantitative and qualitative development required them to offer technical, and sometimes financial, assistance. As a result, subcontractors could not merely be used as 'shock absorbers'. From the subcontractors' perspective, working for large firms with access to the latest technology and management ideas had its benefits. And with steadily increasing orders the dangers of dependence had to be weighed against the opportunities for growth which this dependence provided.

By the end of the 1960s, technical levels of *keiretsu* subcontractors had clearly risen. This presented problems for those who insisted on a causal

---

[31] Nakamura *et al.* (1981,74); Chusho kigyo kenkyujo (1987, 155).
[32] Watanabe (1985); also Watanabe (1983).

link between subcontracting exploitation and low technical levels. An initial reaction, exemplified by a case study of Hitachi, was to maintain that large firms with their *keiretsu* had indeed become globally competitive, but that *keiretsu* relations were still based on exploitation.[33] More recent work has argued that mutual commitments and investments laid the foundations for the growth of stable, long-term subcontracting relations. Buoyant economic conditions of the high growth period provided a favourable environment for their establishment, and they in turn facilitated rapid growth and diversification of output. Organisational innovations occurred within relational subcontracting, such as the ranking of suppliers and restricting the number in the first tier, and adoption of more 'objective' methods to set prices, payment, and risk. They also contributed to information sharing and joint problem solving through value analysis and value engineering techniques applied to meet target costs for final products.[34]

The common caricature of *keiretsu* pyramids, moreover, with the dominating assembler at the apex and neat tiers of subcontractors underneath, was never an accurate depiction, and probably became progressively less so. Some have used a 'mountain range' analogy, to point to common overlaps in lower tiers, but even in the mid 1960s, more than 30 larger suppliers simultaneously belonged to the suppliers' associations of arch rivals Toyota and Nissan. For less direct competitors, the number was much bigger. *Independent* suppliers played a vital role in both the automobile and electric machine industries.[35] Examples of the latter include companies like Murata Manufacturing, Mitsumi Electric, and Alps Electric.

Problem children no longer

Nakamura pointed to such firms as a 'third type' in his attack on dual structure orthodoxy. Leading medium-sized enterprises (LMEs – *chuken kigyo*) were neither large and monopolistic, nor small, backward, and exploited. He argued that LMEs were a vital part of Japan's industrial structure, at the cutting edge of new technology and organisational development, and becoming more important with the qualitative development of the economy. Nor were they simply responding to market developments and structural changes in the economy; they were often instrumental in creating these. Almost half of listed companies, he later showed, were started

---

[33] Chuo daigaku keizai kenkyujo (1976); see Watanabe (1985).
[34] See Nishiguchi (1994), also Smitka (1991), Asanuma (1989) and Miwa (1994), for English-language accounts of the automobile industry.
[35] Watanabe (1985). See Sako (1996) for the role of independents in the automobile industry.

after World War II, the majority of them independently of large companies.[36]

Changes in the labour market, others claimed, were undermining the dual structure. In 1957 there were between 0.3–0.4 job openings advertised for every job searcher. A decade later the ratio was 1:1, and it continued to rise. The first signs of a labour shortage, however, appeared as early as the late 1950s. In 1959 the pattern of higher wage rises in large companies disappeared as smaller firms pushed up their wages, particularly starting wages, in order to attract highly coveted school leavers, or young workers. The gap between large and small companies in welfare provision remained large, but wage differentials began to decrease. Small firms (and, indirectly, large firms) used to relying on cheap labour were forced to adjust or sink in this new environment.

Much interest also focused on another 'third type' – the micro-firm or 'micro-management' (with less than ten or five employees, including self-employed), which contrary to expectations had increased throughout the high-growth period (table 2.2). This third type was typically considered an intermediate structure between capital and labour, where there was little separation of ownership, management, and labour, or of business and daily living activities. 'Micro-management' existed precariously on the basis of very long working hours and its need to secure only a subsistence income. Another interpretation, however, insisted that the rise in this stratum was a healthy phenomenon, pointing to the dissolution of the dual structure rather than its perpetuation. Surveys in the late 1960s by the Peoples' Finance Corporation highlighted positive reasons for startup, innovativeness, and high levels of remuneration in a sizable number of startups. They were suited to the new economic environment, and replaced others which could no longer adapt. Kiyonari, who championed this view, and Nakamura then pointed to the rise in 'venture business' – small, growing companies started by highly educated founders to exploit new technologies and changing markets, devoting a high proportion of turnover to research and development. Nakamura in particular saw this not simply as a negation of the dual structure thesis, but evidence of a newly emerging industrial structure. As Japan became a post industrial, 'knowledge-intensive' society, its markets would fragment, the era of mass production and marketing would end, and, with it, the dominance of large firms in favour of fleet-footed LMEs and venture businesses.[37]

---

[36] Nakamura (1962, 1990, ii). Eight hundred and one of the (non-financial or insurance) 1,721 companies listed in 1989 were started after World War II, 522 of them as SMEs. I have borrowed the translation 'LME' from Evans (1995).

[37] Nakamura (1970); Kiyonari *et al.* (1971). There are clear similarities between this view and the recent 'post Fordist' vogue.

Table 2.2 *Employment structure by company size, 1960–1994 (manufacturing)*

	1960	1970	1980	1990	1994
Self-employed	9.9%	10.8%	11.8%	9.4%	7.6
Family employees	6.7	6.2	5.2	3.8	2.9
Employees 1–4[a]	} 24.7	} 22.1	3.4	3.2	3.3
5–29			20.5	19.9	19.3
30–99	14.9	14.7	16.2	16.9	17.0
100–499	13.8	16.3	16.2	18.3	18.9
500+[b]	26.2	30.1	26.9	28.2	30.9
Total[c]	100	100	100	100	100
	(9,510,000)	(13,770,000)	(13,670,000)	(15,050,000)	(14,960,000)

Notes:
[a] 1960 and 1970 size categories are for 1–29 employees.
[b] includes public sector employees.
[c] Total=self-employed+family employees+employees. Figures do not necessarily add up to 100 because of rounding and inconsistencies in the original data.
Source: Somucho (ed.) (respective years), *Rodoryoku chosa* (Labour Force Survey).

Dual structure writers were quick to point out the limited evidence for such claims and question some of their assertions. Was not the rise in micro-businesses attributable to small firms, unable to pay rising wages, shrinking to their core workforce, on the one hand, and subcontracting out to other self-employed or family businesses started by older workers facing wage ceilings in employment, on the other? Was not the self-exploitation that enabled them to survive much more representative than creativity and high productivity? Where was the evidence of a narrowing productivity gap with large firms anyway, and were not wage differentials starting to increase again?[38]

Moreover, SMEs faced serious challenges in the late 1960s and 1970s. Tariff reductions in the wake of the Kennedy Round hit small firms, as did increasing competition from NIEs in the US market, leading to the declining share of exports relative to large firms noted earlier. The 'Nixon shocks' and currency realignments of the early 1970s (the yen rose from ¥360 = $1, the rate fixed in 1949, to ¥308 = $1, and when floated in 1973, to ¥280 = $1) sparked rumours of impending ruin in provincial SME consumer good

[38] E.g., Takizawa (1971).

industries (*jiba sangyo,* localised industry), just as they were expected to play a new role in regional development.[39] Government expenditure aimed at heading off recession added to inflationary pressures, on top of which came the first 'oil shock' of 1973. There followed a period of 'crazy prices' and industrial turmoil. In 1974 as the economy recorded its first negative growth in the postwar period, bankruptcies hit a new high (11,681 companies with debts of more than ¥10 million, 99 per cent of which were SMEs. The following year the figure was still higher, at 12,606).[40]

The worst apocalyptic fears, however, failed to materialise. In the second half of the decade SMEs not only increased their share of employment, but if anything narrowed the productivity gap with large firms, again demonstrating a positive contribution to the economy during a difficult period. The 1970s, too, marked the decisive emergence of the machine industries as the main powerhouse of the Japanese economy, and powerful competitors on the global stage. Subcontractors, which were particularly numerous in these industries, managed to simultaneously reduce their prices and improve productivity through frantic rationalisation, including the purchase of CNC machine tools. Working to finer tolerances and reducing defect rates, many became self-certified suppliers, meaning their 'parent' assemblers did not inspect their work. Delivery times were drastically reduced. Larger suppliers became responsible for subassembly or assembly work, and design work as well, culminating in 'black box' design, in which the assembler supplied the overall specifications and performance criteria for new products or components, and the supplier did everything else.[41]

A growing proportion of subcontractors in the 1980s rated their technological capabilities as equal or superior to their 'parent' companies in their specific area of expertise (over half according to a survey in 1982). The latter had clearly become more reliant on their 'children' over time, and there was a tendency to avoid terms like 'parent' and 'child' and the hierarchical connotations of *shitauke* (subcontracting) in favour of more neutral terms like 'maker' and 'supplier' and 'transactional relation', depicting a more equal, mutual relationship. Not only did larger 'suppliers' develop their own technology, but the number of joint (with the 'maker') or sole patent applications increased as well. Formerly it was more likely for these to be taken out in the 'parent's' name.[42]

Further proof of the improved position of subcontractors was seen in the diversification of order sources in the second half of the 1980s. Between

[39] To give some indication of the importance of this sector, in 1980 *jiba sangyo* accounted for almost a half of manufacturing establishments, a third of employment and a fifth of output; Chusho kigyo kenkyujo (1987, 431).
[40] Nakamura *et al.* (1981, 255–7).   [41] Nishiguchi (1994).
[42] Shoko chukin (1983); this happened even in small factories in Ota Ward – cf. chapter 5.

1987 and 1990 the proportion of subcontractors dependent on a single company for over 90 per cent of their orders allegedly plunged from 34.5 per cent to 15.8 per cent, while those whose six biggest customers accounted for less than 70 per cent of orders rose from 2.4 per cent to 9.4 per cent. Obviously the booming economy was a factor in this, but a growing number were also using their greater technological and managerial strengths to launch their own products. More than a third of subcontractors surveyed in 1989 claimed some type of design facility; a quarter said they carried out R&D. In 1990 a quarter claimed to have their own product; for those whose six biggest customers accounted for less than 70 per cent of orders, the figure was one half.[43]

Finally, the steadily rising trend in the proportion of SME sub-contractors was reversed: 55.9 per cent of manufacturing SMEs did some form of subcontracting in 1987, down from 65.5 per cent in 1981 (80.1 in electrical machinery, down from 85.3 per cent; 79.9 per cent in transportation equipment, down from 87.7 per cent). This was partly the result of *datsu shitauke* ('escaping' from subcontracting), partly the demise of uncompetitive smaller subcontractors.[44] By linking up in 'networks' (a buzzword of the 1980s) it was thought that small firms could overcome many of their size handicaps, combining technological, financial, marketing, and management resources to exploit opportunities in the rapidly changing economic environment.

The changing view of SMEs can be vividly traced in government publications of the past two decades. In its 1972 report the SME Policy Deliberation Council recognised the limitations of past modernisation policies which indiscriminately encouraged capital accumulation and scale production. Diversity amongst small firms was belatedly recognised. Eight years later, the Council's 1980s 'Vision' (entitled 'Rediscovering SMEs') argued that the majority of SMEs were not premodern and destined to decline, but were in fact modern, rational, and vital. The 1990s 'Vision' went further. Subtitled 'seedbeds of creativity', it stressed the positive role of SMEs in generating economic vitality, competition, individual and community wellbeing, and even in fostering grass-root internationalisation. Policy swung to support this role in the 1990s, and 'venture business', champion of the new age.

Swinging pendulum

It would only be a slight exaggeration to say that a new orthodoxy emerged in the 1980s which saw small firms in a mainly positive light. Even within

---

[43] Chusho kigyo cho (ed.) (1990a, 160; 1992b, 62–5).
[44] Chusho kigyo cho (ed.) (1993a, 253; 1990a, 157–8).

the traditional approach, the influence of Marxism declined. These shifts partially reflect the changing circumstances of small firms, in terms both of their accumulated managerial and technological resources and of the economic environment in which firms today operate. Some would say that there was a lag between these changes and their belated recognition owing to the lingering influence of the old orthodoxy. Others would argue that the image of SMEs has changed much more than their objective circumstances; one subgroup that the dual structure still exists or, on the contrary, that it never existed.[45]

Retrospective reappraisals are interpreting the lot of small firms and the dual structure in a more favourable light. Hwang, for instance, looks beyond cheap wages to the efforts of *machi koba* owners to improve their competitiveness in Osaka between 1900 and World War I. He also stresses the positive roles of *tonya*.[46] Hondai argues that the dual structure allowed for the simultaneous growth of both large and small firms, which optimised capital and labour resources, and enabled small firms to raise their technical levels through specialisation and economies of scale, as well as through technical assistance from 'parent' firms. He contrasts this with the situation in many developing countries where much of the production is carried out in capital-intensive factories with little linkage to labour-intensive small firms.[47]

Perhaps the last step in the process will be a reappraisal of the contribution of small firms to Japan's industrial culture. Instead of being referred to in derogatory terms, perhaps the efforts of so many to raise their own little flag (*hito hata o ageru*), to be lord of their own castle (*ikkoku ichijo no aruji*), and to accumulate skills to do this, will be seen as an important alternative current in Japan's modern industrial history to the 'salaryman' in the major corporation. This, according to Mori, is precisely why Japanese industry has prospered; it is not remarkable that companies like Matsushita, Sony, and Honda grew from such tiny factories, but that they retained much of their small firm vitality. Others have been trying to rediscover it through flattening their hierarchies, spinning off subsidiaries, and nurturing 'intrapreneurship' to ward off the debilitating 'large firm malaise'.[48]

There is a danger, of course, of the pendulum swinging too far, that the new orthodoxy will be just as partial as the old one. It is prone to overgeneralisation from success stories, and economic rationality is stressed (or assumed) at the expense of historical observation. Mori himself is pessimistic about the prospects of small firms or *machi koba* in Japan, claiming that *their* culture is being lost. It is they which are being forced to behave

[45] Takada (1989), is an example of the former, Miwa (1990), an example of the latter.
[46] Hwang (1993).   [47] Hondai (1992).   [48] Mori (1991a).

like large firms. Their tremendous capital investments of the late 1980s were cause for alarm, not celebration. The subsequent recession demonstrated his point; many owners were unable to service their loans and became insolvent.[49] Japan's old small firm 'problem' (too many tiny, 'backward' small firms) is gone. In its place a new small firm problem is emerging – how to incubate and nurture small firms and revive a culture supportive of them.

[49] Mori (1991b).

3 Industrial districts

The 'rediscovery' of industrial districts has aroused considerable interest amongst Western scholars, but little is known about such districts in Japan, and even less about Japanese studies of them. By default, people look to Italy for models of industrial districts, and to Japan for subcontracting networks. Sakaki is an exception, but is only one type of district, and a relatively small one at that.[1] Yet there are hundreds of small firm agglomerations called *sanchi* (literally industrial districts), which produce traditional or semi-traditional goods ranging from cloth to Buddhist altars and gloves. Some, on the other hand, produce high-tech. goods using high tech. methods, like Sabae, famous for its spectacle frames. *Sanchi* tend to be located outside the main urban centres, but large cities and their suburbs can have their own localised industry (*jiba sangyo*) as well.

Within the machine industries, several types of industrial district can be found as well. Some are dominated by large assemblers such as Toyota and Hitachi. They have a large number of small firms, but the predominant mode of transacting is vertical. There are also districts in which the key players are medium-sized manufacturers of own brand or OEM products, which subcontract some of their work locally, but do more in house because the local supplier base is limited both in scope and sophistication. A third type is the vast concentrations of very small firms in the metropolitan centres of Tokyo, Osaka, and to some extent Nagoya. The large firm presence in these centres has become indirect as a result of relocations, but the small workshops have persisted, encouraged by specialisation and external economies. These are arguably Japan's grand Marshallian industrial districts. All three types have been vital for Japan's machine industries.[2]

Machine industry districts are not islands unto themselves, but are nodes in a broader geographical configuration of industry which encompasses

---

[1] Friedman (1988). It is unclear from this account, furthermore, how Sakaki fits into Japan's broader industrial structure.

[2] Attempts have been made to create industrial districts, too, the most famous being the 'technopolis' projects.

most of Japan, and in recent years has spilled out into Asia. Core-periphery models of this configuration are only partially appropriate, but they rightly point to the key role the metropolitan districts acquired in the process of industrialisation.

This chapter looks at the geographical or locational characteristics of Japan's industrialisation, especially in the machine industries. It then provides case studies, first of Ota City and Kiryu (in Gunma), and second of Ueda City and Sakaki (in Nagano), showing how these fit into the broader configuration of the machine industries as well as their industrial district characteristics. (The district of Ota Ward/south Tokyo is taken up in chapter 4.) Finally, it briefly considers the process of internationalisation, the development of a broader configuration in east Asia, and the serious impact this is having on districts within Japan.

Locational aspects of industrialisation

Much of the industrial growth of the early Meiji period occurred in provincial Japan, in textiles, traditional, and hybrid industry. Kyoto led the industrial output tables, followed by Gunma, then Osaka, Aichi, Yamaguchi, Tochigi, Nagano, and Niigata. Tokyo was ninth, with only about a quarter of the industrial output of Kyoto.[3] During the Meiji period, some centres of textiles and light industrial production rose to prominence while others declined. Osaka's rise was conspicuous; by 1894 it boasted 42 per cent of the country's spinning needles, and was dubbed the 'Manchester of the East'. By the end of the century, Aichi (Nagoya) had become the major growth centre of textiles and light industry, second only to Osaka in the number of factories.

As for heavy industry, the Meiji government inherited a number of arsenals and shipyards from the Tokugawa shogunate and individual domains, and launched a number of model enterprises, most of which it later sold off, such as its shipyards in Nagasaki and Hyogo to the Mitsubishi and Kawasaki *zaibatsu* respectively. Around these, and close to major ports and population centres, four core heavy industrial regions were established by the end of the Meiji period: Keihin (Tokyo-Yokohama/Kanagawa), Hanshin (Osaka-Kobe/Hyogo), Chukyo (especially Nagoya/Aichi), and Kita Kyushu (Fukuoka, centring around the giant Yahata steel mill, but incorporating Nagasaki, a major shipbuilding centre). Hanshin by far outstripped Keihin in industrial output, but the picture is different if shipbuilding and textiles is excluded. Machine production in 1909 accounted for only 5 per cent of total industrial output, but almost half of this, including 90 per cent of electric machines, was produced in Tokyo alone (table 3.1).

---

[3] Murata (ed.) (1980, 51); Tsujimoto *et al.* (eds.) (1989, 8).

Table 3.1 *Geographical distribution of machine production, 1909 (¥1,000)*

	Tokyo	Kanagawa	Osaka	Hyogo	Kyoto	Aichi	Nagasaki	Fukuoka	Other	Total
Machines										
generators and accessories	1,393	15	730	148	23	185	157	190	Saga 123 Niigata 211	3,461
electric machines	1,853	6	245	–	32	–	–	–	–	2,135
metal working machines	63	10	18	–	8	–	–	–	–	100
woodworking machines	1	4	1	5	2	18	–	–	Shizuoka 4	35
weaving, dyeing machines	84	12	483	–	12	220	–	–	Mie 47 Gunma 23	1,050
agricultural machines	5	–	–	–	–	–	–	–	Niigata 1	6
mining, refining equipment	178	–	6	7	19	–	–	330	Niigata 461	1,057
other	3,510	288	522	1,813	14	230	15	218	Niigata 146	7,273
subtotal	7,086	334	2,004	1,972	109	652	173	738	Niigata 830 Saga 242	15,147
Shipbuilding	94	1,001	1,885	8,498	3	1	4,657	–	Hokkaido 273 Mie 196	16,787
Vehicles										
locomotives, rolling stock	415	–	450	–	–	220	–	1		1,117
(horse-drawn) carts, carriages	19	–	–	–	–	–	–	–		19
(person-drawn) rikusha	252	–	45	–	–	–	–	–		297
luggage, freight carts	25	–	34	22	8	8	–	8	Okayama 5	127
other	173	–	15	4	–	22	–	2		254
subtotal	883	–	545	25	8	250	–	11		1,813

Equipment, Instruments

scientific	57	—	—	—	166	—	—	—	243
medical	55	—	—	—	2	—	—	—	57
watches, clocks	600	—	46	—	—	753	—	—	1,398
photographic	7	—	—	—	—	—	—	—	9
electric machine appendages	616	25	196	—	3	—	—	—	840
other	1,440	21	1,155	239	102	322	6	61	4,315
subtotal	2,775	46	1,397	239	273	1,075	6	61	7,145
TOTAL	10,838	1,381	5,829	10,734	393	1,978	4,835	810	39,893

Note:
Figures do not always add up due to rounding and non-inclusion of small-scale production areas.
Source: Takeuchi, 1983, 56 (original source: *Kojo tokeihyo*, 1911).

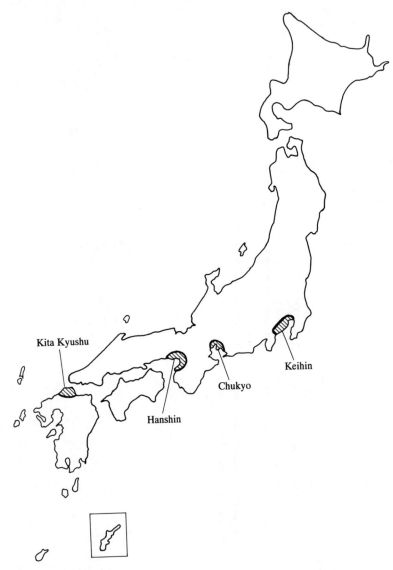

Figure 3.1 Four main industrial regions in pre-war Japan

The Keihin Industrial Belt resulted from the northwards thrust of heavy industry from the south (Kanagawa), and the south-westward thrust of industry from Tokyo. The former included the Yokosuka naval shipyards, and shipbuilding, oil refining, and machine repairs which developed rapidly around the Yokohama port in the 1890s. Industry spread into Kawasaki, where swampy land around the mouth of the Rokuro (Tama) River was reclaimed and industry was encouraged to move in. Key electrical machinery factories, including Yokohama Electric Cable (later Fuji Electric) and Tokyo Electric's Kawasaki factory, were established around the turn of the century, and NKK's steel plant was built there in 1911.

On the Tokyo side, industrial production began from a low base, mainly traditional artisan manufacture in the east of the city. Early factories were established in the east, too, but new engineering factories were subsequently established further west, in Kyobashi and Shiba, where the government's Akabane factory, which produced 46 types of machines, was located. This and a telegraphic equipment repair and production factory played a vital role in technology diffusion in the machine industries. Tanaka Hisashige built his repair shop in Shiba, which eventually became Toshiba, and other key factories such as Miyoshi Electric, Meidensha, the forerunner of Oki Electric, as well as machine tool maker Ikegai, were built nearby. By the end of the Meiji period several would-be car makers had set up operations, and shortly afterwards Kaishinsha began producing the Dat, forerunner of Datsun. This factory belt expanded southwards, eventually meeting up with the belt moving north from Kanagawa.[4]

In the boom years of 1914 and 1919, 47 per cent of new factories and 58 per cent of factory employment growth took place in the four core regions, especially Osaka and Tokyo.[5] If units with less than five workers were included, the figures would probably be higher still. Large factories played a critical role in technology diffusion, but the rapid increase in small factories and workshops was due to other factors. The major cities were by now absorbing the bulk of the population increase; those coming from rural farms and towns typically worked for several years to acquire some capital and skills before setting out on their own. The 'fission' process was facilitated by electricity, the presence of merchants, and the growing concentration of other small firms. A tiered structure emerged in the machine industries, with those in the lower tiers trading mainly amongst themselves, with or without *tonya* coordination.

With the rapid growth of the engineering and chemical industries during the 1930s, large-scale production became more pronounced, but in industries such as precision equipment, electrical machinery, and machine tools,

[4] Takeuchi (1983 and 1988).   [5] Takeuchi (1988, 29–31).

workshops also flourished. Yamanaka and colleagues, who studied small-scale industry from its locational characteristics, painted a somewhat different view of their persistence than scholars like Arisawa, whose views were mentioned in chapter 2. In explaining urban small-scale industry, they emphasised labour availability and market proximity, but also the benefits of external economies, which helped such small firms start out from doing, for instance, machine repairs.[6]

Like Yamanaka et al., Komiyama contrasted urban small-scale industry with that of provincial Japan, pointing to constraints on growth in the latter. He quoted a military officer who listed four problems in raising the level of small factories in the provinces: difficulties in getting materials, fierce competition, exploitation by brokers, and insistence on carrying out the whole process (or lack of specialisation, the absence of external economies). He held that their general technical level was lower, machines less advanced, with very few milling machines in particular compared with the large cities.[7] This dichotomy may have been somewhat overstated, since smaller districts did emerge outside the core regions organised around textile, agriculture, and mining equipment production. Technology transfer through the relocation of urban factories towards the end of World War II also stimulated industry in such areas, laying the basis for postwar growth, but they did not have the enormous concentrations and the fine division of labour that grew up in the core industrial regions.

Concentration and dispersal – core and periphery?

Wartime factory relocations, designed to reduce vulnerability to air raid damage and large-scale air raid devastation itself, led to a significant decline in core region employment by the close of the war. In the following years, many new industrial cities sprang up, with heavy industry spreading along the Pacific coast, and machine and light engineering factories spreading inland, even into remote farming communities. After the early postwar hiatus, however, the pull of the core regions again proved irrepressible.

Kita Kyushu never managed to regain its former status. Chukyo held its own with new heavy industry factories, and automobiles (Toyota) took over from textiles as the leading industry. After the postwar flourish of lighter industry, Hanshin slowly began to lose ground to Keihin, although it still possesses a vast number of factories. Between 1955 and 1960, almost one third of the total rise in Japan's gainfully employed occurred in Tokyo

---

[6] Yamanaka (ed.) (1944); Mitsui (1985). Yamanaka et al. attempted for Japan what Florence did in the UK shortly afterwards, namely measuring locational effects on small firm size, but they were faced with data constraints.   [7] Komiyama (1941, 114–20).

alone.[8] Its position further strengthened, first with the growth of machine industry output (accounting for 26.5 per cent of total industrial output in 1965, 29.8 per cent in 1975, and 39.6 per cent in 1985), then as the increasingly dominant financial, service, and international centre of Japan (not to mention the political centre). Concentration after 1960 occurred not necessarily in Tokyo itself but within the broader capital region as the metropolis sprawled ever outwards. The magnetism of the capital region is expressed in the term 'monopolar concentration' (*ikkyoku shuchu*).

The government responded to the resultant congestion with several sticks, beginning with the Industry Restriction Law of 1959, which effectively banned the rebuilding or extension of factories with a floor space of 1,600 m^2 or more in most of Tokyo and large parts of Kawasaki and Yokohama. (This was later reduced to 500 m^2, and 1,000 m^2 in Osaka.) Two other laws and a Tokyo ordinance applied to semi-industrial zones placed further restrictions on factories. Carrots were introduced to encourage relocation under the 1972 Industry Relocation Law.[9] Just how much these measures were responsible for factory relocations may be debated. Large factories had their own reasons for moving, namely cheaper land and labour as they expanded their production capacities. What is clear is that Tokyo's share of industrial output declined from 16 per cent in 1959 to 12 per cent in 1965. The number of factories with 300+ employees peaked at 499 in 1963, and thereafter rapidly declined.

Relocations produced successive rings of industry, pushing out into the Kanto plain. Tokyo and the three prefectures of Kanagawa, Saitama, and (inner) Chiba came to constitute one large industrial region, and industry spilled even further afield into the northern Kanto plain prefectures of Ibaragi, Gunma, and Tochigi, thence into northern Japan. In Osaka, too, factories first spread within the region into Higashi Osaka, then into neighbouring Shiga, Hyogo, Mie, and eventually into all of the Chugoku region. But in two important respects, this was not a simple 'donut' phenomenon, with a hollowing out of the inner cores.

First, the large factories usually maintained a presence on their original sites, either as their headquarters, or as research and development facilities after moving their headquarters into central Tokyo. (More than a third of Japan's new R&D facilities were built in Tokyo and Kanagawa in the boom years of 1983–5, and two thirds in the capital region.[10]) Communications equipment and computer giant Fujitsu, based in Kawasaki, is a good example. Originally the telephone department of Fuji Electric, it became independent in 1935. It established its first factory outside Kawasaki in

[8] Kakinuma (1988, 11).   [9] Nihon keikaku gyosei gakkai (ed.) (1987); Tokyo to (1989).
[10] Kakinuma (1988, 34).

1959, in Tochigi, and now has 15 base factories nationwide, mostly in east Japan. Its production headquarters building and base development factory stand on the original site, and its business headquarters is located in down-town Tokyo.

Second, while some of the larger subcontractors moved with their 'parent' company, the vast majority of small factories remained. Workers of large factories who did not want to move stayed behind as well, and set up their own factories. Personal reasons were important, of course, but many small factories did not subcontract for a single relocating parent, and their owners felt that moving out of the urban centres would narrow their business opportunities and leave them isolated. In other words, they would be forfeiting the advantages their industrial districts offered.

Yet to these small factories the relocation of so many major factories posed a problem potentially as fundamental as the worker shortages and rising wages of the 1960s. If they were simply adjuncts to the large factories, their numbers would almost have certainly declined. In fact, their numbers *increased* for the next 20 years, attesting to the benefits of their concentra-tions, their independent culture, and the efforts of their owners to diversify order sources, launch their own products, and become specialised in higher value added processes. At least that may be said of small factories in Tokyo:

In the case of Tokyo, even though large factories moved, the number of small firms increased, and there was an increase in SMEs escaping from dependent sub-contracting relationships and becoming independent by relying on high level skills, as well as R & D factories. By contrast, small factories were severely affected by the moving of large factories in Osaka, and could not arrest the decline in manufactur-ing. In the capital region, too, a similar tendency can be seen in the coastal areas of Kanagawa.[11]

The vitality of small firm concentrations, especially in Tokyo, attracted growing interest. Industrial geographers pointed to the diversity of the industrial base which included all the key processes for the machine indus-tries, and how these 'complex areas' were being upgraded less through the activities of particular large factories than through improvements in the technical capabilities of smaller firms.[12] Small firm specialists pointed to horizontal links between small firms in addition to vertical subcontracting links, and the role of 'organisers'.[13] And out of these urban concentrations were born innovative small firms, with high productivity and paying high wages, adaptable and adapted to a changing economic environment – 'venture business'.[14]

[11] Nihon keikaku gyosei gakkai (ed.) (1987, 221–2).
[12] E.g., Itakura *et al.* (1973); Ide *et al.* (1977); Takeuchi (1978).
[13] E.g., Sato (ed.) (1981).   [14] Kiyonari (1972); also Furukawa (1985); and Mitsui (1985).

Relocating large firms were themselves influenced by these concentrations. As the supplier bases in the areas they moved to were smaller in scale and less sophisticated, they left purchasing departments at their old sites, and located their factories within (overnight truck) transportation distance from the centres. The outward expansion thus depended on an improving transportation infrastructure as well as on the hunger for new land and labour. To give another example, Tokimec (formerly Tokyo Precision Instruments, a major measuring and control device, aero, marine, and power equipment maker established in Ota Ward in 1896) was late to move partly because of its reliance on local specialist, low volume subcontractors. After divisionalisation in 1968, it relocated its production facilities to Tochigi, leaving behind its headquarters and R&D facility. Ten per cent of its suppliers relocated to Tochigi, too, but it still relies on small suppliers in Ota, one third of which were started by former employees. The choice of the Tochigi sites reflected not just favourable land and labour conditions there, but the need to maintain its Ota supplier base.[15]

According to one estimate, at the end of the 1970s, 42 per cent of Nissan, 60 per cent of Isuzu, and 42 per cent of Mitsubishi's second tier suppliers were located in south Tokyo; if Kawasaki is included the figures rise to 65 per cent for Nissan and 60 per cent for Mitsubishi.[16] Some of these suppliers, however, also established branch factories outside the Keihin Belt for similar reasons to those of the large factories, leaving behind their headquarters and low volume precision work. Initially located in nearby Kanagawa, by the late 1980s these branch factories were being built as far away as Tohoku (north-east Japan). In other words, a spatial division of labour was established not just within large firms, but eventually within suppliers and smaller product makers as well. With the broader spread of industry and expanded output, orders to suppliers based in the core regions did eventually decline, of course. More than 20 per cent of Isuzu's main suppliers were local Ota Ward companies in 1957, but by the early 1990s the figure was less than 10 per cent.[17] The smaller number, however, were involved in critical parts or processes.

Factory relocations had important consequences for industry in the recipient areas as well. At first they were welcomed, since they brought new investment, employment opportunities, and promised to spur local industrial growth. In time, however, the blessings proved to be mixed. In some cases a complementary relationship with local industry and *sanchi* broke down as competition for labour intensified. Moreover, assembly factories by themselves did not create high-level machining districts, especially if they continued to be supplied with key parts from elsewhere. For better or

[15] Interview, procurements department personnel July 1990.
[16] Takeuchi, A. (1983, 70–1).   [17] Ota kuritsu kyodo hakubutsukan (1994, 56).

for worse, local industry was increasingly integrated into wider production configurations:

Local industrial concentrations in both surrounding and more peripheral areas have been swamped by this wave. In some cases textile factories have converted to subcontracting, in some cases they do simple assembly work. And sometimes you can even find textiles in one part of the factory and parts assembly in another. Thus provincial industry is becoming integrated into the network of industry from the metropolitan areas.[18]

The government, of course, attempted to promote regional development. The First Comprehensive National Development Plan (CNDP, 1962) designated 15 New Industrial Cities and over 100 Underdeveloped Region Industrial Development Areas, providing incentives for industry to locate in these areas. Some New Industrial Cities such as Koriyama have become important industrial centres, although, again, just how much this owes to government policy is open to debate. In recent years policy makers have sensed that new high tech., information, and related service businesses will also have to be promoted, as well as the deconcentration of functions such as R&D if young people are to be encouraged to stay in local cities or return ('U-turn') from the core regions and provincial industry is to be revitalised. Such thinking was incorporated into the 4th CNDP of 1987.

It was also one strand of the Technopolis concept, proposed by MITI in its 'Vision for the 1980s'.[19] The original version envisaged the creation of several new high tech. model cities characterised by 'rural serenity in the city and urban activity in the country'; vanguards of the twenty first century. In its less utopian version, projects have to be located near a 'mother city' of at least 150,000 people, there has to be a nearby university engaged in high tech. teaching and research, and some high-tech. industry has to exist already in the area. A Technopolis Law was enacted in 1983, and, by 1994, 26 projects had been approved. In addition, eight other national projects had been launched under five ministries and agencies, as well as some 130 'technopark', 'intelligent cosmos research concept', 'innovation plaza', etc., schemes funded by local and prefectural authorities.[20] No authority wants to be left out (including metropolitan centres, of course, which have their own schemes).

Sceptics doubt that regional policy can bring about industrial (re)generation. Projects likely to succeed – like the Hamamatsu Technopolis – will do so because of their favourable locational characteristics and existing nearby industrial concentrations.[21] Hamamatsu, centre

---

[18] Itakura (1988, 245–6).   [19] On the Technopolis concept, see Tatsuno (1986).
[20] Kagaku gijutsu cho (ed.) (1993, 2, 89–90).
[21] E.g., Itakura (1988); Takeuchi (1983).

of Japan's motor bike and musical instruments industries, had indeed developed a formidable concentration of industry by the late 1960s (with relatively little influx from the Keihin Belt), as had other cities in intermediate (neither metropolitan nor remote) regions, offering considerable potential for self-generated development. The earlier metropolitan–provincial (*toshigata –chihogata*) dichotomy was replaced by a graduated, concentric ring conception, seen in terms of technology, sophistication, value added per part produced, in-house spatial divisions of labour, and so on.[22] Most of Honda's development work, for instance, is done at its Sayama factory near Tokyo, special vehicles are made in Hamamatsu, volume cars in Mie, and mature, volume cars in Kumamoto, each further and further away from the capital region.[23] In terms of subcontracting, south Tokyo factories handle one-off or small batch work; the largest batch sizes are 10,000 parts. This increases to 25,000 within a 50 km radius, 200,000 within a 100 km radius, and up to several million within a 200 km radius.[24]

The metropolitan-centred, graduated conception sees dynamic upgrading of each ring as a response to competitive pressures and further expansion. As each new ring is added, each moves up a notch. It is helpful if not taken too literally. Interregional linkages bypassing the centre have been increasing, and there is no guarantee that the metropolitan-led orderliness implied by the model can be maintained, as we shall see.

Industrial districts in east Japan

Table 3.2 summarises locational trends in Japan's machine industries between 1985–90. It shows that, while the core regions still have the largest concentrations, they are either shrinking or growing less rapidly than other prefectures, both in terms of establishments and output. They also show the general concentration and growth in eastern Japan. These trends are even more pronounced if we include other data. From 1975–80, Gunma was the fastest growing prefecture in terms of manufacturing output, followed by Ibaragi and Nagano. From 1980–5 electronics growth pushed Nagano into first place, followed by Gunma and Kanagawa. By 1985–90 manufacturers (including many SMEs) were investing further afield; the number of machine industry factories in the northern

---

[22] There are similarities here with Britain's 'locational hierarchy spatial structure' (Massey (1979); Massey (1984); Heim (1983)), only this structure is more pronounced in Japan, and has moved further down the size scale of firms.

[23] K. Sakamoto, mimeo and interview, December 1992; cf. also Nihon ritchi senta (1993, 17).

[24] Kokumin kin'yu koko (ed.) (1989, 120–1).

Table 3.2 *Fifteen main machine industry prefectures, 1985, 1990*

Prefecture	Machine industry establishments			Output		
	1985	1990	% change 1985–90	1985	1990	% change 1985–90
1 Fukushima	2,385	2,730	14.5	1,776	2,485	39.9
2 Ibaragi	3,641	3,874	6.4	3,588	4,996	39.2
3 Tochigi	3,022	3,255	7.7	3,568	4,838	35.6
4 Gunma	4,424	4,738	7.1	4,113	5,385	30.9
5 Saitama	10,685	11,642	9.0	6,796	9,435	38.8
6 Chiba	3,290	3,549	7.9	2,618	3,452	31.9
7 Tokyo	20,109	17,125	−14.8	8,881	10,890	22.6
8 Kanagawa	10,386	10,726	3.3	14,753	18,058	22.4
9 Niigata	4,429	4,699	6.1	1,544	2,268	46.9
10 Nagano	5,484	5,541	1.0	3,673	4,669	27.1
11 Shizuoka	7,462	8,036	7.7	5,560	8,243	48.1
12 Aichi	13,055	14,246	9.1	16,693	23,717	42.0
13 Osaka	19,436	19,339	−0.5	9,062	10,401	14.8
14 Hyogo	6,236	6,373	2.2	4,653	6,585	41.5
15 Hiroshima	3,221	3,402	5.6	3,438	4,840	40.8
Japan	151,786	157,392	3.7	118,686	158,315	33.4

Note:
Establishments with four or more employees are covered. Machine
industries=metal products, machinery and equipment, electrical machinery,
transportation equipment and precision equipment. Output is measured in ¥1,000
million.
Source: Tsusansho (ed.) (1987, 1992), *Kogyo tokei hyo* (Census of Manufactures;
Report by Cities, Towns and Villages), pp. 19–23.

prefectures of Fukushima, Miyagi, and Yamagata increased by over 10
per cent and output by over 40 per cent, while even further north in Iwate,
Akita, and Aomori they increased by over 20 per cent and 50 per cent
respectively.[25]

In this section we will look at industrial districts in Gunma and Nagano
which, as we have just seen, were at the forefront of machine industry
growth in the 1970s and 80s.

[25] Kokumin kin'yu koko (ed.) (1989, 248); Tsusansho (ed.) (1987, 1992).

1 Fukushima
2 Ibaragi
3 Tochigi
4 Gunma
5 Saitama
6 Chiba
7 Tokyo
8 Kanagawa
9 Niigata
10 Nagano
11 Shizuoka
12 Aichi
13 Osaka
14 Hyogo
15 Hiroshima

a Ota City
b Ueda City

Figure 3.2 Fifteen main machine industry prefectures

Ota City and Kiryu[26]

Ota City (not to be confused with Ota Ward in Tokyo) is the leading industrial city of Gunma Prefecture in the northern Kanto plain. For a long time
an important textile centre in Japan, Gunma also developed a military-ori-
ented engineering base before World War II. Ota was home to Nakajima
Aircraft, which at its peak made almost a third of the country's aircraft
engines and employed a quarter of a million workers in factories throughout east Japan. After the war, some of the engineers and workers stayed on
with Fuji Heavy Industries (FHI), which took over several Nakajima factories and produced first the Rabbit scooter, then Subaru cars. Other
Nakajima engineers founded local companies like Ogihara and Miyatsu,
both major non-*keiretsu* automobile diecast makers, while former blue-
collar workers founded local subcontracting companies.[27]

During the 1980s around two thirds of Ota's industrial output came from
transportation equipment alone. Around 30 per cent of firms in the
machine section of the Ota Chamber of Commerce were registered under
this industry, but many other firms making plastic products, metal parts,
and so on were also connected with the industry, and ultimately with FHI.
While not as pronounced as cities like Toyota and Hitachi, Ota shares some
characteristics of a company town. Since FHI is a relatively small car
maker, and was late in launching production, there are few large first tier
suppliers in and around Ota. These are spread more widely in the Kanto
plain, and are usually suppliers to Nissan, which is FHI's largest shareholder.[28] Many of the smaller factories in the area, however, produce exclusively for FHI or its first tier suppliers.

Efforts have been made to modify this vertical orientation since the
second half of the 1980s – when Subaru sales began to flag and the company
advised its subcontractors to diversify order sources – yet the tradition of
vertical dependence compromised attempts to gain orders from outside the
district according to local government and Chamber of Commerce officials.
The same applies to slowness in forging links amongst themselves to
develop new business. The vulnerability of many firms was evident in the
early 1990s. In 1992 there were 1,370 factories in Ota and neighbouring
Oizumi cho, 86 per cent of which had fewer than 30 employees. Three years
later there were some 200 less as a result of closures or conversions, most of
these being small factories. From a chronic labour shortage, resulting in one
of the highest proportions of foreign workers in the country (officially 16

[26] Unless otherwise stated, information here comes from interviews with Ota City and
Chamber of Commerce officials in November 1992, and T. Sonoda.
[27] Companies like Honda, Nissan, and Prince also actively recruited former Nakajima engineers.   [28] Cf. Sheard (1983).

per cent of workers in firms with four or more employees, but higher unofficially) there were growing fears of unemployment.

The high quality of the labour force has been a major factor in attracting large factories from outside the district, principally the Keihin Belt, over the past 35 years. These factories include Sanyo Electric, Mitsubishi Electric, Nissan Diesel, Meidensha, Niigata Tekko, and Gunma NEC. This influx deepened the industrial base and accelerated concentration in the machine industries. Labour was drawn away from localised industry, which includes button production (one company alone claims over one third of the Japanese market) and knitted goods. The latter was a postwar creation, although it drew on the area's traditional textile strengths. It thrived in the early postwar years, but labour shortages, trade friction, and the rise of the yen from the late 1960s forced the industry to contract. From a peak of 2,237 firms in 1967, the local knitted goods association had contracted to less than 1,000 firms by the late 1970s.[29] The industry today is characterised by a few medium-sized firms plus many small producers, with a division of labour organised to produce small-batch fashion-oriented garments for rapidly changing markets. It was much less affected by recession in the early 1990s.

Ota is attempting to develop a high tech. industrial core. The first phase of a research park was completed in 1994 with other facilities to be added in 1997. In addition to local firms, it was hoped that R&D facilities from Tokyo companies would be attracted. It is still too early to judge how successful this project will be.

Ota forms one corner of the triangular textile weaving district known as Ryomo, the other corners consisting of the more traditional textile towns of Kiryu and Tatebayashi. The latter, being on flatter land closer to main access roads, converted to machine production relatively early on, leaving Kiryu as the main textile centre. Even here, the vigour of textiles has declined – 30 per cent of workers still worked in the industry in 1992, but it accounted for just 20 per cent of Kiryu's manufacturing output. National government money was granted to establish a research facility and introduce advanced technology design methods, but this does not appear to have reversed the decline.

By contrast, machine production accounts for almost three quarters of manufacturing output (table 3.3). There are four major firms with several hundred employees. All were founded with local capital, but are to varying degrees linked with outside assemblers such as Nissan, Hitachi, and Honda. They have one or two local affiliates, but otherwise do not have substantial subcontracting links with local firms. Most of their work is done in-house. There is, however, another notable local industry, namely the

[29] Sonoda (1991).

manufacture of *pachinko* pinball machines, and here the leading firms do
have substantial subcontracting links with small local factories.

Ueda and Sakaki[30]

Nagano Prefecture has a tradition of indigenous entrepreneurship which
some have linked to poor farming conditions, which forced its inhabitants
to engage in side businesses, as well as to a general enthusiasm for education and industry. Like Gunma, it has long been a major textile producer,
and its early machine production was in textile machines and their repair.
Kiyonari pointed to this indigenous base, as well as to wartime and postwar
relocations, such as those of Seiko and Olympus, as the main ingredients
for the rapid expansion of the precision and electric machine industries in
Suwa City.[31] Here I will look at one of the prefecture's other major industrial cities, Ueda, which (with adjoining towns Tobu and Maruko) has
roughly 10 per cent of the prefecture's 17,000 factories, as well as nearby
Sakaki.

Ueda's industry is not dominated by a single large company. Most of the
core factories have fewer than 1,000 employees, and most derive from
wartime relocations. Nagano Precision Instruments, for instance, was set
up by Tokimec. Indigenous entrepreneurship, however, is represented not
only by the vast majority of small firms, but by Art Kinzoku and Shinano
Kenshi. Although started in Tokyo, the founder of Art was a local man.
After studying aircraft engineering he decided that automobiles had greater
immediate potential, and started a repair shop in 1918. By 1926 he had
developed a lightweight alloy piston. The factory was evacuated to Ueda
during the war, stayed, and now has the largest annual production of
pistons in the world. Art has traditionally had strong links with Honda –
Honda Soichiro was its most famous apprentice – and Mitsubishi, but
recently Toyota, has acquired a major stake in the company.

Shinano Kenshi was also started in 1918 by a newspaper foreign corre-
spondent who returned home to set up a factory, spinning silk waste into
yarn. The company still makes yarn, but in 1962 branched out into small
precision motors, and then into audio electronics in 1972. Shinano Kenshi's
competitive advantage lies mainly in its ability to make small motors (for
VTRs, copiers, etc.) in high volume (units of millions). It has factories in
the US, China, and Thailand.[32]

As in Ota City the majority of factories are in the machine industries,

---

[30] Information here comes from local interviews in December 1992 unless otherwise stated.
[31] Kiyonari (1975).
[32] Organ Bari also branched out from textiles. It still makes over 80 per cent of Japan's sewing
machine needles, but has moved into electronics.

Table 3.3 *Machine industries in Ota City, Ueda City and Ota Ward, 1990*

	Metal products	Machinery & equipment	Electrical machinery	Transportation equipment	Precision equipment	Total manufact.
Ota City						
establishments						
4–9 employees	92	97	39	32	4	479
10–299	51	65	40	35	1	351
300+	–	1	2	6	–	12
employees	1,773	3,094	3,014	11,060	31	26,567
output	35.8	85.6	133.2	734.7	5.2	1,169.1
Ueda City						
establishments						
4–9 employees	30	66	60	18	14	335
10–299	17	42	73	18	6	269
300+	–	1	4	3	1	11
employees	622	2,279	7,197	3,440	706	20,532
output	8.1	55.4	150.1	92.2	12.9	510.5
Ota Ward						
establishments						
4–9 employees	652	774	379	105	90	2,760
10–299	288	401	287	74	58	1,545
300+	1	4	5	1	1	17
employees	10,501	17,802	14,317	3,683	2,221	69,907
output	175.6	415.6	353.7	111.8	48.8	1,729.2

Notes:
Establishments with four or more employees covered. Output measured in ¥1,000 million.
Source: Tsusansho (ed.) (1992), *Kogyo tokei hyo* (Census of Manufactures; Report by Cities, Towns and Villages), pp. 122, 173, 205.

but, whereas in Ota transportation equipment alone accounts for two thirds of industrial output, in the Asama region, which includes Ueda, electrical machinery accounts for only one third, and all the machine industries combined account for two thirds of output. The industrial structure is thus more diversified. Like Ota City, some 85 per cent of all factories have fewer than 30 employees, but there are quite a few in the 40–60 employee size range which do design, machining, and subassembly work, as well as a number of small OEM product makers, whose output is marketed under the labels of more famous large companies. Technical sophistication allows the OEM makers to produce in large volumes competitively.

There is a contrast with the small, cramped workshops in south Tokyo which specialise in one or two processes like internal grinding, white metal machining, slotting, and so on. Here the factories are larger, more spacious, and handle higher volume work and more processes. They are much more self-contained, doing processes in house which would be subcontracted out in Tokyo. Less than 15 per cent of Shinano Kenshi's turnover, for instance, is subcontracted out.[33] Thus there is neither the strong vertical subcontracting orientation characteristic of company towns, nor the very fine but diversified interfirm division of labour found in metropolitan districts. Nonetheless, this type of district, in which a number of high volume product or subproduct makers produce for a variety of customers, is critical for Japan's machine industries.

The best-known traditional industry is Ueda *tsumugi* (a type of non-silk kimono), which was especially famous in the mid-Tokugawa period. Although easily the largest *tsumugi* producer in Nagano, however, by 1981 there were only 35 businesses in the weaving cooperative, and most had fewer than ten employees.[34]

City officials and industrialists are very concerned about Ueda's future, and about how to prevent the haemorrhage of youth to the metropolitan centres. Asama has become an official Technopolis project, which aims to build on the existing mechatronic and parts industries, as well as to develop biotechnology. By late 1992 a new research park in the south of Ueda had attracted eight software companies, a subsidiary of Seiko Epson and a large new Art Kinzoku factory, in addition to a new vocational college.

Sakaki lies nearby to the north-west of Ueda, and exemplifies Nagano's rural entrepreneurial tradition. It gained fame as a relatively poor agricultural community which developed a sophisticated industrial concentration in a remarkably short period of time.[35] In the mid 1980s Sakaki

[33] Watanabe (1992) and Nihon ritchi senta (1993) see a gradual diminution in policies of self-reliance.   [34] Sasaki (1986).   [35] See Friedman (1988).

boasted 365 factories. Only 14 factories had more than 100 employees, 75 per cent had fewer than ten, and over two thirds of production was in the machine industries. Three factories have spawned the main product makers. The first was originally a sewing machine company which moved from Tokyo after the war, and is now a major OEM typewriter manufacturer. (It maintains its R&D facility locally, but the official headquarters and new product development centre have been moved to Tokyo.) The second was started by soldiers returning from the war as a shoe horn subcontractor, and grew into a world-class plastic injection mould machine maker. The third is a tester maker (also originally from Tokyo, now moved into Ueda). These companies and one or two of their offshoots devote a large portion of turnover to new product development and R&D. There is also a major OEM and own brand mini back hoe maker, which started out manufacturing auto parts.

In addition to these final product makers, there are two tiers of parts makers. One consists of larger factories, which manufacture parts for companies like Honda and Nissan. The second tier consists of the bulk of small factories, which are involved in work like machining (111 factories), press (33), diecast (24), and welding (9). Many in fact are little more than workshops attached to houses, and the owners still have farming interests, but these factories and workshops allegedly housed 1 per cent of the nation's CNC machines in the mid 1980s. They attract orders from far beyond the prefecture's borders. All three tiers in fact are outward oriented. Finished product makers procure only 14 per cent of their parts within Sakaki. Parts makers deliver 51 per cent of their parts to Kanto factories, and only 11 per cent locally. Forty four per cent of their subcontracting is done locally.[36] There are close linkages within the parts maker strata, but weak links with the finished product makers.

Like Ueda, Sakaki is quite different from both the company town-type of industrial district, and from the metropolitan industrial districts, and this is its strength. The degree of horizontal cooperation in the form of information exchange and local policy efforts to improve the industrial base are noteworthy. (Industry and local government have much closer links than, for instance, in Tokyo's Ota Ward, where the local government has to represent a wider range of divergent interests.) Its rural location, too, suggests similarities with districts in the Third Italy. But in terms of scale and interfirm trading relations, Sakaki is not Japan's leading Marshallian industrial district by any means.

---

[36] Takeuchi and Mori (1988).

Internationalisation and industrial districts

Industrial districts within Japan are affected by the internationalisation of the economy, including foreign direct investment (FDI), which we shall consider briefly. FDI has accelerated markedly in recent years, spurred by strategic corporate expansion, threats of trade friction, and the spectacular rise of the yen. The 1989 level – $68 billion – was five times that of 1985. By 1992 FDI had halved to $34 billion, but then picked up again after further currency appreciation. Less had been directed towards Asia than either North America or Europe by 1993, but the proportion was rising, and, in terms of investor numbers, the proportion was well over half. (This is because almost half are SMEs, which since the early 1990s have invested mostly in Asia, especially in China.)[37]

The economic vitality of Asia and the emergence of a 'regional division of labour' in east Asia have been the focal point of many study tours and much debate. In its optimistic (simplistic) form, this 'regional division of labour' is an extension of the graduated domestic conception. High value added and advanced technological work is done in Japan, medium value added and technology work is done in the NIEs, and so on through ASEAN, Vietnam, Cambodia, and Myanmar. Through participation in the 'flying geese formation', all benefit from rising technological standards and economic levels. Coincidentally, the lives of mature, volume products and the machines that produce them are extended as they move offshore from Japan.

This view evaporated in the 1990s as accelerated development and rapidly rising technological levels in the NIEs and ASEAN, coupled with further rises in the yen, threatened its orderly assumptions. 'Hollowing out' pessimism spread in its place. In the 1980s, Matsushita produced multi-functional, high quality, small batch products in Japan, and standard, volume products in Malaysia. It made its split-type air conditioners in Japan, and most window-type conditioners in Malaysia, for sale in ASEAN countries and the Middle East. Subsequently, however, more sophisticated products have been moved to Malaysia – some split-type air conditioners were moved there in the early 1990s, 90 per cent of them for export back to Japan.[38] It took 20 years between the time Sony started selling colour TVs in Japan and assembling them in Asia. It took six years for the Walkman, but only seven months for the FST TV, including its tube. According to one director: 'There's nothing we can't produce in our Singapore factory.'[39]

[37] Keizai Koho Senta (1994); Chusho kigyo cho (ed.) (1995a).
[38] Shibata, Ishiro, and Ogihara (1992).   [39] Cited in the Asahi shinbun, 6 January 1995.

Some product development is also being relocated overseas. Aiwa, for instance, which already produces 80 per cent of its output abroad, has R&D and procurement facilities in Singapore. According to an SME Agency survey, only 15 per cent of assemblers did product planning, design, and development abroad in 1993, but the proportion was expected to treble within five years.[40]

At the parts level, supply bases in Asian countries are also developing, and increasingly sophisticated parts are being exported into Japan. The same is happening at the basic process level: '[A] shift is occurring from the 1980s entry into the region by Japan's assembly sector in pursuit of cheap, plentiful labour to the 1990s trend that is seeing Japan's basic formative material sectors, such as casting, moving outward with the nation's fundamental knowhow.'[41]

Industrial districts within Japan are affected differently by the rise of the yen, internationalisation, large firm restructuring, and economic development in Asia. 'Peripheral' districts in which standardised, volume goods are produced are more at risk than 'core' districts with a high proportion of low volume, prototype, non price-sensitive or rapid turnaround work. Small firms in company towns with a high degree of dependence on a few peak firms are especially vulnerable if those firms move production offshore. By contrast, small firms in districts less reliant on large, peak firms, and with diversified order sources are in principle less vulnerable. Larger concentrations, or 'complex areas', offer greater opportunities for diversification than small ones.

As predicted by the graduated model, there are some parallels between the problems facing small firms in provincial districts in the 1990s and those faced by small firms in the metropolitan districts with factory relocations and rising costs in the 1960s and 1970s. The latter responded by pursuing higher value added strategies, diversifying order sources, technical specialisation, and own product strategies. Small firms in intermediate districts such as Ota and even Ueda have been attempting to make this transition in the past ten years, with increasing urgency. Already these districts have considerable concentrations of industry, which hold out the potential for spontaneous development, but they are smaller than the metropolitan centres, and forging stronger links with other districts is vital.

Metropolitan districts are also vulnerable, however, for similar reasons

[40] Chusho kigyo cho (ed.) (1994a).
[41] Seki (1994, 31). As the industrial bases in other Asian countries grow, moreover, there is an increase in intraregional trade without coordination from the 'centre', which is implicit in the graduated model.

to Japan in the 'regional division of labour'. The amount of work flowing into them has declined, partly because of recession and large firm restructuring, as the following comments from Ota Ward suggest:

You know what restructuring is? It's making a slight modification on the blueprint and demanding that the work be done for half price. The Fair Trade Commission can't censure them if they've made a change.

We're actually busy at the moment. We're making machines so the manufacturer can take in work it used to subcontract out. Others may curse us, but there's no other work we can do.

But it is also as a consequence of intensifying competition *between districts*:

We're having to compete with people over in east Tokyo now. Before, we did precision work, but we could charge a higher price. Now we're having to do the same work for a low price. We'll end up hanging ourselves.

There was this part for a large car maker. ¥200 was a fair price, but I said ¥120, because that's the way things are. A broker in west Japan got it for ¥85.[42]

Small firms are not simply passive victims of internationalisation, of course, and such pressures act as a spur for further innovation. A survey of almost 5,000 client companies by the Small Business Finance Corporation in 1994 showed that just over 6 per cent had themselves established production facilities abroad, and a further 20 per cent were either contemplating it, or felt the need to do so. A smaller survey by the SME Agency of SMEs in Ota Ward suggested that roughly 10 per cent were producing abroad.[43] Small firms have established their own 'regional division of labour' through trading and manufacture abroad, either individually or in consortia. A small Osaka-based construction materials company with 15 employees is a good example. It imports parts from Korea and Taiwan, 'finishes' them in Osaka and markets the products as Japanese goods. The owner now sees himself as more of a merchant than a manufacturer, but in 1993 was considering setting up a manufacturing plant in either Vietnam or China, the newly favoured direct investment destinations.[44]

In the end he did not go ahead, which may have been just as well. Surveys show that many small firms either pull out or 'fade out' (sell part of their investment) of their foreign investments, with serious consequences for the company.[45] There have also been many casualties of internationalisation and restructuring in the economy, as well as intensifying interregional

[42] Interviews, September 1993.
[43] Asahi shinbun, 25 December 1994, 12 November 1994.
[44] Interview, May 1993. Osaka's machine industry companies have traditionally been more export oriented than those of Tokyo.   [45] Fukushima (1991, 70–1).

competition. Major metropolitan districts may offer small firms greater opportunities to adapt, but they are by no means immune from these pressures, and, as we shall see in the next chapter, have additional problems of their own. The adaptability of industrial districts and their small firm owners is being tested to the limits in the 1990s.

4 Small firms and industrial districts: Ota Ward

Ota and Ueda are sizable industrial districts, but as table 3.3 showed, they are far smaller than Ota Ward in Tokyo in terms of factory numbers. The proportion of micro-factories with four to nine employees is also less. If micro-factories with one to three employees were included, both differences would be even more pronounced. Japan's metropolitan concentrations are remarkable, both for their scale and their high proportion of very small firms. In fact they are without parallel in the industrialised world, but they do not feature in most writings on small firms and industrial districts.

Several candidates could be listed to redress this neglect. Osaka and Tokyo have the largest machine industry concentrations, and, within these, Higashi Osaka City and Ota Ward stand out. They are administrative districts, of course, but are key parts of their respective industrial belts. They share a number of features; both were late industrialisers within their regions, and grew to a peak of almost 10,000 factories. The proportion of small factories increased in both, and, by the mid 1980s, 80 per cent had fewer than ten employees. Both are highly concentrated in the machine industries, particularly in the staples of metal products and machinery and equipment.

Ota Ward was chosen because of the prominence of Keihin and east Japan described in the last chapter, its pronounced restructuring from the 1960s, its reputation for technological preeminence, and its industrial goods orientation (often contrasted with a consumer goods orientation in east Tokyo; Higashi Osaka has both). The account that follows is thus to some extent representative of other metropolitan districts, but to some extent unique. This uniqueness is justifiable because of Ota's important position in Japan's machine industries, and because it has frequently been the vanguard of change within them.

This chapter provides an overview of industry in Ota Ward, looking first at its industrial development both before and after World War II, then at the main characteristics of its industrial structure. It then looks at how work flows between the factories, entering the district through its larger factories, and then filtering downwards *and sideways*. Specialisation is important, but is not the only source of flexibility within the district. Despite Ota's formidable strengths as an industrial district, there are serious threats to its continued vitality. In this chapter we shall consider locational demerits, deriving from Ota's location in inner Tokyo.

A late industrialiser

Ota Ward lies in south Tokyo, bounded on the east by Tokyo Bay – into which Haneda Airport and several reclaimed islands protrude – on the south and west by the Tama River, beyond which lies Kawasaki City in Kanagawa Prefecture, and on the north by Shinagawa, Meguro, and Setagaya Wards (figure 4.1). Its 54 km^2 covers about one tenth the total area of the 23 inner wards, one fortieth of all Tokyo, and includes prime residential areas, parks, and ponds in the north-west, and densely factoried areas in the south and south-east. The residential population is 650,000. Roughly 350,000 people are employed in about 40,000 establishments, around 20 per cent of these in manufacturing. It is Tokyo's leading ward in terms of factory numbers, employment, and output. In the early 1990s Tokyo had some 10 per cent of Japan's factories, and around 10 per cent of these were located in Ota Ward. It was not always preeminent, however. In fact, it was a late developer.

At the beginning of the Meiji period the district consisted of a group of villages dispersed around what became Ebara County, supplying agricultural and fishing produce for Tokyo.[1] It was also well known for its straw souvenirs. Although the main Tokaido and Kamakura roads passed through the district, as well as the first railway, which opened between Tokyo and Yokohama in 1874, early industry was primarily an extension of these traditional activities. Plaited straw goods, especially hats, enjoyed a boom, and earned valuable export revenues. The largest producer employed 80 women and 40 men in 1891, and in 1900 there were 118 members of the local producers' association. When the industry peaked in 1916 it was Japan's leading plaited straw goods producer, but by 1931 the industry had disappeared, a casualty to rising suburban wage costs and rural competition, replaced by the rapidly expanding engineering sector.[2]

With the exception of one or two canning enterprises, factory development in the Meiji period was sporadic. The strength of the fishing and

[1] For the sake of simplicity Ota Ward is referred to retrospectively. The district's nine main villages had become towns by the 1920s. These were grouped into Omori and Kamata wards in 1932, which were amalgamated to form Ota (from Omori and Kamata) Ward in 1947.

[2] Ota ku (1951).

Figure 4.1 Ota Ward, south Tokyo and the Keihin Belt

seaweed industries impeded plans to develop the coastal area along the lines of Kawasaki across the river, and opposition by local residents prevented several companies from setting up factories. Late development was not just a consequence of equidistance between Tokyo and Yokohama. By the second decade of the century, however, the growing need for land for larger factories proved irrepressible, and industry began to converge from both the Tokyo and Yokohama sides. Early key factories were the Tokyo

Gas Omori factory (1909); Kurosawa Trading at Kamata (1911), which made typewriters and office equipment; Japan Special Steel (1915), which spawned many factories through craftsmen becoming independent; Tokyo Gas Electric Machines (1917), reputed to have the largest number of craftsmen in Japan, incubator of Hino and Isuzu as well as numerous small factories; Niigata Tekko at Kamata (1918), Japanese pioneer of marine diesel engines; as well as pump and turbine makers Ebara and Dengyosha.

Still the rural serenity was far from overwhelmed, and machine factories were a small minority of the influx. Of the 51 factories with five or more employees in 1918, only eight made machines, one tenth the number of neighbouring Shinagawa. In the north-west, Den'en chofu was launched as a venture in 1918 by leading industrialists who were becoming alarmed at the growing urban labour movement and social unrest, and sought to create Japan's garden city (*den'en toshi*) on the edge of Tokyo. Kurosawa Trading, too, was a utopian complex (named *Warera no mura*, or Our Village) which in addition to the factory included housing, school, gardens, and recreation grounds. Nearby was a ceramic art factory 'set amongst the flowers'. Shochiku Kinema sought to create a cinematic paradise there. Beside it was a perfume factory, and nearby was Sanseido's model print works, dubbed 'Kamata Girls' School'.[3]

Two events firmly established Ota's position in the machine industries (and sunk hopes for a pastoral modernity). The first was the Kanto Earthquake of 1923, which resulted in an influx of population and factories from the devastated older parts of Tokyo. By 1928 there were 158 factories with five or more employees, and almost half were in the machine industries. The second was the Manchurian Incident in 1931, which sparked a massive buildup of heavy industry and armaments. Production ballooned (table 4.1) and Ota became 'alive with the sound of sirens, hammers, motors, and trucks from morning to night'.[4] A new wave of key factories dated from this period, including Ando Electric (1933), Hokushin Electric (1934), Nihon Seiko (1934–5), and Mitsubishi Heavy Industries' Shimomaruko factory (1937), many of them located in the west of the ward.

In 1936, when engineering overtook textiles in employment in Japan and Keihin overtook Hanshin in industrial production, Ota surpassed Shinagawa in factory employment and production (though not factory numbers) to claim its place as the centre of the Keihin Belt. It still had less than 5 per cent of Tokyo's factories, but accounted for 10 per cent of factory employment and production. Of the 1,000 factories with five or more employees, three quarters were in the machine industries. Over half the

---

[3] Chiiki shinko seibi kodan (1978); Ota kuritsu kyodo hakubutsukan (1994); Ohama (1989).
[4] Ota ku (1951, 65).

Table 4.1 *Factory growth in the 1930s, Ota Ward*

Year	Factories	Employees	Production (¥m.)
1932	1,112	15,547	49.2
1933	1,324	21,688	70.5
1934	1,493	28,992	92.2
1935	1,673	35,372	120.4
1936	2,034	46,481	161.2
1938	2,872	103,658	446.0
1941	5,148	159,626	938.3

Source: Ota ku (ed.) (1951) pp. 965–7.

factories had fewer than five employees (a figure not so different from today), however, and only a quarter of those were in the machine industries (compared with three quarters today). In 1936, too, Shochiku Kinema gave up trying to make talkie movies amidst the sound of hammers and machines, and moved out of the district. Complaints about air pollution were voiced, but curbing pollution was less important than serving the nation's war effort. One quarter of Tokyo's designated (important) military factories were in Ota, producing everything from tanks, armoured vehicles, and howitzers to collapsible bicycles and precision instruments. More than one in ten of Japan's designated aircraft companies had factories in Ota.

Belated attempts were made to disperse industry towards the end of the war, but the bulk of the factories were destroyed in air raids, beginning in 1942 and culminating in almost complete destruction in April 1945. Ebara's company history records 24 250kg bombs hitting its Haneda factory in a single night, destroying not only the factory, but all the machine tools which were outside awaiting relocation. Japan's first attempt to become a world power lay in ruins.

Out of the ruins, makeshift factories were erected to make pots and pans and lunch boxes. In vacant lots in between, vegetables were grown. The 1948 statistics show just 2,488 factories in Ota, less than half the number of 1941. The following year the figure rose to 2,742, making it third amongst Tokyo's wards in terms of factory numbers and highest in terms of employees, but only sixth in terms of production, the gap attributed to the depressed state of the postwar machine industries and stagnant investment. 'Don't let the smoke from the chimneys die out', was the message from demonstrating Keihin workers, while small factory owners demonstrated against crippling taxes.[5]

[5] Ota ku (1951, 968); Ota kuritsu kyodo hakubutsukan (1994, 50).

Special procurements for the Korean War breathed new life into the ward's industry, with production trebling between 1950 and 1951, and doubling again by 1953. After a brief slump, Japan entered a prolonged period of high growth. Industry in Tokyo boomed, and Ota recorded even higher growth rates, and, with them, the former problems of congestion and pollution. One consequence was described in chapter 3. From the 1960s the larger factories began to relocate their production facilities outside Tokyo, where land and labour were more plentiful. In 1960 there were 63 factories in Ota with 300 or more employees; by 1975 the number had declined to 33, and by 1990 to a mere 16. Some moved completely, but many retained a local presence. Canon, for instance, moved production to Ibaragi and Fukushima, and its local factory subsequently became an R&D lab. Niigata Tekko moved its diesel engine factory to Ota City, leaving behind an engineering centre and housing land. But the land from Mitsubishi Heavy Industries' bulldozer factory, which was moved to Kanagawa, was eventually sold to the religious sect Soka Gakkai. Japan Special Steel, a pillar of Ota industry, was absorbed by Daito in 1976 in the post Vietnam War special steel slump, and its former site is now used for housing and a park.[6]

On the other hand, the long-awaited bayside and reclamation work was able to proceed unimpeded when in 1963 the government bought out the fishing rights of the local fishermen. Land which was formerly used for drying seaweed was converted by its owners to small rental factories – sometimes the owners took up machining work themselves – or housing for factory workers. This contributed to the growth of factory numbers. At the same time, polluting factories were encouraged to relocate to the reclaimed islands from 1967. Thus government policy guaranteed a continued presence for basic processes like forging, casting, heat treatment, and press work.

Limited subcontracting bases in the new destinations forced relocating factories to continue relying on Keihin subcontractors. Moreover, craftsmen in the Keihin Belt had established a reputation for being able to handle difficult work that could not be done elsewhere. This created 'invisible roads of work' leading into the district. A former vice president of the giant IHI, for instance, recalls that when his company began making jet engine parts under licence in the late 1950s: 'We had none of the jigs and tools and special machine tools necessary to make the complicated three-dimensional engine parts, the likes of which I had never seen before. Every day I had to get out the phone book and look up SMEs in Kamata [Ota] and Kawasaki to find someone to do this work for us.'[7] Large firm production strategies

---

[6] Ota ku (1986, 17–19).
[7] Tokyoto shoko shidojo (1993, 8); orig. Nihon keizai shinbun sha *Nihon no seizo gijutsu: tsuyosa no himitsu* (Japanese Manufacturing Technology: Secrets of Its Strength). The reference to 'invisible roads of work' comes from Koseki.

were also increasing the availability of work. These included increased sub-contracting and product diversification, leading to 'large varieties in small lots' (*tahinshu shoryo*) and prototype work.

In brief, the environment for employees who for one reason or another – factory relocation, realising a dream, company closing down – wanted to start out on their own was very favourable. Many came from outside Tokyo, mass-recruited by the Keihin factories after graduating from middle school or high school. Dubbed the 'golden eggs' of the high growth period, many 'hatched' after an incubation period in which they gained the necessary craft skills.[8] Startup costs were still low, they could rent small local facto-ries, and work was plentiful (at least in the 1960s). To give two examples:

I had been planning to become independent for about three years. It happened in 1964, the year of the Olympics, when there was a lot of work about. I was the sales manager for a company and had to drink a lot. I became ill, and was in hospital for four months. When I came back I found someone else in my seat. I thought about taking another job, but all my friends said I should use the chance to start out on my own.

I was single, and doing ship work at Tokimec, which was going to be moved to Tochigi. I like to sleep in the morning and work when I want. I decided to quit. I only got about ¥350,000 in severance money, not enough to buy a machine, but you could get them easily enough through monthly instalments. I rented a room in a building with a broker a friend had introduced. The broker gave me a bit of auto-mobile work, which wasn't so bad then, even though it was 1974. I couldn't draw any pay for several months, but I scraped through.[9]

Such people were forced into making a choice, but it is worth noting that up until the early 1970s, when the rapid climb in factory numbers began to level out, they could easily have got jobs in other factories, given the severe labour shortages. The fact that they chose independence is not simply attributable to a favourable environment, but to incentives to become inde-pendent (freedom, higher income, etc.) and a culture which saw this as being normal and desirable. These factors are behind the two trends shown for the period 1960–75 in table 4.2: the significant increase in factory numbers and the rising proportion of micro-factories.

Of course there were many closures as well, and the ranks of micro-fac-tories were swollen not just with startups, but by companies shrinking to their family core in the face of recruiting problems, management problems, and rationalisation pressures from customer companies. Sometimes shrink-age was a precursor to closure, but conversely it sometimes coincided with increased production and profits as a result of technological innovation and

---

[8] More precisely, 'golden eggs' referred to the diminishing supply of middle school graduates.
[9] Interviews, August 1990.

Table 4.2 *Trends in factory size composition, Ota Ward, 1960–1990*

Factory size (employees)	1960	1975	1990
1–3	20.1%	39.0%	45.0%
4–9	21.5	38.5	35.1
10–19	25.4	12.1	10.3
20–29	11.5	4.0	4.9
30–299	20.3	5.9	4.4
300+	1.3	0.4	0.2
Total factory N	4,987	8,311	7,860

Note: Figures do not necessarily add up to 100 because of rounding.
Source: Tsusansho (ed.) (respective years), *Kogyo tokei hyo* (Census of Manufactures).

moving to higher value added work. Expanding firms, moreover, could not simply build larger factories on their existing premises, given congestion and legal restrictions. They either hired or built small factories nearby – likened to octopus legs, where the original factory is the head – or established larger branch factories outside the district, beginning in Kanagawa in the late 1960s and 1970s, and further afield in the 1980s. For all these reasons, the number of micro-factories increased and, with increasing competitive pressures, resulted in an extremely fine interfirm division of labour which we shall now look at. The number of factories in Ota Ward continued to increase throughout the 1970s, albeit more slowly, peaked at 9,190 in 1983 according to official statistics, and then declined to 7,160 in 1993.

Ota's industrial structure

In 1960 one third of Ota's factories had more than 20 employees. By 1990 the proportion had declined to less than 10 per cent (table 4.2). The number of large- and medium-sized factories had declined conspicuously. Conversely, there was a spectacular increase in the proportion of micro-factories, especially those with one to three employees. A further significant trend has been increased concentration in the machine industries (table 4.3). In 1949 approximately half of Ota's factories were in the machine industries, the same proportion as in 1936. The proportion rose steadily after that. Between 1965 and 1985 almost 90 per cent of new factories

Table 4.3 *Trends in Ota's machine factories, 1960–1990*

	1960	1975	1990
Metal products	19.7%	23.3%	22.2%
Machinery and equipment	20.3	25.4	31.7
Electrical machinery	15.2	14.9	13.9
Transportation equipment	9.6	6.0	4.6
Precision equipment	5.9	4.7	3.6
5 industry total	70.7	74.3	76.0
Total factory N	4,987	8,311	7,860

Note:
Figures show share of respective industries in total (manufacturing) factory numbers, and are rounded.
Source: Tsusansho (ed.) (respective years), *Kogyo tokei hyo* (Census of Manufactures).

belonged to these industries.[10] Their share is the highest in Tokyo: twice the average of 39 per cent in 1990, and two and a half times the national average of 32 per cent.

Within the machine industries, there has been a further concentration, in metal products and even more markedly in machinery and equipment, the latter rising from 17.7 per cent of the ward's factories in 1955 to 31.7 per cent in 1990 (37.4 per cent of one to three employee micro-factories). Roughly 27 per cent of Tokyo's – and 4 per cent of the nation's – machinery and equipment factories were located in Ota in 1990. The decline of vehicles and vehicle parts reflects the fact that most volume work has been relocated outside Tokyo, but in 1990 Ota still had one quarter of Tokyo's transportation equipment factories. Precision equipment also shows a decline, but some of these factories may have been reclassified as industry boundaries blurred. Ota is not a leading district for volume automobile part production and assembly, and other districts have become more specialised in electrical machinery and precision equipment, but some of the key parts and moulds for these industries are still made in Ota.

Ota's concentration in metal products and machinery and equipment is seen as a source of flexibility rather than of rigidity associated with, for example, Ota *City's* concentration in vehicle-related factories. It is linked to the growth of micro-factories; as workers set up on their own doing lathe, milling, grinding, etc., work, they were classified under general machinery

[10] Seki and Kato (1990, 31).

and equipment rather than under the industries their parts are machined for (which may have been a variety of industries, anyway). More specifically, they come under the subcategory of 'metal processing', which comprises one third of all machine and equipment factories. In turn, the growth of micro-factories has facilitated the emergence of another subcategory, 'industrial machine and equipment manufacture', under which a quarter of the industry's factories are grouped. Even very small factories with limited manufacturing capabilities can launch their own products by having much of the work machined – and designed – by factories around them. These tend to be customised machines for industrial use. It is not unusual for subcontractors to have developed machines for their own work, and then to have moved into the commercial manufacture of those machines (cf. F. Industries in the next section). In other words, the concentration has been in areas which have allowed for the progressive generation of new products:

In recent years in districts which have forged high level concentrations in the machine industries, such as Ome and Hachioji in the capital, the share of electrical machinery and precision equipment factories has risen (measuring instruments using electronics technology is especially high), but metal products and machinery and equipment have not kept up, and this often inhibits the spread of product development. In the case of Ota Ward, these two industries account for more than half the factories, and the proportion has increased. Combined with the remarkable development of electronics technology in recent years, this will enable even richer product development.[11]

Another critical feature of Ota's industry, according to these observers, is that *all* the processes needed to make machines are found within the ward, whereas there are gaps in the districts in western Tokyo (Ome, Hachioji, etc.), including materials, basic processes, basic parts, and plastic moulds. This is difficult to demonstrate under the standard industrial classification, so they developed an alternative according to processes the factories actually carry out, and grouped their survey respondents as shown in table 4.4.[12]

More than a third of the factories surveyed were engaged in machining. If makers of jigs, tools, precision diecasts, and moulds, which are essential for the machine industries, are added, the proportion rises to 44.5 per cent. A second staple for the machine industries is the basic processes, accounting for slightly less than one third of Ota's factories. Many of these are considered 'bad neighbours', and, while their numbers have been depleted in

---

[11] Seki and Kato (1990, 32).
[12] The survey was carried out in 1985, and covered all of Ota's factories. There were 3,575 responses (36.8 per cent), of which 3,029 (84.7 per cent) were in the machine industries. A 1994 survey using this classification but with a slightly lower response rate gave similar figures, except that only 7.4 per cent of factories were classified as product makers; Ota ku (1995a, 31).

Table 4.4 *Ota's industrial structure by process, 1985*

	Factories (%)	Employees (%)
Product makers	10.6	40.3
Heavy processes		
shearing, welding	2.8	1.9
sheet metal processing	9.2	5.0
press	8.1	6.0
casting	2.4	2.0
forging	0.6	1.1
heat treatment	0.5	0.4
painting	2.1	1.1
plating	2.9	3.7
subtotal	28.8	21.2
Machining		
machining	36.7	18.2
moulds, jigs	7.9	4.9
subtotal	44.5	23.0
Related processes		
plastic moulding	4.9	4.3
PCBs	0.1	0.5
piecework assembly	2.0	1.9
basic parts	2.3	1.5
raw materials	2.8	1.5
other	4.1	5.7
subtotal	16.2	15.4
Survey *N*	100 (3,029)	100 (48,229)

Note:
Basic parts include nuts, bolts, condensers, etc.
Source: Seki and Kato (1990) p. 115.

other parts of Tokyo, they have survived on Ota's reclaimed island sanctuaries. Ota has more than half of the capital's forgeries and a third of its casting factories. Third, there are a variety of related processes which are also essential to the machine industries, such as plastic moulding, basic parts, and printed circuit boards. Some of these do not need to be in immediate proximity, and only 16 per cent of Ota's factories carry out these processes, but those in Ota tend to be at the complex and high value added end of the spectrum, catering for prototypes and new rather than standard products, according to the authors.

This breadth and depth have facilitated the expansion of the final category: product makers, which comprised one tenth of the survey total but 40 per cent of employment. Machining factories averaged just 7.9 employees, and more than half had three employees or less. The average product maker, by contrast, had 36 employees. Nevertheless, it is worth noting that two thirds of product makers had fewer than 30 employees.

Table 4.4 categorises factories according to their *main* activity, but it does not tell us the *range* of activities they are engaged in, or the degree of specialisation. Another survey conducted in 1988 focused on factories with fewer than 30 employees. It used similar process categories, and showed that two thirds of the micro-factories (fewer than ten employees) carried out one process only, compared with one third of the 10–29 employee factories. An average of 90 per cent of turnover was in this core process, compared with 75 per cent for the larger factories. Thus there appears to be a high degree of specialisation, especially within the micro-factories, although just how specialised they were *within* the process categories was not made clear. The authors argued that the vast concentration of factories, high factor costs, and competition have led to a very high degree of specialisation and technological upgrading to support this specialisation.[13] In other words, Ota Ward is a highly 'flexible specialised' industrial district.

According to the same survey, however, such specialisation only provided a distinct competitive advantage for between 20 per cent and 30 per cent of the factories. Another more numerous type of factory provides the district with a different type of flexibility. This is the *nandemoya* (will do or machine anything), jobbing shop, or recently dubbed 'convenience factory'.[14] Two thirds of the micro-factories had five or less employees, were subcontractors, and reported no product or special technology, hinting at the extent of this type. They are particularly important in dealing with rush orders, overflow orders, and low volume but non-specialised work. The authors labelled them 'terminal factories' since they are at the end of subcontracting chains.

Disavowing a particular competitive advantage may of course reflect owners' modesty as much as anything, and many factories are in fact semi-specialised, or a mixture of specialist and *nandemoya*. Specialisation helps to reduce price-cutting competition and losing work to cheaper provincial centres, while retaining broader capacities is useful when downturns affect specialised work. Owners have been encouraged to specialise in recent years, but their instincts for survival often lead them to maintain backup

---

[13] Ota ku (1989, 13, 21). The survey covered just over 2,000 factories with a 49.4 per cent response rate.

[14] 'Convenience factory' is a play on 'convenience store', which is a mini-market situated conveniently, stocking convenient goods, and open at convenient hours.

capabilities. Owners may also call themselves *nandemoya* because they can make their own jigs and fixtures, or accept a difficult order for the challenge as well as for the possibility of new work. Many *nandemoya* therefore have high technical levels and specialised or semi-specialised skills.

T. Technology (six employees), for instance, does machining work to tolerances of three microns for a semi-conductor machine company in one workshop, and variety of milling and turning work in another. J. Precision does slotting work to 2.5 microns for the same semi-conductor machine maker in one factory (eight employees) and in another (four employees) does pre-finishing CNC work. The specialised work in both cases could only be done in two or three other factories in Japan, but the owners took on jobbing work as well. F. Metal (26 employees), to give a further example, specialises in white metal work, but also does other heat treatment, ingot manufacture, casting, post-casting rough machining, and recently even precision machining.[15]

These examples suggest the high degree of adaptability which has been required of Ota's factory owners, allowing them (a) to weather downturns, such as when their specialised line of business enters a slump, (b) to adapt to long-term changes in the economic environment – their sideline may become their main line of business over time – and (c) to develop their own proactive strategies, such as when jobbing is used to subsidise the development of a specialisation or a new product. The combination of flexibility and specialisation *within individual firms* (as well as across firms) has in turn endowed *the district* with a flexibility, durability, and adaptability, as well as an upgrading dynamic. It does not just result from specialised firms interacting flexibly. These characteristics are reinforced by other sources of flexibility as well, relating to the ownership and management of these factories (chapter 7).

Invisible roads of work

Ota's industry has been described as a 'spatial FMS' (flexible manufacturing system). How does work flow through this 'FMS'? The surveys mentioned in the previous section provide a fairly coherent picture, as follows. The larger the factory, the greater the number and geographical spread of its customers. The smaller the factory, the fewer the customers, and the more likely they are to be located within the ward (table 4.5). As far as *placing* orders goes, the trends are similar. The suppliers of larger factories are more numerous and distributed more widely; those of smaller factories are fewer and local (table 4.6). There is an asymmetry between placing and

---

[15] Interviews, August–September 1990.

Table 4.5 *Location of customers by factory size*

Size (empls.)	Ota	Shin. Meguro	Other Tokyo	Kawa-saki	Other Kanag.	Other Kanto	Outside Kanto	N	Av. no. of customers
1–3	52.2	8.8	11.9	8.2	12.7	4.3	1.9	1,074	6.2
4–9	34.6	8.3	17.1	8.3	8.9	10.2	12.6	935	16.0
10–19	28.0	6.9	19.4	7.1	10.6	11.3	16.7	352	27.1
20–29	15.6	6.1	24.2	5.8	8.3	10.9	29.2	194	64.1
30–49	11.3	5.4	23.8	6.6	11.3	20.2	21.4	112	76.1
50–99	6.9	6.0	23.6	4.3	8.4	14.2	36.7	82	91.0
100–299	2.5	2.1	32.9	4.3	13.4	20.0	24.8	28	230.6
300+	5.5	2.9	21.2	5.5	13.7	18.2	33.0	7	438.1
All	21.8	6.3	21.4	6.5	10.3	12.8	20.9	2,784	24.8

Note:
Shin.=Shinagawa; Kanag.=Kanagawa.
N=number of factories surveyed in each size category.
Source: Ota ku (ed.) (1986, 150).

receiving orders, however. In all size categories customers are more geo-graphically dispersed than suppliers. The asymmetry is most pronounced in the largest factories. One third of their customers are outside the Kanto region, but less than a fifth of their suppliers. Conversely, only 5.5 per cent of their customers came from within Ota Ward, but 20.7 per cent of their suppliers. Small factories tend both to receive and place orders locally, but they, too, place more orders locally than they receive. (This applies to both volume of orders and the number of customers and suppliers.)

Given that they are larger, it is not surprising that product makers' customers are widely dispersed – more than a third come from outside Kanto, and a mere 3.9 per cent are located within Ota. A third of their suppliers come from within Ota, however, and just 10.7 per cent from outside the Kanto region. Factories doing machining work are smaller, but even here, one in eight of their customers come from outside the Kanto region. More than a third come from within Ota, however, and almost 60 per cent of their suppliers. Many of the basic processes likewise tend to have both local customers and suppliers, with more local suppliers than custom-ers. In brief, the larger factories, often product makers, operate on a national or international scale. Many in fact belong to companies which have factories outside the district, and receive orders from, and place orders with, these. Activities like piecework assembly are done almost entirely outside the district. The larger factories rely on smaller local factories,

Table 4.6 *Location of suppliers by factory size*

Size (empls.)	Ota	Shin. Meguro	Other Tokyo	Kawa-saki	Other Kanag.	Other Kanto	Outside Kanto	N	Av. no. of suppliers
1–3	69.0	8.1	9.0	5.9	4.9	1.9	1.1	551	4.6
4–9	61.2	7.5	11.4	6.7	5.5	5.1	2.6	718	8.5
10–19	50.5	9.0	14.4	8.0	8.1	6.5	3.5	319	15.4
20–29	50.2	10.2	13.0	8.4	5.8	7.4	4.9	176	22.7
30–49	37.2	9.2	15.7	9.6	10.0	13.9	4.4	110	22.3
50–99	33.0	8.4	23.6	7.3	6.1	11.4	10.3	82	41.6
100–299	26.6	7.9	22.1	7.3	9.6	14.0	12.6	29	57.1
300+	20.7	9.7	16.4	6.5	15.8	12.5	18.5	10	132.5
All	48.2	8.7	14.9	7.5	7.2	7.9	5.6	2,002	13.2

Sources and notes: As for table 4.5; av. no.=average number for those which have suppliers/subcontractors.

though, for a substantial portion of their subcontracting, while small factories, which are often engaged in machining, are embedded locally both with respect to receiving and placing orders.[16]

The following examples illustrate the role played by Ota's 'new key' product makers, and the importance of local subcontractors to them. F Industries had 75 employees in 1990. The founder started out after the war machining parts for vehicle makers Mitsubishi and Isuzu. In the mid 1950s, based on his own experimentation and improvisation, he decided to launch a product – a machine for making those parts. He gradually reduced his subcontract machining and became a full-time manufacturer of customised machine tools for vehicle makers nationwide, with exports to Korea as well. Taking orders from these companies, in 1990 F. Industries subcontracted out work to about 100 factories, three quarters of which were located in Ota.

S. Machines had only 12 employees in 1990. It was founded by a draughtsman who moved to Tokyo after the war, worked for Ota-based machine tool maker Mitsui Seiki, then a smaller company before becoming independent in 1958 at the age of 42. His first work was designing pipe benders and oil seal testers, and having them made by other small factories. From the third year he started to design press-related machines, bringing critical machining work in house when he could hire some craftsmen. He now gets orders from major press makers around the country, and sub-

[16] Seki and Kato (1990, 180–210).

contracts out work to 15 regular subcontractors – 10 in Ota and the rest in Kanagawa – as well as another 60 he calls on occasionally, most of them local.

S. Ltd, with 100 employees in 1990, started out as a tool trading company before the war, and after the war took on some machining work for its biggest customer. In 1957, also at the customer's request, it made a machine for an assembly line. It has since grown into one of Japan's top three firms in automated assembly line equipment, receiving many orders for large firms' overseas transplants. From a small number of subcontractors each with around ten employees, it now has a large network of subcontractors (some of them further subcontract work), the largest with 30–50 employees, mostly located in south Tokyo.[17]

The 1988 survey, once again, focuses on smaller factories, contrasting micro-factories with factories with 10–29 employees. Customers of the latter were much more dispersed and larger, normally product makers. Two thirds of the top three customers were not local (from Ota, Shinagawa, Meguro, or Kawasaki), and three quarters had more than 100 employees. Two thirds of their orders were described as regular, although this proportion was lower for product and mould makers. By contrast, the customers of micro-factories were closer and smaller. Two thirds of the top three customers were local, and only one quarter had more than 100 employees. Fewer customers were product makers. The majority were factories involved in the *same process*, and almost half provided irregular or spot orders.

As for *placing* of orders, the larger group subcontracted out a quarter of their turnover to an average of 14 companies. Three quarters placed orders for special work which complemented their own processes, but 70 per cent also placed orders for the same work as their own (overflow work or work involving several processes, including their own speciality). Almost one fifth – mostly assemblers or product 'makers' with little or no in-house manufacturing capability – farmed out all work except the final function they performed, whereas only 10 per cent did not subcontract work out. By contrast, 40 per cent of the micro-factories did not subcontract work out, and those that did had an average of only four subcontractors, but it also comprised a quarter of their turnover. Much of the work was complementary, but there was overflow work as well. For both groups the majority of work was described as a 'wide variety of small batches' (*tahinshu shoryo*).[18]

---

[17] Interviews, August–September 1990. S. Ltd had also established two branch factories in Kanagawa to do high volume work, and a sister company in the founder's hometown in Gifu which assembled car radios.   [18] Ota ku (1989, 14–18, 27–33).

This survey shows that work coming into the ward filters downwards *and sideways*. The smaller factories rely on the larger factories, particularly for regular orders, but also place a lot of orders with each other, both supplementary to their own specialities, and overflow work. This is called *nakama torihiki*, or confrere trading. Micro-factories, therefore, are not necessarily 'terminal' factories, and the commonly held view of strictly hierarchical (in terms of size) subcontracting chains only partially reflects the flow of work in Ota. This view is partial in other respects, too. First, a quarter of the micro-factories had direct links with factories with more than 100 employees. It is not unusual for Ota's micro-factories with specialist technology to have direct links with giant firms, although more commonly there are 'cushions' in between. Second, small factories sometimes take in more work than they can handle, not just in terms of volume, but in terms of processes, knowing that it can be done with the cooperation of other factories nearby. This contributes to the lateral flow of work. Third, merchants or brokers still play a role in introducing work to micro-factories, as we saw with the former Tokimec lathe operator who liked to sleep in. They can have far more extensive networks of customers than small owners struggling to make ends meet can hope to cultivate. A survey from the late 1970s suggested that for micro-factories with one to three employees, they play almost as important a role as personal acquaintances in securing orders.[19] Sometimes they provide capital assistance, but more often their role is limited to placing orders and information provision.

As a 'spatial FMS', Ota Ward is quite distinct from the industrial districts of Ota and Ueda Cities. Large factories have been important, but no single factory has had a dominant role. Like Ueda (and Sakaki) orders are brought in from far and wide by many of the factories. There are also small- to medium-sized product makers (called 'new key' makers above, since they have emerged in the past 20–30 years, and have been critical in making up for work lost through factory relocations), but in Ota Ward they produce in far smaller volume, and rely to a far greater extent on the local subcontracting base, giving a high density of interfirm linkages. High land and labour costs have contributed to these differences, but the enormous base of specialist and generalist *machi koba* is also critical. These small factories and workshops carry out a substantial amount of trade with each other.

---

[19] Chiiki shinko seibi kodan (1978, 110–12).

Locational demerits and hollowing out

In 1986, industrialists in Ota Ward issued a 'National Technopolis Declaration':

In order to maintain and develop our outstanding industrial concentration based particularly on SMEs, and make Ota Ward the leading-edge industrial district of the next generation, we industrialists of Ota Ward declare the following:

1 We shall further upgrade our industrial concentration and promote networking, product development, and prototype-responsive companies, establishing a pivotal position in our country's industry.
2 Using our proximity to Haneda International Airport, we will aim to become a world-class leading industrial district.
3 We will promote congruity between industry and housing, becoming a model district for the co-existence of housing, industry, and commerce unparalleled in the world.

The declaration was more than chest-beating, or an attempt to create a distinctive image for business reasons. It was a product of concern that the vitality of the district was being undermined, and a plea for greater understanding on the part of policy makers and residents. The number of factories had begun to decline, and the indications were that this trend would accelerate. The reasons are complex; here we will focus on locational *demerits,* which have come to weigh heavily on individual firms, counterbalancing the merits of being located in an advanced industrial district.

The first major demerit is the mixture of factories and residential housing. There always has been a mixture, and, if most residents work in the factories, the potential for conflict is minimised. Indeed, it can be a great asset, since it helps to nurture an industrial community. But there were also local farmers and fishermen before industry became established, and, as Ota became part of inner Tokyo, the proportion of residents working elsewhere also rose. Indeed, as land and apartment prices soared, factory workers and their families were virtually priced out of the local housing market.

As we saw, complaints about noise, smell, vibrations, and pollution were voiced as early as the 1930s. Such complaints increased in proportion to economic recovery in the postwar period. The official response to pollution and congestion was to encourage the separation of industry and housing, and to place restrictions on industry. From the late 1960s, smaller factories which caused pollution were encouraged to move to three reclaimed islands which were set aside for exclusive industrial use. By 1990 these islands were home to 250 factories. These relocations and other anti-pollution measures resulted in a decline of complaints lodged with the ward authorities, and secured a future for the factories within the ward. But pressure on factories remaining in the original neighbourhoods increased, since the vacated land could not be re-used for factories, and was often used for housing. The factories that moved were the more dynamic ones; many small firms were not able to, despite favourable loans. Thus the vulnerable were made even more vulnerable.

Large factory relocations out of the district also left plots of land which generated conflict. Even when the land was in an industrial zone, there was pressure from local residents for more park and recreation space, and other amenities. Figure 4.2 shows the dramatic change in the once heavily factoried Higashi Kojiya near Haneda Airport between 1964 and 1985. Much of the area still coloured black comes under the only exclusive industrial zone apart from the reclaimed islands, but even within this zone, large white patches have appeared.

By the late 1970s fears were beginning to be expressed about the long-term viability of remaining industry, given that many of the larger and more active factories had moved, and housing 'encroachment' was becoming more and more visible. Policy emphasis began to shift from separating housing and industry to 'harmonising' the two. One means has been the building of 'factory apartments'. The first of these, consisting of ten factories on the ground floor with seven stories of apartments above, was completed in 1985. In addition, a private venture arising from discussions between the Tokyu Corporation and the Kowakai (a local industrialist's association) resulted in a complex of housing, leisure facilities, and some 25 small factory units in a separate building. The Kowakai has been very active in pushing for the western part of the ward to be designated a 'model district' of factory and housing harmony. Its plan features an 'urban industrial park' with rental factories, conference, and leisure facilities, etc. An initiative is also under way to provide temporary factory space for owners while their aging factories are rebuilt.

Such efforts have been relatively small in scale and have not solved the basic problem. Rocketing land prices in the second half of the 1980s exacerbated it. Fishermen who had built rental factories in the 1960s were encouraged by developers to sell or convert their property to new apartment buildings. Some landlords were also said to be exploiting tenant vulnerability to extract higher rents and one-off fees and rents when contracts were renegotiated.[20] The smallest factory owners, again, were most vulnerable. They were the most likely to rent factories, which were disappearing, and least able to buy property, prices for which were soaring. Those who owned their own land and factories were in a much better position, since soaring land prices provided collateral to secure loans to invest

[20] Cf. Jichi roren (1993).

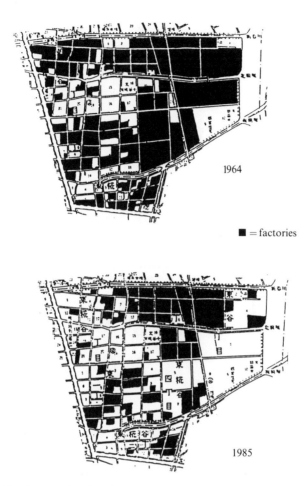

1964

■ = factories

1985

Figure 4.2 Disappearing factories in Higashi Kojiya
Source: Ota ku (1986, 238).

in new plant and equipment, but it also tempted some to sell up or convert their property, again increasing pressure on those remaining.[21]

Table 4.7 gives an indication of the location-related problems faced by owners in the mid 1980s. Almost a third of those surveyed expressed a desire to move, mostly within the ward, but sometimes outside it. Many are torn between the industrial district and community merits, and locational demerits. Locational problems contributed to a decline in factory

---

[21] Cf. Inagami (1989a, 148).

Table 4.7 *Ota factories' problems with current location*

Size (employees)	Aging plant	Cramped	Expansion difficulties	'Parent' relocation	Rented premises	Residential neighbours	Pollution complaints	Roads, transport	Land use/ zoning	No particular problem
1–3	25.9	43.7	25.2	3.9	33.8	20.0	16.0	8.1	3.8	22.9
4–9	27.9	50.1	33.3	4.0	25.9	22.2	16.8	7.3	6.6	17.0
10–19	32.5	49.1	35.5	3.8	19.0	29.8	15.7	7.9	8.4	14.6
20–29	26.7	49.2	29.8	4.2	15.2	22.0	11.0	9.9	7.9	22.5
30–49	23.5	46.2	34.5	1.7	7.6	28.6	12.6	9.2	14.3	21.8
50–99	27.7	41.5	34.0		3.2	25.5	13.8	11.7	19.1	24.5
100–299	20.6	52.9	17.6	2.9	8.8	20.6	11.8	5.9	14.7	26.5
300+	11.8	35.3	23.5		5.9	29.4	5.9	11.8	23.5	35.3
All	27.2	46.9	30.0	3.6	25.2	22.7	15.5	8.1	6.8	19.9

Note:
The figures are percentages, with multiple answers.
Source: Ota ku (ed.) (1986, 279).

numbers of 22 per cent between 1983 and 1993. This decline affected most size bands. The decline in larger factories is attributable to continued relocations and branch factory establishment, shrinkage, and in some cases conversion to apartment housing, since larger plots of land are more attractive to developers than the tiny plots of micro-factories. The decline in micro-factories is attributable to location problems compounded by other problems, such as loss of business, postwar founders retiring without a successor, and the dearth of new startups (see chapters 5 and 7). But for existing businesses expanding into vacated premises during this time, the decline of micro-factory numbers would be even more pronounced. These problems combine to cast a shadow over Ota's position as a 'national technopolis'. A sober assessment in 1995 concluded that its distinctive strengths are being eroded by factory closures, succession problems, retirement of skilled workers, and partial replacement of skills by new technology which can be used equally well in other – cheaper – industrial districts.[22]

'Hollowing out' became a buzzword in Japan in the 1990s. One type was discussed in chapter 3 – the relocation of production overseas by larger factories. There are other hollowing out scenarios, however, including at least two variants of 'hollowing out from below'. First, the number of micro-factories is rapidly decreasing. Many are livelihood businesses, and *nandemoya*, or jobbing shops. Their closure will gradually affect the district's flexibility, although it will be a slow process since there are a lot of them. Second, the basic process base is vulnerable. Although they found a haven on the reclaimed islands, their work is considered '3K' (*kiken* dangerous, *kitsui* demanding, *kitanai* dirty), and they find it very difficult to attract and retain young workers. Average employee ages are very high, and many skilled workers are nearing retirement. There has been a conspicuous lack of employees starting out on their own, and successor problems, hence a lack of rejuvenation. This hollowing out is linked to the hollowing out of critical process skills.[23] To a lesser extent, the same may be said of machining. The spectre is looming, then, of thin patches if not holes appearing in Ota's industrial structure, which may compromise its role as a 'spatial FMS'. Some see these as a manifestation of an even more fundamental hollowing out, namely of the productionist spirit or tradition. Minimising locational demerits and bringing about a rejuvenation are as important as keeping ahead of economic and technological change. In fact, they are closely linked. This is well recognised in Ota's new 'Industrial Vision', which calls on the ward to become a '*global* technopolis' by becoming more outward looking and open. At the same time, it must become inwardly

---

[22] Ota ku (1995a).   [23] Ukai (1990, 1992); Tokyoto shoko shidojo (1993).

attractive, and foster a modern, progressive image of manufacturing if it is to become an incubator of industry for the twenty first century.[24] In the meantime, factory numbers will most probably dip under 5,000 by the turn of the century.

---

[24] Ota ku sangyo bijion iinkai (1995). The committee which produced the Vision was chaired by Nakamura Hideichiro, author of the LME theory, discussed in chapter 2.

5   Interfirm relations 1: 'vertical'

Subcontracting is widely seen as a key to the success of Japan's machine industries, and has attracted great interest in recent years. The focus of this attention has been on relationships between major assemblers and their first tier suppliers in the automobile and consumer electronics industries. Moving down into the second and third tiers, and out into other industries, the picture is murkier. Subcontractors, moreover, tend to be approached through their 'parent' assemblers, compounding the potential for partiality, and reinforcing the view of small firms as appendages of large firms. To avoid these biases I decided to look at small firms in the context of industrial districts, and subcontracting from the perspective of small firms (even at the risk of introducing a new bias – Ota Ward is a distinctive industrial district, with greater flexibility in interfirm relationships than in many other districts).

In the small-firm-as-appendage view a major reason for so many small firms in Japan is that large firms have a use for them. In the past this use was seen as exploitative. Large firms externalised labour and product market uncertainties on to small firms, using them as 'shock absorbers', enabling their own employees to enjoy the benefits of higher wages and secure employment under 'Japanese style employment'. The lower wages of subcontractors helped them to compete successfully on world markets. They could have their cake and eat it because they could force compliance on subcontractors without having to bear the costs.

Objections to this view and the Marxist approach which informs it mounted. Large firm strategies have necessitated *willing* compliance from their subcontractors, it was pointed out, which means cost and risk sharing. Cooperation instead of exploitation has been the key characteristic. The greater responsibility assumed by subcontractors – in product development, for instance – means that dependence was mutual. It all adds up to a rational way of producing things.

There is a danger of the pendulum swinging too far, with subcontracting idealised, and small firms still left out of the picture. It is true that over half of manufacturing SMEs are subcontractors (over 40 per cent are not), but the appendage view might be turned on its head, with some historical justification. In other words, the reason subcontracting is so prevalent in Japan might be because of the existence of so many small firms. A chicken and egg situation, perhaps, but it does bring home the point that small firms are not simply pliable objects of large firms.

This chapter begins with an overview of subcontracting, then looks at subcontracting from the perspective of small owners in Ota, how they establish and maintain subcontracting relations, the degree of symmetry or equality, and what happens when conflict arises. It considers recent changes brought about by socioeconomic developments and competitive pressures. The changes are not simply a move towards spot markets. They also result in the exit by many small firms from volume or mass production networks and in the attempt to join or create what have been called 'skill concentration' networks.

Subcontracting in Japan: an overview[1]

Around 56 per cent of manufacturing SMEs derive some income from subcontracting in Japan. The small-firm-as-appendage view is understandable in a way because the proportion is much higher in industries commonly studied, such as textiles and machines. In electrical machinery and transportation equipment around 80 per cent of SMEs subcontract. The smaller the firm, the more likely it is to engage in subcontracting, and the higher the proportion of its income it derives from this. The smaller the firm, too, the more reliant it is on a smaller number of customers. One third of SMEs obtain subcontracting orders from a single customer; for micro-factories with one to three employees the figure is almost a half (table 5.1).[2]

This points to an interfirm division of labour in Japanese manufacturing in which a high proportion of final turnover is accounted for by intermediate inputs. In electrical machinery and transportation equipment this proportion rises neatly with establishment size, suggesting smaller subcontractors feeding larger contractors or subcontractors which ultimately feed product makers or assemblers. By contrast, in industries such as food and chemicals, the proportion of intermediate inputs declines with

---

[1] Subcontracting here means the manufacture or repair of materials, parts, or products according to the customer's specifications or with the customer's brand, with the assumption that the subcontractor is smaller than the customer. This is similar to its use in Japan's subcontracting laws.

[2] The figures are somewhat dated, but are the most comprehensive available.

Table 5.1 *Subcontracting in Japan (1987, manufacturing and machine industries)*

Firm size/industry	Proportion which do subcontracting	Of which, proportion of turnover from subcontracting	And average number of 'parents'	And percentage reliant on a single parent for 70% or more of subcontracting
Manuf. av.	55.8%	74.3%	5	52.4%
1–9	58.3	88.5	4	54.9
10–29	48.3	79.6	7	39.8
30–99	47.5	76.9	10	41.9
100–299	44.7	75.5	14	43.5
300–999	34.0	72.7	20	44.7
1,000+	17.8	59.5	27	36.2
Metal products	71.0	80.7	6	41.3
Machinery and equipment	74.8	80.6	5	44.6
Electrical machinery	80.1	87.0	4	57.9
Transportation equipment	79.9	90.0	4	55.2
Precision equipment	70.4	83.7	4	54.6

Source: Calculated from Chusho kigyo cho (ed.) (1990e), *Dai nana kai kogyo jittai kihon chosa hokokusho* (Report on 7th Industry Conditions Basic Survey), Tokyo: Tsusan tokei kyokai, pp. 158–9, 166–9. (Manufacturing *N*=679,662 companies.)

increasing establishment size (as it did in the machine industries in the early part of this century).[3]

A survey in 1991 by the SME Agency asked why customers contract or subcontract work out. The main responses were: first to reduce costs (47.1 per cent), to make use of the subcontractor's specialist technology (42.2 per cent), to enable flexible response to fluctuations in demand (30.6 per cent), out sourcing of small lot or low volume processes (17.1 per cent), and preventing a decline in organisational efficiency which would accompany expansion of capacity (12.5 per cent; multiple answers). Asked why they accept subcontract work, suppliers cited stability in work volume (58.7 per cent), difficulties in developing own products (25.3 per cent), difficulties in marketing or gaining new orders (20.4 per cent), limitations in product design ability (19.1 per cent), and little fear of bad debts (13.5 per cent).

The stability in work volume response is noteworthy, and leads to the next point; in addition to a limited number of transaction partners, relationships tend to be long term. According to a survey in the mid 1980s, two thirds of subcontractors had never changed their 'parent', and over half had been doing business with their main 'parent' for at least 15 years.[4] In the above SME Agency survey, 97 per cent of relationships exceeded five years. The main reasons for long-term relationships cited by 'parents' were trust (83.6 per cent), stability of supply (50.8 per cent), subcontractors' specialist technology (38.9 per cent), quality (32.8 per cent), and cheapness (27.7 per cent).[5] A further feature is legal informality. Surveys in Tokyo show that less than two thirds of subcontractors have basic contracts – which tend not to be particularly detailed in any case – with customer companies, and the figure is lower for smaller subcontractors (table 5.2). Over a third of subcontractors say they accept orders without any prior form of agreement, the overwhelming reason given being long-term trading relationships.

Subcontracting is now seen to offer significant competitive advantages, whereas once it was considered a sign of industrial backwardness. First, it results in an efficient *division of labour*:

The division of labour in Japan made possible the enormous expansion of volume in the process-assembly industries during the high growth period, and contributed to the maintenance of economic vitality during the stable growth period through outstanding efficiency. In this division of labour the myriads of processes are handled by different companies which are linked according to the flow of work.

---

[3] Chusho kigyo cho (ed.) (1992a, 84–6).

[4] 'Parent' company is used in the Japanese sense here, indicating a major customer, often without ownership or personnel ties.

[5] Whether this meant all subcontracting relationships, or just main relationships, was not clear. Chusho kigyo cho (ed.) (1992a, 87); Chusho kigyo cho (ed.) (1988a, 60–1).

Table 5.2 *Extent of contracts reported by Tokyo subcontractors*

	N	Proportion with basic contract	Order form (formal)	Order slip	Verbal understanding	Scrap of paper	No prior agreement	Because			
								of long-term trading	difficult to ask customer	no opportunity to arrange one	risk losing work
Metal products	1,052	32.6	52.9	28.6	12.5	5.2	38.2	89.6	7.2	3.7	4.0
Machinery & equipment	407	29.5	54.1	26.8	12.3	5.7	33.4	87.5	2.9	5.2	2.2
Electrical machinery	543	58.4	69.6	35.4	8.1	3.5	19.7	87.9	5.6	3.7	3.7
Transportation equipment	134	61.9	65.7	49.3	13.4	5.2	23.9	93.8	–	–	–
Precision equipment	502	45.2	62.2	33.5	13.7	4.8	25.1	86.5	8.7	4.8	2.4
Survey	3,697	39.1	55.3	30.3	11.9	4.7	32.8	89.0	5.4	3.7	3.2

Note:
Other industries surveyed were ferrous and non-ferrous metals, and textiles.
Source: Tokyo chusho kigyo shinko kosha (1993), *Heisei 4 nendo shitauke torihiki joken to jittai chosa hokokusho* (Survey report on subcontracting conditions in fiscal 1992).

Each company devotes its energies to its process, appropriate scales for each process are realised, and this makes for an extremely efficient production structure overall.[6]

Second, the subcontracting *process* or relationship is seen as efficient. From the transaction cost perspective, savings are made in search and negotiation costs. And as game theory would show, since the relationship is ongoing, there is a built-in propensity to cooperate, and books need not be balanced with each transaction. Relationship-specific investments which offer long-term advantages are encouraged without the fear that asset specificity will be used against the investor. Further, what is lost in terms of spot market allocative efficiency is more than compensated for by 'X-efficiency' or by the benefits of 'goodwill'.[7] Subcontracting relations have been a vehicle for technology transfer, at least in the past. Although somewhat dated, a survey in 1984 suggested that 45.1 per cent of SME subcontractors introducing new technology received technical assistance from their 'parent', 37.7 per cent received information, 28 per cent were loaned or leased equipment, 24.2 per cent received training for their employees, and 14.1 per cent received financial assistance.[8]

Cooperation is flavoured with competition, however, and pressure to perform. Failure to do so results in penalties, and ultimately a demotion in subcontracting status, jeopardising orders. The fact that such a high proportion of assembler turnover comes from intermediate inputs almost guarantees that the relationship will be stressful. If the assembler wants to become more competitive, it must seek performance improvements from its subcontractors. It is a different kind of stress, however, from the uncertainty of spot-market relationships.

The line between cooperation and coercion may be a fine one in such circumstances. Assemblers do depend on their subcontractors, but the degree of dependence in the relationship is seldom symmetrical. Assemblers which act in arbitrary and unfair ways may suffer from damaged reputations and jeopardise future cooperation from their subcontractors, but not to the extent which some have claimed. Some major assemblers have a bad reputation in Ota for beating down prices, imposing conditions or terminating orders 'unfairly', but still get a lot of work done in the ward. Small subcontractors are seldom totally indispensable, but they may not be able to change their 'parent' easily.

To those who would emphasise coercion over cooperation, hence exploitation, the following rebuttal is often made: 'Comparing industries

---

[6] Chusho kigyo cho (ed.) (1992a, 89).   [7] Leibenstein (1966); Dore (1983b).

[8] Chusho kigyo cho (ed.) (1985a). These were probably not very small subcontractors. Over three quarters said they introduced the technology to raise their own levels, but 40 per cent were urged to do so by their 'parent'.

with high proportions of SME subcontractors and those with low proportions, we find that in the latter case sales profits rise with increasing firm size, whilst in the former there is little change according to firm size. Thus we can see that in industries where the division of labour is spread wide, the profits are also dispersed more evenly.' Norms about cost and risk sharing do exist, and sometimes in the case of assemblers and large subcontractors, they are formalised.[9] The more demanding the assembler, too, the greater the ultimate benefits of cooperation, in terms of improved management and technical capabilities, and of reputation, which may be called upon should diversification become necessary. The order, cleanliness, and efficiency of Toyota suppliers is legendary, and these suppliers have been the main beneficiaries of increased inter-*keiretsu* trading in recent years.

On the other hand, there is another dynamic related to stressful relationships, more common amongst small subcontractors hence not widely noted. Here in response to 'parental' pressure, subcontractors upgrade their technical levels, diversify order sources, and sometimes stop subcontracting by launching their own product. Two examples from south Tokyo are fairly typical. S. Electronics (20 employees) did PCB mounting work for a major electronics company, but constantly had its prices pushed down. In an effort to make ends meet, the founder developed a new machine to do some of the work, and this machine ultimately enabled him to realise his dream of quitting subcontracting and marketing a product under his own brand name. M. Precision (nine employees) machined parts for major consumer electronics companies in the 1970s, also had its rate cut frequently, and was unable to pass on rising material costs. The owners decided they had had enough of being 'rats on a treadmill', severed ties with these companies and moved into higher value added work for new key companies like S. Ltd (mentioned in the last chapter). The large firm appendage perspective would see such firms as unable to keep up with parent company demands, and falling by the wayside. For the small firm owners, it was a rational decision, and a matter of principle. The survival of many small firms in Japan at the moment depends on making this transition.

Visible roads of work

The last chapter described how orders come into Ota Ward from throughout Japan and overseas, filtering downwards and outwards. They do this in various ways, sometimes through intermediaries – brokers or 'cushions' – and sometimes directly; sometimes they come 'cold' through telephone

---

[9] Chusho kigyo cho (ed.) (1985a); Miwa (1994). Profit distribution has been cited against the monopoly capital/ exploitation theories since the early 1960s, though technically the two are not incompatible.

directories, subcontracting association advertisements, or even the on-line O-Net, but more often through established links. In this sense, the 'paths of work' are visible, not invisible, and their paving is quite intricate. This may be seen both in the building up and in the maintenance of relationships. Let us look at the building up of relationships first.

When M. Precision severed links with its major customer, the owner was able to find new work with S. Ltd because his wife was a former employee there, and he had a friend there. T. Technology (specialist + *nandemoya* introduced in the last chapter) was also having trouble with its 'parent' company, and the owner was introduced by his cousin to a new semi-conductor machine maker wanting specialist work done. F. Manufacturing (mould maker, six employees) was introduced to a major electrical contractor by a friend. The contractor's work required secrecy, and the common hometown of the owner and purchasing manager further helped to establish the trust necessary for the initial order to be placed. Wife, cousin, and friend were not just neutral conveyors of information, but were known and trusted by the parties concerned. They had a (non-financial) stake in a successful outcome which helped to smooth over any initial barriers. Another way in which subcontracting relationships are established is when workers become independent and do work for their former companies, or have work introduced by them. One survey showed that more than a quarter of subcontractors do work for their former employer, and another 15 per cent have had customers introduced by them.[10] The personal relationship is already established, and the parties are well known to each other.

Likewise, in the majority of cases, work is introduced through or to known parties. This reduces uncertainty and search costs, and, to use Sako's terminology, helps to determine competence, and establish goodwill and contractual trust.[11] Competence and contractual trust are important requirements; goodwill above and beyond contractual obligations helps to cement the relationship. Nonetheless, subcontracting relations tend to be established gradually, with more orders placed as the relationship is established. As the owner of F. Manufacturing commented, this requires a distinctive ('soft') 'technology', which in addition to trust building includes the twice-yearly giving of gifts – being able to calculate how much to spend on them and who to give them to – golf and social gatherings, and so on. In his case, it included lending his jeep to one of the contractor's managers.

It is worth looking at F. Manufacturing in more detail. The company was founded in 1952, and initially made moulds for biscuits and cakes before moving into autopart and electrical component moulds. In 1963 it

---

[10] Chusho kigyo cho (ed.) (1990a, 123). An earlier survey of Ota industry gave similar figures – Chiiki shinko seibi kodan (1978, 128).   [11] Sako (1992, 37–40).

was introduced to the contractor, which was looking for someone to make thin moulds for a new type of circuit board. The owner gave a competitive quote, and his relationship with the contractor's purchasing manager – they came from the same town in Hokkaido – helped to secure the initial order. Within F. Manufacturing, though, there was a debate. The work was awkward, it required new tools and equipment, and would tie the company up when other work was plentiful. The owner accepted the order on the condition of cash payment, in order to purchase the necessary machinery.

The companies have been doing business ever since, and a deepening of the relationship meant that F. Manufacturing became dependent for 100 per cent of its orders from the contractor, through which its moulds find their way into almost every major vehicle and electrical manufacturer in Japan. The relationship was cemented with good social relations as well as good quality moulds. The owner's son became friends with a former purchasing manager who was promoted within the company. This friendship was at the same time a strategic investment. In the mid 1980s the contractor established a factory in Thailand, and asked F. Manufacturing to train three Thai workers (not employees) with the object of transferring the mould technology to Thailand. This posed an obvious threat to F. Manufacturing, but it was obliged to cooperate. The son appealed to his friend to compensate them for any lost business, and was introduced to harness work from an affiliated company. (Some of the mould work was later brought back from Thailand, because delivery dates and defect reduction targets were not being met.) Without the long-term relationship *and* this close tie, it is doubtful whether he would have got the new work.

A similar company, C. Manufacturing (13 employees), was not so lucky. It was founded in 1953 and made moulds for plastic toys and then for electrical goods. Its relationship with a major assembler started in 1970, and expanded with work for video cameras. In 1980, 20 per cent of work came from this customer, but by 1986 the proportion had risen to 70 per cent. C. Manufacturing was in the process of filling a major new order when a rival assembler came out with a radically different video camera. A strategic decision was made within the first assembler's group to switch to this new type, and to consolidate production. The assembler would cease to assemble video cameras. 'It happened so quickly. We'd done two months design work on the new model, and we were compensated for that, but the order was cancelled. I guess some companies – in the supplier's association – might have been compensated for future losses, but not us. I had good relations with the general manager, but even they didn't help when I tried to get new work. We were left high and dry. It would never have happened at H. [rival group].' The outcome was a sudden drop of over half the company's turnover, and a vow never again to become dependent on a single customer for more than 25 per cent of orders.

These two examples point to the complexity of 'interfirm relations'. Legally, and in a number of important respects, the relations are indeed *'interfirm'* relations. But in a practical sense, the two small firms were subcontracting for a particular *factory*, and if that work dried up, they would not necessarily be introduced to work from another factory in the same company, which would have its own set of long-term relations and prior obligations. Furthermore, *interpersonal* relations can be critical. The owners know it is prudent to maintain relations beyond the customer factory's current purchasing personnel, and to watch personnel developments within the customer's company carefully. If F. Manufacturing's owner had simply asked the incumbent purchasing manager to introduce new work, he would probably have got none. Luckily his key contact had been promoted high enough to use his influence in an affiliated company. However, even a general manager-level contact was insufficient in the case of C. Manufacturing. Some large assemblers have a reputation of being 'dry' or brutal (unmoved by particularistic considerations, forgetful of past relations).

Normally, a mental ledger of obligational debt and goodwill credit is built up and is known to certain personnel within the customer's company. The owner of K. Grinding (ten employees), for instance, recalled a visit by a purchasing manager from a consumer electronics major who obviously had cost-cutting targets to meet. 'I almost had a fight. He was asking me to do a low volume pin gauge for ¥1,000 when a standard volume gauge costs ¥1,300. I told him he had to be joking. He asked me to put this one on his bill.' By accepting the order, K. Grinding's owner was creating goodwill credit for future use. The purchasing manager would meet his targets within the company, and he [or his successor] would try to repay the obligational debt at a later date.

The purchasing manager had visited K. Grinding with a 'cushion' – in this case a broker intermediary. The broker was well connected, and had introduced work from several divisions of the same company. Small factory owners may be happy to have such people take a slice of the subcontracting rate in return for providing the 'soft' technology input. Intermediaries often have more time for this, have a wider range of contacts, and hence may be able to provide work more consistently and under better conditions. The intermediary can watch for emerging market trends and technological shifts in a way that the small firm owner, tied to his machines for much of the day, cannot. This is the advantage of the broker. First, second, or third tier suppliers act as intermediaries or 'cushions' as well, of course, sometimes with beneficial and sometimes with detrimental consequences, as the following example suggests.

C. Manufacturing also makes moulds for camera makers. It either gets orders directly from the maker (assembler) and delivers their moulds to the company which will actually use them (the 'moulder'), or the moulder acts as the intermediary. 'We get both types of orders. Ideally, we would like to be under a strong moulder, which can provide a powerful wall on prices and delivery. By strong I don't mean big – 100 employees is enough – but with specialised skills and not in a *keiretsu*. But if the moulder isn't strong, we prefer a direct relationship. Nothing is ever 100 per cent the first time. Something has to be changed. Most makers know this, and will pay for modifications after the first trial – they even put that in writing. It's in the modifications that you make a profit, but if you get a weak moulder in between they'll say they can't ask the parent for that, and you have a Japanese-style wishy-washy situation. If you have a direct relationship, too, nothing gets creamed off in the middle.'

Thus, subcontracting is a complex socioeconomic relation involving 'hard' as well as 'soft' technological competence. Mastery of the latter may be construed by some as self-interested, profit-maximising behaviour, but it must be understood in terms of the social embeddedness of sub-contracting in Japan. This does not mean that all suppliers, domestic and foreign, are bound by a rigid set of practices that they must observe in order to get work. Different expectations are built into different relationships. In terms of analysing these relationships, size is an important variable – relations between large companies become routinised and bureaucratic, while amongst smaller firms, personal relations tend to play a larger part, and obligational debts and goodwill credit remain subjective evaluations. The nature of the work is important – low volume versus high volume, high precision versus low precision, continuous versus one-off work – as well as the nature of the market – stable versus volatile, and growing versus mature, and so on. Any general theory of subcontracting in Japan would have to take such factors into account.

Vertical relations?

The degree of symmetry in subcontracting relations is a controversial issue. 'Vertical' in this chapter's title, and the definition of subcontracting used – between larger and smaller firms – implies a basic asymmetry, but is this really the case? Non-Marxist scholars have repeatedly pointed to the evolu-tion of cooperative mechanisms and risk sharing which limit the potential for abuses of power by the 'parent' company. Technological upgrading on the part of subcontractors has resulted in mutual dependence.[12] Furthermore, it has resulted in greater subcontractor independence. As we

---

[12] Cf. Miwa (1994). Nishiguchi refers to 'symbiosis' in his criticism of dualism, but in an oblique criticism of flexible specialisation, also argues that dominant–subordinate relations between large and small firms have not been reversed (1992, 210).

saw in chapter 2, the reliance of subcontractors on a single 'parent' dropped conspicuously in the late 1980s (partly as a result of the boom economy, but also as a result of a longer-term trend), and there was a growing trend for subcontractors to develop their own product as well.

Some see greater transactional equality resulting from these developments. There has been a move to abandon terms like parent and child company (*oya gaisha, kogaisha,* also *shitauke,* translated as subcontracting) because of their hierarchical connotations in favour of more neutral terms, such as manufacturer or maker and supplier.[13] According to a senior manager at Minibea's Ota factory:

> If I were to characterise the differences between the 1960s and now in polar types, I would say that in the 1960s the subcontractors said please let us do some work and we deigned to give them some. It was a matter of cost, and minimising risk for us. We planned for mid cycle, and when it got busier, we farmed work out. They absorbed the fluctuations. Now they have improved their technical levels, and we seek their cooperation. They have fought their way through difficult times. Technical demands are much higher now, and we want to do business with those companies that can meet the demands.[14]

Large firm managers are happy to use alternatives like *kyoryoku gaisha/kojo* (cooperating company/factory). Subcontractors have been more cautious, even at the height of the 'bubble' boom when there was a marked improvement in their technology and negotiating power. Abandoning parent–child terminology raised apprehensions about another trend, namely towards 'drier' relations: 'They have become weaker, but also a lot drier. We could use the word *otokuisan* (special customer), but I suppose we're reluctant to abandon "parent" because we hope they'll show special consideration in hard times.'

The owner of T. Technology consciously used 'otokuisan'. He machined work to tolerances of three microns in a temperature-controlled factory, and claimed: 'Our special customer can't do this work. I guess large companies have broad technological power but not much depth in specific work.' In his view changing subcontracting relations were not just related to technological improvements on the part of 'cooperating factories' but also to a generational change: 'New companies now don't borrow tools from their "parent." Those that do are still "child" companies. If we got an

---

[13] Asanuma (1989, 1990) uses these terms, though partially in order to overcome the particularism of the Japanese terms. Y. Kume, president of Nissan, asserts; 'From now on unreasonable demands for rationalisation and threats will not get anywhere. While maintaining this division of labour, we must reform our vertical consciousness of parent and child, up and down' (*Nikkei Business,* 27 January 1992, 14).

[14] Interview, T. Hirayama, July 1990. The factory has about 300 employees, makes a wide range of military and civilian equipment, and has about 100 regular and 100 non-regular local subcontractors.

order for ¥10,000 and a tool we needed for it cost ¥5,000, my father's generation would go and borrow the tool from the "parent." My generation would go out and buy it. We can use it again in the future.'

Despite his company's technological strength, he was not optimistic about being able to renegotiate trading conditions. 'You would have to be sure you could make a viable business out of your technology. You could quite easily find the relationship ended.' His caution was well placed. According to another owner: 'I was doing work for ¥2,500 an hour. The price had been dropped after the yen rise in 1986. I hesitated because there was a cushion [a larger subcontractor] in between and there was another company getting work through the cushion which I didn't want to get into trouble. But I eventually made a list of requests for rate rises of between 30 per cent and 150 per cent. The cushion took it to them and they said not a yen more.' The relationship was temporarily severed. Diversification of order sources is said to have made subcontractors less vulnerable to pressure from a single parent, but it certainly did not help this owner negotiate better conditions.

Greater technological ability, mutual dependence, and subcontractor independence, therefore, do not mean transactional equality. The institutionalisation of subcontracting relations over the past 40 years has also institutionalised asymmetry. Trying to negotiate prices upwards where periodic cuts are the norm (and requests to have promissory notes with shorter sight dates, or a larger proportion of cash, etc.) risk sending the message that the subcontractor is fundamentally dissatisfied with the relationship, or may even have serious management problems. The imbalance of power has also been institutionalised through such practices as just-in-time (JIT). Although relatively few owners in Ota are still involved in volume production, hence JIT, in their view the costs for inspection work, more frequent deliveries and stock storage (sometimes hidden, sometimes in a warehouse near the assembler, but necessary because of high penalties for late delivery) have to be borne by the subcontractor. Sudden shifts in production can result in extraneous stock, which the assembler is not committed to purchasing. Such views, indeed, were a factor in the avoidance of this kind of work.

At the height of the 'bubble' boom, and even amongst SME subcontractors which rated their technological level as superior to other firms in the same industry, only a quarter considered that subcontracting rates strongly reflected their wishes.[15] In the subsequent recession, the majority of Tokyo's subcontractors were forced to make cuts in their prices.[16] Interestingly, a recent Fair Trade Commission survey suggested that more

[15] Chusho kigyo cho (ed.) (1992a, 97).   [16] Tokyoto chusho kigyo shinko kosha (1994).

subcontractors complied because they thought the parent company was in trouble as well than because they feared losing orders, indicating continued cooperation and trust, but these were predominantly larger sub-contractors.[17] Small factory owners in Ota have been more bitter about pressures during the severest postwar recession: 'With their words they say please [reduce your rates], but the reality is *dokkinho* [Antimonopoly Law – forcing unfair rates]. We know very well they'll take the work elsewhere if we don't drop the price.' 'They say VA, VA (value analysis), but that's *dokkinho*, too.' The recession has accentuated the asymmetry of dependence, but in the views of some subcontractors it has been exacerbated by assemblers implementing reforms that they had long planned, anyway.

Do subcontractors ever act collectively to strengthen their bargaining position? This is rare. In late 1992, subcontracting association members of a major press maker approached their parent to ask for more work, asking in effect for it to build up stocks. Since the stocks would cost money to store, they indicated they would be prepared to accept a 15–20 per cent cut in rates for that work. The press maker allegedly responded that after due consideration of their difficult situation, it had decided to go along with the proposal, but on one condition – that the rates on all their other work be cut by the same amount as well![18] Most subcontractors are unequivocal – if a 'parent' company perceived any attempt by subcontractors to exert collective pressure, it would swiftly act against them. Supplier association members might be in a strong position to get new orders, and may at times apply subtle pressure to discourage parents from placing orders with outside companies, but they do not bargain collectively.[19]

Conflict and the law

To put the above discussion in perspective, only (or as many as) one in eight subcontractors in Tokyo reported trouble with their main customer in 1993, during the trough of the recession. (This was double the proportion in 1990.)[20] That does not mean the other seven were happy, of course, since as mentioned, subcontracting relations are bound to be stressful. If there were disagreements, however, they had not gone as far as open trouble.

Overt problems in subcontracting are as likely to stem from non-contractual causes as the subcontracting work itself, and are often the end

---

[17] Kosei torihiki iinkai (1995, 28).

[18] T. Koseki, personal communication, November 1992.

[19] See Sako (1996), for a study of suppliers' associations in the automobile industry.

[20] The most common problem was unfair rate reductions, followed by delayed payment, difficulties in collecting payment, and goods returned after delivery: Tokyoto chusho kigyo shinko kosha (1994, 39).

result of a sequence of smaller grievances. Large firms are seen as 'dry' or 'cold' when they fail to recognise sufficiently all those rush deliveries which require weekend work at no extra cost, when a cut-rate job is not recognised in the rate for a new order, and so on. In other words, discrepancies arise when the unofficial ledgers of obligational debt and goodwill credit do not match. This can happen when personnel in the 'parent' firm are moved around, when incumbents are constrained by overriding performance targets, or when people see things differently. Obligational debt may be a major matter to a small subcontractor, but a minor consideration for the large firm, and special considerations must be weighed against the dangers of setting precedents and undermining established procedures.

If conflict does arise, then, it is often difficult to redress by legal means, but a legal framework nonetheless exists. Cultural norms deem that the more powerful party in asymmetrical relationships should not use that power to pursue its own interests at the expense of the other party. This finds expression in labour law, as in other countries, but is also distinctively incorporated into the main laws pertaining to subcontracting – the Antimonopoly Law, the Law for the Prevention of Delay in Subcontracting Rate Payment and Related Matters (Delayed Payment Law – DPL), and the Subcontracting Promotion Law.[21] The background to the DPL is as follows. Immediately following the Korean War special procurements boom in the early 1950s, there were widespread instances of large firms delaying payments to small firms, and cancelling or returning orders. In 1952 the Occupation ended and the Antimonopoly Law (AML) was revised and 'Japanized'. References to unfair competitive practices were replaced by references to unfair transaction practices, and firms were prohibited from using their superior position to enforce unfair transaction terms, but the AML by itself was considered insufficient to deal with the nuances and abuses of subcontracting. After a lot of wrangling, the DPL was passed in 1956.[22]

This law, which has been modified several times, equates size with the ability to enforce unfair trading conditions, hence the subcontractor has to be smaller than the firm which places the order, according to several size

---

[21] A delayed payment bill was introduced into the British parliament in February 1996 after widespread instances of 'subby bashing' in the construction industry and a CBI survey in which up to one in five small firms claimed that late payment was a threat to their survival. In opposing the bill, Deputy Prime Minister Heseltine seemed unable to grasp the signifi-cance of large contractor–small subcontractor asymmetry, or how it could be incorporated into law. Small firms, he argued, need the flexibility to string along their creditors, and late payment is part of the culture of British business (*Independent*, 4 February 1996).

[22] Shoya (1988). The construction industry is covered by a separate law. It is possible to liti-gate under the AML as well as civil law, but this only happens in rare cases, usually when the subcontractor has gone out of business.

categories. The definition of subcontracting is similar to that given in the first note of this chapter. Duties are placed on parent companies, as well as prohibitions, as shown in figure 5.1.

Breaches of the first two obligations may lead to a token ¥30,000 fine, and breaches of prohibitions may lead to public disclosure of the 'parent's' name. Neither has ever happened. The real intent of the law is not punitive, but to encourage good practice. Subcontractors can lodge complaints with either the Fair Trade Commission (FTC) or the SME Agency. In most years no more than 100 do so, the reason being that they are afraid to complain for fear of reprisal, prohibition no. 7 (figure 5.1), and a guarantee of anonymity notwithstanding. In effect they must be prepared to risk severance of the relationship.

There is another means of uncovering infringements, though, namely through annual surveys of 'parents' and subcontractors by the FTC and the SME Agency. Between them they surveyed roughly 50,000 parent companies and 100,000 subcontractors in 1990, and uncovered over 6,500 offences by just under 5,000 parent companies. Over half were the failure to issue an order form, which makes it difficult for a subcontractor to prove its point in case of a dispute. Delayed payment (taken as more than 120 days in most industries) and promissory notes not discountable have declined over the years, but still accounted for 22 per cent of the offences.[23] Warnings are issued to offending companies, and on-the-spot investigations are commonly carried out. Very occasionally more formal warnings are given.

The Subcontracting Promotion Law was passed in 1970, following initiatives in Osaka and Tokyo, which set up associations to act as a medium for introducing subcontracting work, for the upgrading of subcontracting and subcontractors, and for dispute resolution. Association counsellors informally mediate or refer problems to a dispute resolution committee comprised of 'parent', subcontractor, and neutral representatives. In 1994 the Tokyo SME Promotion Public Corporation (as it is called in Tokyo) dealt with 90 cases, five of which were referred to its committee. Occasionally, intractable cases are referred to the FTC.[24]

It is difficult to evaluate the effectiveness of exhortation, and of educational campaigns (such as the 'Better Subcontracting Month' in November). The subcontracting laws are sometimes called *zaruho* (sieve laws). Parents frequently reoffend, as new people are placed in purchasing departments after personnel reshuffles. The laws may discourage gross offences, but Minsho (People's Chamber of Commerce) claims that they do not protect the most

---

[23] Kosei torihiki iinkai (1992, 141).

[24] Tokyoto chusho kigyo shinko kosha (1995, 6). The size stipulations of the Delayed Payment Law do not apply here, and a lot of the dispute resolution work of subcontracting associations is between small companies.

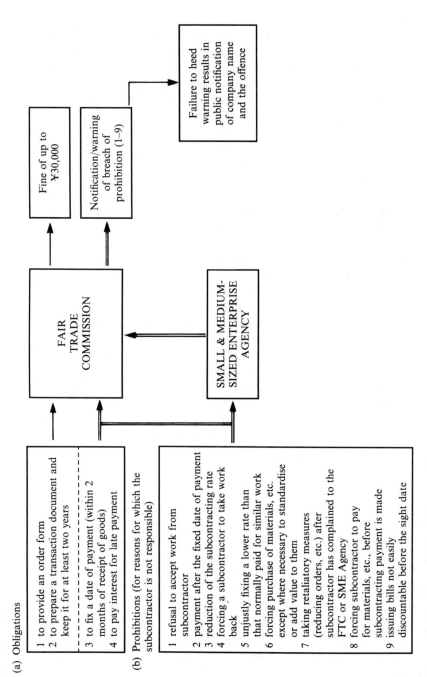

(a) Obligations

1 to provide an order form
2 to prepare a transaction document and keep it for at least two years

3 to fix a date of payment (within 2 months of receipt of goods)
4 to pay interest for late payment

(b) Prohibitions (for reasons for which the subcontractor is not responsible)

1 refusal to accept work from subcontractor
2 payment after the fixed date of payment
3 reduction of the subcontracting rate
4 forcing a subcontractor to take work back
5 unjustly fixing a lower rate than that normally paid for similar work
6 forcing purchase of materials, etc. except where necessary to standardise or add value to them
7 taking retaliatory measures (reducing orders, etc.) after subcontractor has complained to the FTC or SME Agency
8 forcing subcontractor to pay for materials, etc., before subcontracting payment is made
9 issuing bills not easily discountable before the sight date

FAIR TRADE COMMISSION

SMALL & MEDIUM-SIZED ENTERPRISE AGENCY

Fine of up to ¥30,000

Notification/warning of breach of prohibition (1–9)

Failure to heed warning results in public notification of company name and the offence

Figure 5.1 Overview of Delayed Payment Law
Source: Chusho kigyo cho (ed.) (1992d), *Shitauke torihiki handobukku* (Subcontracting Transaction Handbook), 4th edition, Tokyo: Tsusan shiryo chosakai.

vulnerable, smallest subcontractors.[25] (It would like to see the laws strengthened, but believes the government is under pressure – from the United States
to make interfirm relations more transparent and open, and from big business,
which wants to free itself from subcontracting obligations – to 'improve' the
laws, making small subcontractors even more vulnerable, for instance by
removing certain transactions from the definition of subcontracting.[26])

One micro-factory owner interviewed had complained about a customer to
the FTC. The customer had cut prices unilaterally, he stopped doing the work
in protest, the customer said it would not pay the last month's bill, and he
lodged a complaint. 'It took me a year to get my money, and then it was a six
month promissory note. Of course I stopped getting orders, but some of that
same work comes to me now through another company.' This incident reinforced the owner's view that it is much better to get work from other small firms
than large manufacturers: 'They pay cash and they don't give you trouble.'

Another had also complained to the FTC about a unilateral reduction in
rates. Said a friend: 'The FTC did an investigation and the customer was
made to pay its suppliers. But they found out who made the complaint –
they do somehow – and gradually reduced the orders. It's very difficult to
prove it's retaliation. In the end the customer's purchasing manager
changed and he's getting his orders again.' Other owners, too, reported
work being stopped after a dispute, but eventually coming in again through
a different route or after a personnel reshuffle at the customer company.
Large customers do indeed depend on their small suppliers more than
many would care to admit, or more than they might even know, but that
does not prevent disputes from arising. Most small firm owners, however,
complain about unreasonable parents amongst themselves, grit their teeth
in the short term, and get on with their work. In the long term, they may
try to reduce their vulnerability.

Networks and the future of subcontracting

Subcontracting relations in Japan are the product of historical evolution,
and continue to evolve.[27] Even in the automobile industry, which provided
the model for Womack *et al.*'s gospel of lean production, significant

[25] These small subcontractors, as well as small shopkeepers, comprise the membership base
of Minsho, which is linked to the Communist Party. Minsho has traditionally seen subcontracting in terms of exploitation by monopoly capital, and class solidarity is an important element of organisational cohesion. There are parallels in Japan with the political
leanings of Italy's small firm owners; cf. Weiss (1988).

[26] Zenkoku shoko dantai rengokai (1993).

[27] That is not to say that they are moving inexorably in a (spot) market direction. They are
undoubtedly becoming more flexible, and performance-related criteria are becoming even
more important. To use the Japanese term, they are becoming 'drier'. But the 'soft' technology necessary for long-term subcontracting relations in the past will not suddenly become
redundant, even if it is streamlined. Nor will unofficial ledgers of obligational debt and goodwill credit, though greater care will be exercised over making entries and keeping them.

changes have been unavoidable in the 1990s.[28] Assemblers began to move production abroad and exports began to decline in the 1980s, but the domestic boom more than compensated for this until 1990. To cater for extra demand and worsening labour shortages, assemblers constructed new, highly automated plants in the far west and north of Japan. When demand slumped in 1991, the assemblers were left operating at well below capacity, placing a heavy strain on profit margins already stretched through increased development costs, diversification, and optional extra provision (for which they had been lauded), not to mention new plant investment.[29]

Major strategic changes were announced by assemblers in 1992. These involved pulling out of some markets and forming joint OEM agreements, reducing the number of models and prolonging model changes, and drastically reducing the number of parts through standardisation (in some cases across companies). The assemblers also became more insistent that they would go beyond their *keiretsu* group suppliers in the pursuit of efficiency, and that suppliers could not expect to be bailed out on the basis of *keiretsu* affiliation. These pronouncements marked a new quest for scale economies, and had significant, negative implications for subcontractors. The alarm generated was captured in apocalyptic book titles such as *All Will Disappear Except Toyota* and *The Day of Mass Bankruptcies Among Automobile Parts Companies*.[30] According to one estimate, around 20,000 fewer automobile industry subcontractors, mostly very small firms, would be needed as a result of parts standardisation alone.[31]

There has been a tendency, partly inspired by the vogue for network analysis and partly by objective developments, to see tightly tiered pyramids – or 'mountain ranges' – giving way to loosely coupled networks. Yet in recent restructuring a distinction must be made between between larger, first tier suppliers and small, often third or fourth tier subcontractors. Relations between assemblers and their first tier suppliers have in fact become stronger in many cases. Some former independents, too, have been drawn into *keiretsu*.[32] First tier suppliers from the stronger *keiretsu* like Toyota have increasingly come to supply other assemblers, even of rival

---

[28] So superior is it that 'the whole world should adopt lean production, and as quickly as possible' (Womack *et al.*, 1990, 225).

[29] JIT, too, came under increasing strain and criticism in the late 1980s. Supplier bases in the vicinity of the new factories were incomplete, and small firms everywhere were having trouble finding workers to produce and deliver parts. JIT was seen as an impediment to the national campaign to reduce working hours and environmentally damaging because it contributed to traffic congestion, exhaust fumes, and general resource waste.

[30] F. Fujitani (1993); Y. Misoue (1993). The strategic shift was also evident in other industries, such as consumer electronics.

[31] K. Sakamoto, interview, December 1992, and *Shizuoka shinbun*, 27 October 1992.

[32] As noted in chapter 3, for instance, Toyota has become the largest shareholder of formerly independent piston maker Art Kinzoku, the strategic reason being joint development work on ceramic pistons. Cf. also Fukushima (1993).

keiretsu, but the relationship with their own *keiretsu* assembler is given priority, and profits from the new orders may subsidise the ultra thin profit margins in that relationship. Competitive pressures, product development competences, and geographical dispersion are driving these changes. Even amongst first tier suppliers, however, casualties are expected, while the top component suppliers are becoming increasingly influential.[33]

For small subcontractors, restructuring has bleaker implications. A survey of small (fewer than 80 employees) car part suppliers in Kanagawa Prefecture in late 1992 showed that three quarters had seen sales slump relative to three years earlier, a third were operating in the red, and a further half reported reduced profits. Three quarters were facing new cost cutting demands and half thought it would be virtually impossible to meet them. At the same time, delivery dates had been shortened considerably. The majority were delivering to the assemblers' new factories in west Japan (10 per cent had factories there themselves), but 40 per cent were not, and faced the prospect of declining orders as production was concentrated in those factories. Only 12 per cent – larger subcontractors, predictably – thought relations with their parent company would strengthen, one third predicted they would remain much the same, one third said they would have to diversify order sources, and one fifth said they would attempt to quit subcontracting altogether. The smaller the factory, the worse the prospects were.[34]

The concentration of orders in larger subcontractors at the expense of smaller ones is not just a product of restructuring, but may be traced to long-term trends. In 1975 purchased parts constituted one third of Fujitsu's turnover, and roughly 20 per cent of this came directly from SMEs. By 1990 purchased parts had risen to 60 per cent of turnover, but the proportion coming from SMEs had dropped to just 10 per cent. These trends may say more about procurement methods than a decline in small firm subcontracting *per se* – orders may reach the same subcontractors, only through first or second tier suppliers – but technological change has also played a part. A lot of the metal parts in Fujitsu's machines have been replaced by integrated circuits and fibre optics. And, according to procurement managers: 'We needed suppliers who could keep up with rapid growth, who had comprehensive abilities from development right through to production, and which could reduce costs. Some SMEs grew with us, others didn't. . . .'[35]

---

[33] Nikkei shinbun, 4 December 1993. Sako (1996) suggests that the 'core nodes' in the industry-wide network 'are increasingly not the assemblers, but the 20 or so major component suppliers, which serve several assemblers at once'.

[34] Kanagawa ken chusho kigyo shien zaidan (1993).

[35] Interview, Fujitsu procurements division managers, November 1992.

Most of the examples cited in this chapter have involved, directly or indirectly, large assemblers. At this point it is necessary to make a distinction between different types of subcontracting networks. A Tokyo government study identified two basic types, according to the product produced by the most influential manufacturer or assembler. The first is the 'volume' type, typified by automobiles and consumer electronics. It relies on JIT production, but is becoming geographically dispersed, with large subcontractors and subassemblers playing an increasingly important role. The second is the 'skill concentration' type, in which a variety of low volume machines, often customised, are produced in operations which are difficult to automate. This type of network is less clearly tiered, and the constituent members change frequently according to the particular machine produced at the time. Such networks are now prevalent in metropolitan regions, and are an important factor in the continuance of factory concentrations, despite otherwise unfavourable locational conditions.[36]

Small subcontractors are seeking – or being forced – to leave 'volume' networks and to become part of 'skill concentration' networks. This trend has been apparent in south Tokyo for the past two to three decades, following the exodus of large firms and rationalisation of the 1970s. The motivation is captured in the words of the owner (successor) of M. Precision:

We were like rats on a treadmill. They [giant 'parent'] used to come around and we would drop the speed from 15 to 20 seconds. They would see through it right away and had lots of ideas on how to speed up to 12 seconds instead of 15. Then during the oil shock they took a lot of the work in house. Some of my friends went under. We lost our trust in them. We had a fight and that was it. Those who gritted their teeth may be better off now. One of our workers who became independent went back to Nagano and made stainless straps for videos. He couldn't leave his machines idle for one minute or the work would end up in Taiwan. No New Year, no Golden Week or other holidays. His family took it in turns to keep the machines working. Finally the parent company said you've done well. We have a new product coming out, and if you get this new machine, there won't be any danger of losing it to Taiwan. They're better off for now – for how long I'm not sure – but I don't want to be reliant like that.

He got work from S. Ltd, one of the district's 'new key' product makers, a top-class automated assembly line equipment producer with a large network of local suppliers, but only 100 employees of its own. The transition to the new low volume, high value added work took two to three years, and was not easy, but was ultimately successful.

Such companies are watching current economic and social trends very

[36] Tokyoto (1991, 81–5).

carefully, trying to get a portion of their work from new growth areas like medical and environmental equipment, where 'skill concentration' networks may have a competitive advantage.[37] Some are seeking to develop their own products for these markets, jointly with friends, creating their own networks. M. Precision set up a development company in which the partners designed a dehydration machine for garbage disposal and a metal cleaning machine which they hope to produce by drawing on local subcontractors.

It appears then, that restructuring in *mass production* networks is not only producing small firm winners and casualties, but is encouraging the formation of *flexibly specialised* (to use Piore and Sabel's terms) small firm networks.[38] These still rely on mass production or volume networks to buy their specialised or customised machines, but they are also becoming established in new, relatively low volume, final good markets. While their price cuts may not be as frequent or oppressive as large assemblers, however, and they are often viewed as more sympathetic to the position of subcontractors, orders from 'new key' factories are less stable, and work tends to be taken in house during a downturn, as was evident during the 1990s recession. 'Skill concentration' networks, therefore, have disadvantages of their own, and are not a panacea for small subcontractor problems.

---

[37] C. Manufacturing, for instance, which lost its video work, began to make moulds for medical equipment in 1994–5.   [38] Piore and Sabel (1984).

6   Interfirm relations 2: 'horizontal'

Relations between small firms in Japan has received scant attention in the past, with the exception of their political activities. Surveys on sub-contracting seldom distinguish between 'vertical' and 'horizontal' relations, and subcontracting is assumed to be vertical while relations between small firms are seen as singularly competitive. As a result, even those who see flexible and cooperative relations between small firms as an emerging alternative to Fordist mass production look to Japan only for its sub-contracting practices.

A distinction was made in chapter 5 between 'volume' and 'skill concentration' networks. Leading companies in the latter are often SMEs, and relationships tend to be less vertical or hierarchical. In districts like Ota, however, there are also extensive trading links between small factories which are *not* product makers, encouraged by specialisation. These are called 'confrere trading' (*nakama torihiki*). Confrere trading and sub-contracting for small product makers is actually preferred by some small firms to subcontracting for large firms, despite the irregularity of orders. In addition, informal or neighbourly cooperation between small firms ranges from lending tools – and workers sometimes – to consultation on technical and personnel matters.[1]

Underpinning this is a sense of community, stemming from common residence, common occupational identity, endurance of economic ups and downs and subcontracting pressures, and general shared interests. *Sessa takuma* is a term which neatly expresses confreral rivalry, of competition tempered by mutual encouragement and assistance, resulting in technical and managerial improvements. As well, cooperative relations are more formally established within a variety of organisations, such as cooperative or

---

[1] The forms of cooperation are similar to those described by Pyke and Sengenbeger; '[I]n a regime of cooperation and trust . . . firms will combine their resources to ensure a collective provision of skills, the collective provision of services already referred to, and the kind of cooperation that takes the form of "good neighbourliness" – lending of tools, helping out with spare parts, passing on of advice, assistance in emergencies, etc.' (1992, 17).

industry associations. These organisations serve important functions of mutual support and in helping small firms to achieve efficiency, scale merits, and upgrading. Cooperative business associations are especially noteworthy for allowing independent small firms, even competitors, to cooperate flexibly in limited areas of their business.

This chapter looks first at informal linkages between small firms in Ota Ward, including *nakama torihiki* and *sessa takuma*. It then gives an overview of small firm associations, followed by specific examples from Ota Ward. Finally, it considers interindustry exchange and 'fusion' groups, which have been vigorously promoted as a new way forward for small firms, and technology-enabled or on-line networks. Horizontal interfirm relations are more important than ever before, but, in practice, they have their own inherent limitations.

Confrere trading and friendly confrere rivalry

It is difficult to know the extent of interaction between small firms in prewar Japan. Apart from the Meiji period, they are portrayed as competing atomistically, with the result of perpetually low wages and little surplus left for capital accumulation. Cooperation is usually considered a recent development, dating from the high growth period when the abundance of work made it easier to share work rather than just compete for it, and rising technical levels and specialisation encouraged a finer division of labour. This historical view is suspect, given the early trading and information links between small firms in urban centres, and the fact that cooperation is as much a strategy for survival as competition. It is not hard to imagine a certain solidarity developing amongst neighbouring and related small firm owners struggling in adverse circumstances, finding expression in various forms of mutual assistance.

Certainly such links became more visible in the high growth period. In Ota Ward, in response to the growing shortage of young workers in the early 1960s, and complaints about welfare conditions, industrialists banded together to make a factory which produced over 20,000 meals a day for SME workers. They also established vocational training schools to impart basic industrial knowledge. Yet back in 1939 a group of 62 local SME owners had founded the Omori Machine Industry Apprentice School (which became the Omori Industrial High School), and this was almost certainly just the tip of the cooperative iceberg.[2]

Rather than pursuing the historical argument, we will confine our attention here to the present, and begin by looking at confrere trading. The dis-

[2] Ota kuritsu kyodo hakubutsukan (1994, 74–5).

tinction between this and subcontracting is not clearcut, but we will take it to mean trading relations between similarly sized firms which are not product makers. Two thirds of the top three customers of Ota's micro-factories (less than ten employees) in 1988 were local (from Ota, Shinagawa, Meguro, or Kawasaki), and half had less than 30 employees.[3] These micro-factories actually received more work from other factories in the same general line of business than from product makers. Much of this work was complementary to that done by the customers themselves, but there was a lot of overflow work as well. This suggests the extent and nature of confrere trading. Small factories accept orders for which they do a limited number of processes and farm out the rest, or take on more work than they can cope with, and farm out the extra to other small factories. The density of factories in Ota, the presence of large numbers of specialists as well as jobbing shops which can do the work quickly, facilitates the horizontal flow of work, and forms the foundations of the district's 'spatial flexible manufacturing system'.

O. Technology (six employees), for instance, receives regular orders from five companies, does the lathe work itself and farms out planing, press, welding, and sheet metal work to ten other local companies. The work it farms out constitutes half its turnover. The owner also shares lathe work with a friend on an informal specialisation basis. They have agreed not to compete against each other directly, and not to buy the same machines. There is some overlap in their capabilities, though, and this enables them to help each other out on rush orders. Small factory owners accept more work than they can handle for a number of reasons. Sometimes processes cannot be neatly separated, and it is more efficient – or profitable – for them to coordinate the different processes themselves. (The customer may not even know the work is farmed out in this way, especially if the work is done in a neighbouring factory, or by a subcontractor working on the premises.) Last minute priority orders come in, or orders which exceed their capacity, but which may lead to substantial future business, and rather than seeing work go elsewhere, they will accept it and farm some of it out. They may do this to repay obligational debts or create goodwill credit amongst confreres as well. As in subcontracting, a special 'technology' must be mastered by small firm owners who engage in confrere trading, an important aspect of which is the ability to master the underlying obligational-debt and goodwill-credit norms. Relations are normally based on personal connections, with technical competence a necessary but often not a sufficient condition.

But, as one owner commented: 'Everyone understands that our trading relations are business relations.' It is common to extract a brokerage fee, or

---

[3] Ota ku (1989); cf. also chapter 4.

'telephone money' when work is passed on. The percentage varies according to the circumstances. Brokers commonly withhold around 30 per cent, but confrere 'telephone money' is commonly in the region of 10 per cent. It may be less for a rush order, or when a favour is being repaid. It may be more when the intermediary is paid by a promissory note, but pays in cash, or when tools are loaned. Sometimes none is withheld, sometimes it is withheld only for the first order, after which the customer and confrere subcontractor deal with each other directly. It is not always clear whether 'telephone money' is being withheld, but recipients have a reasonably good idea of the rate, and do not appreciate it if excessive 'telephone money' makes them go under their own normal rate. They expect large factories to try to exploit them, but resent it more when small owners try to do the same.

'What I do,' said one owner, 'is ask them how much they will do it for. If I'm getting ¥1,000 and they say they'll do it for ¥700, then fine, I'll give it to them. I might give them more so they'll keep the delivery date, and I loan tools to one or two as well.' On the other hand: 'In our association, non-ferrous casters introduce work to ferrous casters, but since there's only a 10–15 per cent margin they usually just pass it on. If they send it over to Kawaguchi [another casting district], they might take a 10 per cent cut.'

About 40 per cent of Ota's micro-factories – the so-called 'terminal factories' – do not subcontract out any work. The owner described in the last chapter who preferred dealing with small firms after bitter experiences with large companies, was one of these. He thought if he subcontracted work out he would end up fixing other peoples' mistakes and losing money out of it. Perhaps his intense aversion to being ripped off (*pinhane sareru*) made him averse to acting as a broker as well. He was first and foremost craftsman, not a businessman, but he had an enormous number of small firm customers.

Next, independent of trading relations, small firm owners share information on matters such as employees and recruiting, 'parent' companies, business trends, management issues, technical questions, and new work. To cite the owner of O. Technology: 'Our customers design the work, but they don't produce it themselves. They can't give us technical advice. I get the blueprint, and if I can't figure out how to do it, I go and ask one of my friends. They come to me sometimes, too. And we look at each other's work and ask how did you do it? How much did it cost?' This, in essence, is *sessa takuma*. Owners exchange information, and use this to improve their operations so that they will not be beaten by others.

T. Technology was saved from a crisis in 1980 when the owner's cousin introduced some new work. The work came from a major semi-conductor equipment maker through an intermediary with 15 employees. The owner was uncertain as to whether he could handle the work, but got the necessary pointers from the intermediary: 'They [his cousin and the intermediary] said why don't you join us for this work. I had to get from 0.01mm [tolerance] down to 3–5 microns very quickly, but they helped me do it.'

Horizontal relations are much more extensive in districts like Ota than is generally recognised, even though there is considerable competition as well. Informal relations can be critical in establishing a company, when small firms face critical turning points or crises, as well as on a daily basis. Ties of blood, friendship, and neighbourliness underlie many of these relations. Many owners live locally, drink at the same bars, belong to the same industrialists' association . . . If information is the lifeblood of modern industry, small firms in Ota Ward have available to them a rich arterial system of horizontal as well as vertical linkages which help them to survive and evolve.

Small firm organisations: an overview

Horizontal relations between small firms are often informal, but even the casual observer of small firms in Japan cannot fail to be struck by the large number of small firm organisations. There are over 45,000 registered SME cooperative and trade or industry associations in Japan; about 600 organisations are listed in the Ota Ward Register of Trade Organisations alone. English language accounts have focused on the political activities of peak bodies like the Chuokai (National Federation of SME Organisations), but small firm organisations play important roles in the daily business activities of small firms as well. It may be argued that the number of organisations exaggerates the extent of actual cooperation between small firms, since many have allegedly been formed to gain access to government loans or to reduce tax bills. But this should not obscure the extent of grassroot cooperation which exists both inside and outside registered organisations.

Guilds have existed for hundreds of years in Japan. In addition, the country's opening in the nineteenth century introduced Western – British and German – models of cooperatives and producer associations. From the late nineteenth century the Meiji government showed an interest in small producer organisations which would establish and raise standards, alleviate the 'traditional industry problem', and promote modernisation. Two main types of organisation were recognised. First, national regulations were issued for trade or industry associations in 1884 following the impact of the Matsukata deflation on 'traditional industry' and an Osaka initiative aimed at discouraging price cutting and falling standards. These were given statutory authority in 1897 and 1900. Second, a law relating to cooperative and mutual associations was also passed in 1900. Most cooperatives recognised under this law, however, were agricultural or rural producer cooperatives, to the chagrin of manufacturers and merchants excluded from its benefits.[4]

Government regulations influenced association activities, but of course could not dictate the degree of small firm cooperation inside or outside them. Credit associations spread from 1917, when they were permitted to discount promissory notes and accept savings. New efforts were made to address structural problems faced by small firms in the 1920s under the 1925 Important Export Product Industry Association Law, which embodied elements of both trade and cooperative association law. Government loans at favourable interest rates were subsequently made available, peak federations were recognised, the range of industries covered was increased and credit activities permitted, resulting in a sharp increase in registered association numbers.

During the 1930s the government tried to extend its influence over these associations. By the end of the decade they had effectively become instruments of control and rationing for the war effort. Attempts – not particularly successful in the urban centres – were made to organise even tiny producers. Voluntary and mutual improvement rhetoric was maintained, but participation was obligatory. Yet, even in the 1930s, government action sometimes followed producer pressure, which had become more effectively channelled through peak federations. A striking example was the establishment of the Shoko Chukin Bank in 1936, funded equally by small firm association members and the government. Some elements of the wartime control associations persisted into the postwar period, but attempts were made to democratise small firm organisations, notably through the new SME Cooperative Association Law of 1949. Trade associations, too, were recognised under a temporary law during the 1952 slump, which eventually became permanent as the 1957 SME Organisation Law. (Recession and rationalisation cartels were recognised by these laws.) Cooperative and trade association laws have been revised periodically, in the direction of greater differentiation of organisation types, expansion of activities recognised, egalitarian and democratic stipulations modified (for cooperative associations), and a greater role for central federations recognised. Supporters of these revisions believe the early postwar requirements were too idealistic, and that small firm organisations became more effective as a result, while critics suggest they have sapped the independent cooperative spirit of small firms.

A survey by the SME Agency in 1990 identified 45,566 SME organisations, divided into seven legal categories (table 6.1). Within manufacturing

---

[4] Zenkoku chusho kigyo dantai chuokai (Chuokai (ed.) 1975). Historical references are mostly from this source, and Momose (1989).

Table 6.1 *Registered SME organisations in Japan*

Type sector	Coop. business assoc. *1	Small coop. bus. assoc. *2	Coop. assoc. federation	Enterprise assoc. *3	Joint activity assoc. *4	Commerce /industry assoc.	Commerce /industry assoc. fed.n
Primary	456		13	58	4		
Secondary	15,557	6	354	778	645	1,165	53
manufacturing	10,541	5	261	587	569	1,050	52
(metal prod.	575		14	21	26	72	5
mach. & equip.	697		6	27	11	6	
elec. mach.	190		3	15	2	1	
vehicles	286		3	3	13	1	
prec. equip.)	110			3	5	4	
Tertiary	20,032	19	379	1,322	769	620	21
'Other'	2,904	25	60	266	17	6	
Total	38,949	50	806	2,477	1,441	1,794	74

Notes:
*1 includes 414 credit associations and 44 fire mutual aid associations.
*2 must have no more than five members.
*3 membership is by individuals and all business activities are conducted through the association, which forms an enterprise.
*4 similar to cooperative business associations, but with less stringent governance regulations (not necessarily one member one vote, nor the principle of entry and exit).
All associations must have at least four members.
Source: Adapted from Miura (1991, p. 278), based on 1990 SME Agency survey.

they are widespread in woodworking, textiles and pottery, although the average size of associations in these industries is small. Organisations in the five machine industries comprise 16 per cent of the manufacturing total, and are most prevalent in metal products and machinery and equipment. Outside manufacturing they are widespread in the retail, wholesale, transportation/storage, construction, and service industries. In some of these industries small firm organisations have been essential for regulatory protection and survival.

By far the most common type of organisation, comprising about 85 per cent of the total, is the cooperative business association (CBA – *jigyo kyodo kumiai*). Two thirds of these had fewer than 30 members in 1990, but some were very big, pushing the average number of members per association up to almost 100. If this figure is multiplied by the number of associations and divided by the total number of SMEs, it would appear that over half of SMEs belong to an association.[5] Without taking this figure too literally, it suggests that CBAs are widespread. Table 6.2 shows that the most prevalent type of CBA is a limited number of SMEs in a single industry acting cooperatively in certain aspects of their business. The other main type is more inclusive in terms of firms organised, but not necessarily as inclusive as a trade or industry association. Together they account for 70 per cent of the total.

The full cooperative (enterprise association) is less common. This is related more to the strength of the 'lord of the castle' mentality of owners than a reluctance to cooperate. With this mentality, the preferred vehicle for cooperation is the CBA, which allows independent owners, even potential competitors, to cooperate flexibly. Irrespective of its original intent, then, it would appear that SME organisation legislation both allows and encourages interfirm cooperation that owners are comfortable with. By contrast, competition policy in the UK, such as the Restrictive Trade Practices Acts, may have inhibited small firm cooperation and encouraged mergers.[6]

Cooperation in some CBAs is extensive, in others it is limited. The most common activities are listed in table 6.3. According to the Chuokai survey, almost half of associations surveyed carry out information gathering and provision, and over 40 per cent do joint purchasing. One third undertake welfare activities for members and their employees, and almost one third engage in education and training. The table probably underestimates joint facility and equipment usage (halls, conference rooms, offices, testing

---

[5] Zenkoku chusho kigyo dantai chuokai (1992, 10). These figures do not consider multi-membership (but on the other hand, the denominator is actually establishments, unadjusted for multi-establishment companies). According to a different Chuokai survey, 58.4 per cent of CBA members belong to a single association, and 37.1 per cent belong to two or more (the rest did not answer; Chuokai 1991, 37).   [6] Hughes (1989).

Table 6.2 *Types of cooperative business association*

Type	Nature	Prop. *n.*
1 Single industry – limited	formed by a limited number of closely linked SMEs in a given or related industry	44.6%
2 Single industry – inclusive	association aiming to include all SME businesses in a given industry within a given area	25.6
3 Joint shop	mainly small retailers using the same premises	4.7
4 Shopping street	inclusive association, mainly of service and small retail businesses from a given street/streets	3.2
5 Industrial estate	factories of a given industrial estate	2.9
6 *Keiretsu*	retailers, etc. of a specific company *keiretsu*	2.8
7 Localised industry	producers in a specific industry in a given locality (*sanchi*)	2.3
8 Subcontracting	subcontractors of a specific 'parent' company	2.2
9 Finance	financial activities	2.2
10 Credit card	small retailers and service businesses issuing credit cards	1.6
11 District	association of a given locality irrespective of business/industry	1.4
12 Interindustry exchange	formed to gain benefit from specialist knowledge/ technology from different industries	1.0
13 Wholesalers' estate	wholesalers of a given wholesalers' estate	0.9
14 Joint factory	association for the joint use of a single factory premises	0.6
15 Distribution estate	distribution/wholesaler businesses of a given estate	0.5
16 'Fusion'	formed to develop new business through the 'fusion' of knowledge from different industries	0.5
17 Welfare	joint meals, lodging and other welfare facilities/ activities	0.5
18 Chain	voluntary and franchise chain business associations	0.5
19 Mutual aid	mutual aid activities	0.4
20 Other	not included in the above (1.6%) or unclear (0.2%)	1.8

Source: Zenkoku chusho kigyo dantai chuokai (1992, 4, 14).

Table 6.3 *Activities of cooperative business associations (by rank order, top 15)*

Activity	Currently carried out	Currently important	Important from now on	
			Existing & new activities	New activities
Collecting & providing information	1	2	1	1
Joint purchase	2	1	2	8
Welfare of members/employees	3	7	4	4
Training & education	4	4	3	5
Business capital loans	5	6	8	11
Joint sales/orders	6	3	5	7
Joint advertising/marketing	7	5	6	9
Fire, etc., aid; insurance agency	8	8	11	17
Surveys/research for members	9	9	7	3
Credit guarantees	10	11	16	25
Joint use of facilities such as conference rooms	11	22	18	18
Office work for members	12	14	13	15
Product/technology R&D	13	10	9	6
Maintenance/management of member facilities	14	12	14	16
Joint storage/transportation	15	15	12	10

Source: Zenkoku chusho kigyo dantai chuokai (1992, 30).

equipment, etc.), which over half of associations reported in a separate part of the survey. As the table shows, activities considered most important were, in order, joint purchasing, followed by information gathering and provision, joint sales, and orders, education and training, and joint advertising and/or marketing.[7]

Association priorities change over time in response to the changing economic environment and member demands, as the last two columns of table 6.3 suggest. 'Joint recruiting and standardisation of employment conditions' was ranked second in new activities (final column), but only 22nd in activities currently carried out. This reflected the chronic labour shortage in 1990, but also a growing strategic concern for recruiting. 'Soft', information-related and strategic activities such as technology development have gained in importance over time, joining traditional 'hard' activities like joint purchasing, sales, and financing, some of which have become relatively less important. These trends are also evident in industry associations.[8]

The above surveys were sent to CBAs. In a separate survey of individual members, the following activities were rated most important: information gathering and provision, bolstering trust (e.g., with outside financing institutions and companies), facilitating loans for investment and operating costs, liaising with other associations, and facilitating technical and market information exchange between members. Members also claimed they benefited from maintenance of harmony and order between companies (in the same industry). The industry-related dimension thus appears to be as important as cooperative activities for CBA members.[9] They also benefit from enhanced trust and image.

These surveys suggest that, at the very least, the cynical view of small firm organisations – that they are formed simply to make use of government handouts – is simplistic, and although their economic contribution cannot be accurately quantified, they serve important functions for their members. Of course some associations are moribund whilst others are very dynamic. The majority lie somewhere in between. This was borne out by interviews with association members in Ota Ward.

Small firm organisations: examples from Ota Ward

The first two examples are taken from limited, single industry CBAs (type 1 in table 6.2). They come from the die and mould industry, which is considered representative of south Tokyo, being mainly one-off or low volume

---

[7] Zenkoku chusho kigyo dantai chuokai (1992). The survey covered some 20,000 associations.   [8] Zenkoku chusho kigyo dantai chuokai (1993).
[9] Zenkoku chusho kigyo dantai chuokai (1991, 75, 108).

work, and requiring high levels of machining skills. Dies and moulds have been vital for the growth of Japan's volume industries, but 90 per cent of manufacturers in this ¥1,000 billion industry have fewer than 20 employees. The two associations of plastic mould (moulds for plastic or plastic-like products) producers we will look at are very active, suggesting the potential for small firm cooperation rather than the representative situation.

The Keihin Plastic Mould Cooperative Association had 18 member companies in Kanagawa Prefecture and Ota Ward in 1989, the largest of which had just under 100 employees and the smallest just six.[10] It was founded by 12 companies in 1970 for mutual assistance, and, initially, for organising favourable loans. Soon after its launch it also began joint purchasing, which has expanded over the years. Fifty three outside firms now belong to an organisation which association members agree to buy solely from in return for substantial discounts. The association takes 3–5 per cent as a handling fee, which helps pay the wages of the four full-time staff.

The head of the office staff is an ex-SME Agency official, and not surprisingly, he has made full use of government programmes. In 1984, 24 CNC machines were purchased on behalf of members with favourable loans and no deposit. In 1986–7 CAD equipment was similarly purchased, and ¥80 million of loans secured under the high yen special relief measures. (A 1 per cent handling fee was taken for these activities, too.)

Another of the association's major activities is taking in orders and farming the work out internally (again, a 1 per cent handling fee). The advantage of orders coming through the association is that customers can be guaranteed a fast turnaround, and the office is better placed than member companies to do marketing. In 1987 the association handled orders worth ¥156 million, on top of which members passed on to each other orders worth ¥85 million. A standardised job order form is used to facilitate this. A further activity is joint study groups, looking at CAD/CAM and the consumption tax in 1989, and, finally, the association handles contributions to the small firm mutual fund and the bankruptcy prevention fund.

The Tokyo Plastic Mould Cooperative Association also had 18 members in 1989.[11] It was formed in 1963, when founding members felt they should lay a base for cooperative activities, even though work was plentiful. In many respects it is similar to the Keihin PMCA. It has two full-time office staff, the head being a former director of a large credit bank. One of its main activities is joint purchasing, including machine tools, as well as financing through government schemes and through the bank in which the

---

[10] Interview at the Keihin Plastic Mould Cooperative Association, March 1989, association mimeos, and Kokumin kin'yu koko (ed.) (1989a).
[11] T. Chikara, interviews (August 1990, November 1992, September 1995) and mimeos.

association's capital is deposited. This fund, and the trust of the association, enables loans at lower interest rates than individual members could otherwise secure, even after the handling fee.

The association does not handle mould orders, however. Some members regretted this: 'I'm an executive of the junior section of the Chuokai. I see some amazing associations. Our 18 companies could be as strong as the largest companies in the industry. Once I suggested we take on Toshiba work and do it between us, but the conservative members dragged their heels.' Informally, some members pass on work to each other, and they attempted to continue this in the recession, but, at the end of the day, the primary responsibility of members is to their company and employees, and sharing work comes after that.

Dies and moulds used to be considered a recession-proof industry, but the industry was severely hit in the 1990s. Its designation in 1995 for 'structural improvement' benefits came too late for many small firms. By late 1995 membership of the Tokyo Association was down to eight – five had been forced out of business and five had closed shop. The situation in the Keihin Association was just as grim.

(In passing, a few words about the industry association – the Japan Die and Mould Industry Association. The JDMIA was founded in 1957, apparently at the urging of MITI, absorbing a number of specialised regional associations which had sprung up after the war. Over the years small members have benefited from access to government loans, a special monthly payment purchase scheme negotiated by the association with leading machine tool makers, factory visits to leading manufacturers, and information exchange. Only one in eight small specialists belongs, however. Small members feel that the association is remote from their daily activities and dominated by large companies for whom dies and moulds forms only a part of their business. Surveys come around for reasons they are not sure of, and research is funded that they derive little benefit from. The association is not a very effective pressure group in their view, either. Thus they are ambivalent about the benefits of membership, and whether this is the best structure for representing their interests.)

Next, let us look at a 'relocation association', which are quite numerous in Ota. These were formed to secure approval and funding for relocation to the reclaimed islands or factory apartments, and are sometimes called 'upgrading associations' since most of the funding has come from the government's structural upgrading programme. The Jonan Casting Cooperative Association is one of 18 associations on Keihin Island.[12] It has 21 members, ranging from one firm with 260 employees to several with four,

---

[12] Interviews with Y. Takeuchi, managing director, August 1990, November 1992.

and one joint activity association in which three self-employed casters share a factory. The size gap between large and small members probably reduces the scope for collective action, since large members would benefit little from some of the activities favoured by small members. The association undertakes no joint purchases, nor does it accept orders. This was tried but abandoned when some members felt the association directors were creaming off the best orders. Joint education has been tried, but largely discontinued.

In contrast to some relocation associations, though, which have no office and have received no further loans after the initial relocation, the JCCA is considered active. It has an office manager and two staff. The office organises loans through various government programmes. In late 1992, for instance, it was helping members to draw up detailed plans for equipment loans under the government's new 'labour securement' programme. Many factory improvements could be justified as improving the working environment to make it easier to recruit workers. The office also handles member payments to various mutual insurance schemes and funds. In addition, the association owns a lot of joint testing equipment with a replacement value of ¥200 million, and members carry out some joint research into material properties.

Finally, local industrialists' associations have been formed in different parts of the ward.[13] The Kowakai – Industrial Harmony Association – had 231 members in 1993 (and its sister CBA, through which members are eligible for advantageous government loans, had 207), representing 70 per cent of factories in Shimomaruko, and 15 per cent in Yaguchi, in the western part of the ward. It was formed in 1948 by 40 small factory owners who wanted to improve communication and solidarity amongst themselves, and its sister CBA was formed five years later, when financial problems were particularly severe, compounded by delayed subcontracting payments. The CBA was able to borrow money from the Shoko Chukin Bank, and have promissory notes discounted more easily.

The Kowakai owns a hall, which was rebuilt in the late 1970s after a new membership drive. Extra revenue is generated by renting out rooms for meetings in the hall, in addition to insurance-related activities (for employees, automobiles, travel, non-life, etc.). Use of the hall by senior citizens and local community groups also fosters closer links with the local community, which are important because of the potential for bad neighbour problems. In addition to representing members' interests to the ward and Tokyo governments, the Kowakai provides a forum in which local factory owners can meet and exchange ideas, gather new information and make new con-

---

[13] See chapter 9 for the political activities of these associations. Information here comes from the July 1993 Kowakai Newsletter, and interviews with Kowakai leaders, September 1993.

tacts, and sometimes new business as well. It is an important pillar of the local industrial community.

These associations by no means exhaust the variety of small firm organisations in Ota. There are tax associations to help members prepare their tax returns, the oldest branch of the Tokyo Chamber of Commerce, with over 3,000 members and a staff of 14, as well as three branches of the left-wing Minsho. . . . These organisations help to diffuse knowledge, promote solidarity, and in some cases undertake joint business activities. According to a Minsho advisor: 'There may be No Entry signs in front of the factories, but our members can walk right in and talk with other members about technical problems, subcontracting rates and the like.' During the recession, Minsho attempted to coordinate information about orders for members whose work had dried up.

Benefits of membership of various organisations have to be weighed up against membership fees and handling charges, but factory owners themselves often rated enhanced horizontal communication, and enhanced trust to outside parties like banks or potential customers, as significant advantages.

Interindustry exchange, 'fusion', and networks

Most of the associations described in the last two sections are confined to a specific industry or related industries, and aim at achieving scale economies as well as instilling cooperation into competition. Where industry borders have been transcended, the organisational objective has still been to reap scale economies in areas such as finance, welfare, and education. A new campaign is underway, however, to foster information exchange between small firms of different industries, bringing together their different perspectives to create new products. The objective is to reap the benefits of economies of scope rather than scale, at least initially. In an age in which industry boundaries are becoming blurred, this is seen to offer a new way forward to small firms seeking independence from sub-contracting relations, and new business opportunities. The groups being formed represent yet another type of producer network in addition to volume and skill concentration types described in the last chapter, since there is no single dominant firm, large or small.

The campaign has been vigorously promoted by the SME Agency and other government institutions, but is in fact a formalisation of small firm activities which were already emerging in the early 1970s. Still today, the bulk of interindustry exchange and cooperative product development by small firms takes place independently of official sponsorship. An example given was the owner of M. Precision setting up a development company with friends to design new products. In one project, the group was seeking the involvement of a larger industrial company, introduced by their bank, for development cooperation and marketing of a dehydration machine for rubbish disposal. Other groups have turned to public funds for these activities.

The history of official interindustry exchange begins with the 1972 report of the SME Policy Deliberation Council, calling for a shift from a 'hard', volume, scale-economy orientation to 'soft', knowledge intensive activities. The SME White Paper of 1973 called for interindustry cooperation in the form of information exchange, market pioneering, and R&D. Groups were subsequently formed with the encouragement of prefectural governments and chambers of commerce.[14] In 1981 the 'technology exchange plaza' programme was launched. This encouraged the setting up of groups of around 30 companies which met monthly to discuss technical and managerial issues, visit model factories, and hear speeches from invited speakers.

Official and unofficial exchange groups were said to number about 700 in 1987.[15] The following year the 'fusion law' was passed to encourage groups to move beyond information exchange into product development, and ultimately marketing. Exchange should lead to 'fusion'. Part of the 'fusion' support package was the provision of 'catalysers' (advisors) as well as funds, tax relief, and access to information and testing facilities. Although only 50 or so new groups are funded each year under this law, the total number of 'fusion' and exchange groups leaped to 1,527 in 1988 and 1,927 the following year, with some 65,000 participating firms.

Ota has several such groups, launched with the ward's backing at two-yearly intervals. OKK1 (Ota ku kigyo koryukai – Ota Ward Company Exchange Group) was started in 1988, RAF ('Random and Flexibility') in 1990, and Joint 92 in 1992, with 18–20 members each. (A further group was started in 1994, and there is a group on Keihin Island, formed without the ward's initial assistance.) Members of OKK1 developed a magnetic alternative to barcoding with 'fusion' funding from the Tokyo government, and after unsuccessful negotiations with a major company, were attempting to market the technology themselves in late 1995. RAF members were interested in environmental products. They first developed a receptacle device for milk cartons, and sold about 100 of these within the ward and some outside it. Next they developed a recycling receptacle for PET bottles. This received good publicity, and customers included a major supermarket

---

[14] Nakaguma (1988); Arita (1990). See also Whittaker (1994).
[15] Kokudo cho (1990). The PD Forum (P = plastic moulding, D = dies and moulds), which members of the Keihin Plastic Mould Cooperative Association played an important part in, was one such group launched in Kanagawa in 1983. A particular characteristic of that group was that the Ps were customers of the Ds.

chain. Joint 92 was trying to develop a new flower pot out of incinerated rubbish sludge, which transmits air but has insulating properties as well. By late 1995 a prototype had been developed, and plans were being made to move into production.

A speaker addressing a combined meeting of Ota's groups in late 1992 summarised the background of exchange and fusion groups, and hinted at their limitations. The owner of a small screw company and a leading member of the Adachi Venture group in east Tokyo, he lamented that he had not been able to raise the price for his screws since the 1960s. Many small factories in the industry had closed, and imports from Asia, where wage costs were much lower, were becoming more sophisticated. He had been berated by an assembler for supplying four defects in two million, and was having to install expensive inspection equipment at his own cost. He and others in the group felt they had reached their limit. Testing times had to be met with imagination and flexibility. Exchange groups had a role to play here. The Adachi Venture group had first developed bicycle parking equipment, which they sold at first to Adachi Ward, and then further afield, notching up 40,000 sales, but they still had not fully recouped their development costs. They were currently developing a new telephone box and a shredder – the ward would probably be the first customer here, too.

Many – not all – of the products developed by exchange and 'fusion' groups cater for niche markets, and more and more groups are seeking products for these. Quite a few depend on the patronage of public bodies. Moreover, information exchange is all well and good, but there are significant organisational problems in the development, production, and marketing phases, which the groups may not be equipped to deal with. These were the main practical problems identified by a Chuokai survey of exchange and fusion groups, as well as an underlying weakness in ideals of cooperation.[16] Indeed, where traditions of horizontal cooperation are weak, as in some company towns, there are difficulties in information exchange, let alone 'fusion'. Nonetheless, participants and coordinators point to less tangible benefits, such as thinking systematically about new developments for small firms, becoming used to interacting with external bodies like industrial technology institutes and universities, being able to talk openly about important issues without fear of it affecting business, learning new viewpoints, and making contacts outside the normal sphere of business. Some older factory owners in Ota had no time for such luxuries themselves, but saw them as a useful part of successor training. The Chuokai survey showed that the longer the group was established, the more likely its members were to engage in other cooperative activities as well. Hence they

---

[16] Zenkoku chusho kigyo dantai chuokai (1994); Tokyoto shoko shidojo (1989).

may be a vehicle for establishing habits of cooperation and creative thinking, especially amongst the new successor generation.

Finally, though perhaps not directly relevant to horizontal interfirm relations, let us look briefly at technology-based information networks.[17] A notable example within Ota is O-Net, a public and private-sector financed on-line network which provides information on Ota's companies for those wishing to place orders, also on those wishing to participate in joint orders, joint research, joint development, and information exchange. The idea originated in 1987 when the Ota branch of the Tokyo Chamber of Commerce invited the president of NTT, Japan's largest telecom company, to address its members. He suggested that, while large companies were making worldwide networks, SMEs in Ota might consider making their own to catch information quickly. A feasibility study pointed to the diversification of transaction partners, the importance of speed in modern business, and successors being more willing than their fathers to use on-line means for new business opportunities.

O-Net was subsequently established on a joint stock basis. The principal shareholders in 1990 were Ota Ward 18 per cent, NTT 15 per cent, Fujitsu 15 per cent, local Chamber of Commerce directors 10 per cent, and member companies, etc., the rest. It is housed in an annex of the NTT building in the ward with a staff of seven, headed initially by a former senior NTT researcher. The data base was built from surveys commissioned by the ward and Tokyo governments, providing information on company details, line of work (including tolerances, JIS certification, and patents), machines used, R&D capabilities, requests for information exchange, joint research and development, as well as joint orders. In late 1992 there were 800 registered subscribers.

Although it had still not broken even by 1995, O-Net has the potential to go beyond simply introducing new subcontracting work, to facilitate more fluid interfirm linkages, and to be used by small firms to forge horizontal relations to jointly enhance their business prospects. Whether this potential will be realised, and whether it will prove commercially viable, remains to be seen.

In addition to subcontracting relations, horizontal relations between small firms are an important dimension of Japan's industrial communities, especially for the smallest firms in metropolitan districts. Cooperation tempers atomistic competition. It does not extend to fixing minimum subcontracting rates, and horizontal solidarity is not strong enough to counteract price cutting pressures from large firms. It can help the smallest

---

[17] In 1991, one in eight of Ota's factories was connected to an on-line network, most commonly linked with customers so that orders and blueprints could be downloaded electronically.

firms overcome some of their size-related handicaps, however, whilst retaining their independence.

Observers of small firm associations often express concern at the level of use by members and the degree of solidarity. Stronger members have grown, and have less need of association membership. There is the question of generational change as well – successors are considered to have a more utilitarian attitude towards associations than their fathers. Such observers fear a vicious cycle of indifference and ineffectiveness, particularly in the light of new challenges such as deregulation and market changes. To the general public, associations tend to conjure up an old-fashioned image, and one of protection of vested interests. Yet, as small firms struggle in a climate of uncertainty, large firm restructuring, overseas investment, and rising imports as well as deregulation, exchange and cooperation with other small firms are just as important as ever. Supporters argue that enlightened, not old-fashioned, small firms will seek new forms of cooperation in a harsh environment, and the way to enlightenment is education, particularly of successors.[18] There are some remarkable success stories to support such views.

Somewhere in between the extremes of pessimism and aspiration lies the immediate future for small firm associations and cooperative horizontal relations in general. In machining districts where horizontal interaction has been relatively weak and where powerful assemblers have dominated vertical forms of organisation, small firms may find it hard to develop basic and sophisticated levels of horizontal cooperation. Even within Ota Ward, the onset of recession prompted owners to take work in house that they would normally farm out.[19] Joint activities have been disrupted through lack of funds and partners going into liquidation. But as one owner put it: 'You can't survive by waiting for orders from big companies and slowly losing your employees. I'm lucky because I know a lot of people, and hear a lot of problems, which is where ideas come from. You need to have new ideas, and to get people together. That's the road to survival.'

[18] Cf. Momose (1989, 1991).
[19] Some have been pressured by large companies to do this: 'When we asked them [the parent] for more work, they said you've got a nerve. Look at you, you're still dishing out work to other firms. You've got it too easy as it is [*otonosama shobai ja naika*].'

7 Founders, entrepreneurship, and innovation

Having looked at interfirm relations, let us turn our attention to the internal characteristics of small firms. Ignoring these results in small firms being seen as doormice, 'small sweatshops which are ready to submit to outside pressures', their 'passive pliability' in stark contrast to the active versatility of small firms in other countries.[1] It also results in a fundamental misunderstanding of Japan's industrial culture. Without the 'lord of the castle' (*ikkoku ichijo no aruji*) outlook of so many would-be founders and owners there would be far fewer small firms in Japan. It has been, and still is, a counterforce against amalgamation into larger units (and full cooperatives, for that matter). *Ikkoku ichijo no aruji* represents a type of individualism at odds with the normal groupist image of Japanese society and industry. It is very similar to Florence's observation of Birmingham's *petit bourgeois* owners: 'They prefer their own little works to having a small share, with possibly very little power in a large amalgamation . . . they like the feeling of running a little property. . . . Finally, the most important reason for their wishing to cling to their own little business is the feudal idea of handing it on to their family.'[2] Of course, it is not an atomistic individualism, but is most fully developed within a framework of cooperation, in great industrial districts.[3]

Similarly, the entrepreneurship of small firm owners is not of a swashbuckling, high-risk–high-return nature. It is more aptly described as craft or productionist entrepreneurship. Moreover, the embeddedness of small firms reduces risk and, in the past at least, allowed average workers to become independent. Although they might not have been highly entrepreneurial in the common use of the word, much effort, innovativeness, and

---

[1] The citations are from Grabher (1993, 18). Miyanaga describes a 'peripheral' individualistic tradition in Japan as opposed to 'core' groupism, and argues that in recent years individualistic entrepreneurship has become a more powerful force (Miyanaga, 1991). A more systematic study, however, would have revealed many antecedents to her 1970s fashion designers and 1980s high tech. designers, and would have assigned them less marginal status.   [2] Cited in Hannah (1983, 129).   [3] Cf. Marshall (1923, 577, 599).

even risk taking at times, has been needed to build and maintain their castles – or 'raise their flag' (*hito hata o ageru*) – in a competitive environment. Many failed, but until recently closures were more than compensated for by new founders seeking to become their own boss.

This chapter looks first at the backgrounds of small firm founders, their motivations and the process of becoming independent. It then looks at their attitudes towards their companies and their attempts to maintain them as viable businesses. Indicators of innovativeness are considered, including the spread of computer controlled (CNC) machine tools. Finally, as the founding generation retires and high costs and technological requirements diminish the opportunities for startups, the issue of succession becomes critical. In addition to whether or not there is a successor, and whether the succession process is handled smoothly, there are questions about whether successors are bringing new attitudes with them, and whether there is a general loss of vigour, as appears to have happened in Britain.

Starting out

Links appear to exist between self-employment and small firms in the manufacturing sector, on the one hand, and the nature of agriculture, on the other. Thus: 'In Italy a basis for the necessary entrepreneurial skills has often been thought to lie in a background of *métayage* or peasant farming.'[4] Capecchi suggests that in Emilia-Romagna the proportion of agricultural wage labourers was relatively low and that '60 per cent of the population working in agriculture had experience of small farm entrepreneurship', forming a key resource for the region's small firms and industrial districts.[5]

Dore has made the same argument for Japan, where farming has traditionally been a small-scale family activity involving managerial skills ranging from purchase of fertiliser, planting through to harvest, and sale of surplus. Hard work and innovativeness were necessary and rewarded.[6] During industrialisation, peasant farmers either maintained their agrarian links and developed side businesses, laying the roots of rural or small town manufacturing, or their migrating children brought rural attitudes and social practices with them into urban manufacturing settings. The former is said to lie behind entrepreneurial traditions in prefectures like Nagano, and the latter is to be found in small firm concentrations in the metropolitan centres.

[4] Pyke and Sengenberger (1990, 5). Urban artisans are said to form another pool.
[5] Capecchi (1990, 24).
[6] In Fukada and Dore (1993, 88–90). He contrasts this with Britain, where there was a higher proportion of agricultural wage labour. See also Smith (1959, 1987).

Where the process of urbanisation and industrialisation is rapid (or rural-based), these features are particularly pronounced. In Japan over half the urban population in 1940 had been born and raised in rural villages. In the large postwar rural–urban migration, too, 'village consciousness' was transported to the cities.[7] Most interest has focused on the community spirit aspects, however, and how these found their way into large firms, rather than the base they gave to independent and entrepreneurial activities in small firms.

Although there is little systematic data, a common image of the origin of small firm founders in Ota is that they were second or third sons of farming families (eldest sons stayed behind to take over the farm) who made their way to Tokyo and worked in factories in the Keihin Belt for a number of years before becoming independent. As one owner said: 'We thought that if we made our way to Tokyo we would find something.' Others were the children of such migrants, or of urban artisans or petty business owners. In fact, owners have a great variety of backgrounds, as the following three examples suggest. The founder of C. Manufacturing came to Tokyo from nearby Chiba in the 1930s and found a job at Meidensha (a famous heavy electrical company in Ota). Before he was called up for the war he quit this job and went to work for a small mould manufacturer for six months. 'I asked my friends what the most difficult type of work was and they said moulds. That's what I decided to do.' When he returned from the war he started out again with some friends, became independent in 1950, and founded his company in 1953. The founder of K. Grinding was born in east Tokyo, but was evacuated to his mother's hometown in Fukushima prefecture during the war. The family returned after the war, and he eventually followed in his brother's footsteps, becoming a trainee grinder in a small firm. In 1960 they left their respective companies and went into business together, and went their independent ways in 1971. The founder of J. Precision came to Tokyo from a rural community in northern Japan during the early high growth period. He was trained as a grinding machine operator and worked his way up through a precision ball screw company to become its manufacturing director. When the company moved to northern Japan in 1984, he took the opportunity to become independent and realise his dream of owning his own factory.

Reasons for founding are equally diverse. In some cases independence was not planned – the factory they were working in was bombed, went bankrupt or the owner died, they lost their job by becoming involved in the labour movement or becoming sick, and so on. The founder had to make a choice between seeking employment again or becoming independent, and, with the help of relatives, friends, or former customers, chose the latter. In

---

[7] Fukutake (1989, 33–4); cf. also Dore (1958); Vogel (1967).

other cases independence was the realisation of a dream, the end result of several years of planning, saving, and acquiring the necessary skills and contacts. Here, too, the final step was often triggered by an event such as relocation or an argument with the boss.

The main motives for independence, according to a number of surveys, have traditionally been: being able to make full use of talents, not wanting to be employed by others, securing a high income, and a lifework of doing something worth devoting oneself to (*ikigai o eru tame*). In a survey on self-employment in Tokyo, too, which stressed the spontaneity of becoming independent, these four reasons topped the list regardless of founding date. The main triggers were: that the time – and the founder's age – was right, preparations were complete, and disagreements with bosses.[8] Thus, founders want to be their own bosses and reap the benefits of their own work. They do not want to bow and scrape to others. They are not stereotypical 'salary men'. 'In other words . . . the self-actualisation dreams and ideals of employed workers are linked to becoming independent. They choose to get out of the company or organisation logic, to become independent and start up on their own.'[9] This is the neglected branch of Japan's industrial culture but a key source of small firm entrepreneurship.

The majority were not stereotypical salary men even in employment. Prior to the 1960s as many as a quarter of Ota's small firm founders had worked in firms with over 300 employees, but as economic conditions stabilised and 'lifetime employment' became established in large firms, and as large firm numbers declined, the proportion becoming independent from them decreased. The overwhelming majority of founders worked in small firms prior to becoming independent.[10] Koike estimated that almost 20 per cent of employees in SMEs with more than 30 employees would become independent in the first half of the 1960s, with the proportion rising to almost 30 per cent later in the decade. For those in SMEs with less than 30 employees, the chances were even greater; for the one to nine employee size category they were almost one in two.[11] The proportions might be surprising, but the link with size is not. Studies in other countries have also shown small firms to be the most fertile incubators. Employees have greater contact with those who have set up firms themselves, and can gain more all-round experience, or at least observe various aspects of business and the markets they operate in.[12]

---

[8] Tokyo toritsu rodo kenkyujo (1992, 50); cf. also Nihon rodo kenkyu kiko (1996).
[9] Kamata (1995, 6).
[10] Chiiki shinko seibi kodan (1978, 47–8). Although dated, according to this survey, until the late 1970s two thirds of Ota's founders had worked in firms with less than 100 employees, with 10–29 employees being the most common size.
[11] Koike (1981a).   [12] Cf. Johnson and Cathcart (1979), on the size of incubators in Britain.

There are two interpretations in the case of Japan. Would-be founders may deliberately seek employment in small firms to gain the necessary experience before becoming independent themselves, or else inferior conditions and limited scope for advancement in small firms encourage them to become independent after they have got the necessary experience. The seven to ten years they commonly work before starting out on their own may be considered an apprenticeship period, or, as one owner said: 'After seven or eight years they start to look around them. They see their boss making a lot more money than them, and they ask why shouldn't I be getting that, too?' This is about the time when wage differentials with workers in large firms are becoming obvious, and family expenses are growing. In many cases the motivation will be a mixture of the two, but surveys have shown that founders had the ambition to become independent from early on, in many cases before they were even employed.[13]

Small firms in Japan have been particularly good incubators. According to one survey, over half of founders received no assistance from their former company upon independence, but this proportion has declined sharply over time. In some cases founders receive customers, technical, or financial assistance, and about a quarter do subcontracting work for their former company upon independence.[14] Such assistance has been traced back to the practice of *noren wake*, whereby merchant houses set up able and faithful employees in a branch business in feudal Japan. Employers have used this prospect to motivate workers, and the help they offer secures them a subcontractor with obligational debts.

Such assistance has made it easier for would-be founders to realise their dream and become independent, but it does raise the question of how independent they really become. An extreme case is an 'internal subcontractor', dependent for 100 per cent of his orders from his old company, working on the company premises with his old machine.[15] Most cases are not as extreme, and even where an ex-employee is highly dependent initially, it may be a stepping stone on the road to greater substantial independence. He may be dependent at that point in time for order sources, but independent in terms of motivational drive. Becoming 'independent' (*dokuritsu kaigyo*) is significant because (to varying extents) the worker has become

---

[13] E.g., Inagami (1989a, 103–4).

[14] Cf. Chusho kigyo cho (ed.) (1986a, 55). A recent survey suggests that three quarters of companies from which workers became independent offered help, two thirds in the form of work; Nihon rodo kenkyu kiko (1996).

[15] According to one viewpoint, this is the epitomy of exploitation. The person is in effect a wage labourer without any statutory protection. In the particular case I am referring to, however, the agreement was entered into voluntarily. The ex-employee worked his own hours and his salary almost doubled (although he had to pay his own social security contributions, of course, and a nominal rent).

his own boss, and has a new social status which can be proudly printed on a name card.[16]

Living, work , and lifework

After taking the first steps towards establishing their 'castle', small firm owners go to great lengths to maintain and develop it. The most obvious manifestation of this effort is long working hours, for which small firm owners have always been renowned. G.C. Allen commented on it in the early 1920s, and his description is still reasonably apt: 'There were numerous small metal and engineering workshops equipped with two or three drilling machines or lathes. In all of them work seemed to go on far into the night.'[17] Again, this may be seen in terms of exploitation. Excessively long working hours are necessary to maintain even a basic standard of living. Without such self-exploitation owners would soon go out of business. But even wealthy owners – measured, for instance, by multiple golf club memberships or luxury cars in their garage – work long hours. That is how they accumulated their wealth in the first place, although wealth is usually not their primary objective.

Allen's observation that much of the work went on in rooms or sheds attached to the owners' homes also largely applies today. Almost half (45.7 per cent) of Ota's factories had housing attached in 1985, and another 10.8 per cent had separate housing, but on the same premises. If we exclude from the picture large factories and factories on the reclaimed islands, where residence is prohibited, the proportion is even higher. Over two thirds of micro-factories had housing on the same premises. These owners do not have to commute. They can simply go downstairs to turn on the machines in the morning, pop upstairs for lunch, come down to change over parts during TV commercial breaks in the evening, do a rush order on Sunday evening. . . .[18] Psychologically as well as physically, living and work are not clearly separated. Work is many owners' living sphere (*seikatsu no ba*), and their lifework. It is a major part of their identity and self-esteem, and is not reducible to simple economic calculation. They are very reluctant to give it up even if the returns are not economically justifiable.

After returning from a trip to Taiwan in 1992, the owner of J. Precision commented: 'The margins here can be anywhere from 5–30 per cent. In Taiwan they won't touch most of it. Why sweat over 10 per cent, they say. Better to change your line of business.' Despite the recession, he had just bought land and proceeded to build a new factory with a house on top. He

---

[16] Again, in these industries it normally is 'his'. The proportion of women who own and run businesses in Japan is increasing, however (see chapter 11).
[17] Allen (1983, 35–6).   [18] Seki and Kato (1990, 337–9); Mori (1982).

shrugged off the notion of risk: 'I will do this even in a recession because I plan to be doing it for the rest of my life. I'm doing it for the future.'

There is a widespread perception that unlike the 'salaryman', small firm owners can get away with all sorts of tax fiddles, writing off personal expenses as business expenses, putting family members on the books however tenuous their contribution, and so on.[19] This is on top of an already lenient tax regime for small firms, as a result of which, many pay very little in the way of taxes. Owners themselves may view it as a natural compensation for the risks and rigours of running a small business, but even when they fiddle taxes, it is not normally to 'milk' the business for other purposes. They may indeed draw substantial wages but then loan money back to the company to lower the overall tax burden. They will also loan it back during difficult times or when a large investment is needed. Such juggling can help maintain stability through good years and bad, reducing the risk, and circumventing the rigidities of the tax system. Even when family and business finances are clearly separated, living and work are not.

An owner's 'lifework' is not necessarily confined to a specific product or line of business. Some do work consistently within a specialisation such as grinding or milling, but others may start off subcontracting lathe work and end up doing press work, or grinding, or even part assembly. They may move into rubber or plastic extrusion products if they offer better opportunities. The ability to make switches is both necessary and commendable, but within limits. An owner who converts his factory into a parking lot or apartments for rent, as some did during the 'bubble' years of the late 1980s, is generally considered to have sold out. He has stopped producing. Thus the distinctive outlook of the *machi koba* owner is in fact a combination of the 'lord of the castle' mentality and a productionist culture (*monozukuri bunka*).

As with the traditional family farm, it is unlikely that the 'lifework' will be sold as a going concern. Mergers and acquisitions are not uncommon amongst Japan's larger corporations, but they are still rare amongst small firms, despite the much trumpeted arrival of the 'age of M&A'. An exception may be where there is no successor. According to managers at the Ota branch of a major city bank: 'It used to be that if the 70-year old president of a small company came and said he wanted to retire with no successor, we would advise him on how to close down. Recently, though, people have

---

[19] The wife is quite often the bookkeeper – 'finance director' – both in practice and for tax purposes. Traditionally the wife has had other roles as well, such as washing overalls and making meals for the employees, but this is less common now, and she may have a job, even her own small business in some cases, elsewhere. The father may be 'chairman' or 'advisor'. Cf. also Patrick and Rohlen (1987) on taxes and small family enterprises.

come to think of the M&A option.' They themselves were consulting on two such cases at the time. The trickle has yet to become a flood. The number of mergers and acquisitions involving SMEs increased from 190 in 1984 to 751 in 1990, according to the SME Agency, but less than half of these involved two Japanese parties.[20]

Most small firm owners in Ota still found the concept remote from their own sense of business. When pressed they were skeptical that it would work in businesses like theirs, or that the network of customers and business contacts that they had built up over the years would be transferable to a third party, or, during the recession, that anyone would want to take on their debts. And, expressing the arguments just made: 'What would be the point? This is where I live. If I sold up, I would have to move away from my living sphere as well.' If they do retire or close down, they usually sell their machine tools to a second hand dealer, and either rent out the factory, sell the land to fund a retirement residence, or more likely, construct a new retirement residence on the premises. They will either lay any remaining employees off, or ask friends to take them on, perhaps with a machine tool thrown in. They might redirect work to acquaintances, but they have not yet begun to sell customer lists, as is common in Birmingham.

Innovation

Small firm founders in the 1960s were typically middle school or high school graduates, often the former. That does not mean they were not bright, or that they were not literate or numerate. One of the successes of Japanese education has been high '3R' standards not just among elites, but in all strata of the education system, and these, according to Patrick and Rohlen, have been an important enabling condition for small firm entrepreneurship:

Insufficient education can be a significant barrier to the generation of small businesses, especially in an advanced economy where such characteristics as illiteracy, poor work habits, or the inability to grasp technological or business complexities preclude successful entrepreneurship. The high average level of education in Japan assures the society a large pool of well-trained potential entrepreneurs.[21]

Small firm owners are normally not thrusting, high-risk–high-return entrepreneurs. Their form of entrepreneurship is craft based or productionist, but it still requires innovation to maintain their castles, and even risk taking. It is quite common to find owners investing heavily during recessions, for instance: 'I decided to gamble everything after the yen rise. If it

---

[20] Interview at Ota branch, Sanwa Bank, October 1992; Chusho kigyo cho (ed.) (1992a, 192).
[21] Patrick and Rohlen (1987, 355); also Dore and Sako (1987); Whittaker (1990).

didn't work I would just have to start over again. I bought an ¥18 million Swiss machine, the first, and then the third and seventh in the country. . . .' The gamble paid off, because it secured him new work.

One type of innovation is product innovation. Roughly one in ten factories in Ota is a product maker. These are often the larger factories, but two thirds have less than 30 employees. Many were once subcontractors. Examples already given include F. Industries, whose founder began by machining parts for Mitsubishi and Isuzu after the war, developed his own machine to do the work, and subsequently grew into a customised machine tool maker. S. Electronics, too, developed a machine to do some of its sub-contracted PCB mounting work, which became its first product. Most are not product makers, however, and process innovation is a better measure of their innovativeness. Possession of mechatronic machinery is often taken as an indicator. (It is a rough one, since mechatronic machines are not suited to all kinds of work, the time spent in programming non repeat one-off work may make them uneconomical, and owners may make rational business decisions *not* to invest in them.) CNC (computer numerical control) machine tools, whose movements are controlled by a programmable computer, are the prime example on the shop floor.[22]

In an earlier comparative study of CNC use, I showed that although large Japanese companies began to introduce the earlier generation NC machines later than their British or American counterparts, the time lag before they found their way into small firms was compressed. Small factories began introducing CNC slightly earlier than their British counterparts, and were on average quicker to make subsequent purchases. They were also more likely to use the technology for unmanned and multi-machine (one operator for several machines) operating. This suggests a willingness to innovate on the part of small firm owners.[23] In 1981 almost one in five of Ota Ward's factories (18.4 per cent) had at least one CNC machine. Two years later the figure had climbed to 22.0 per cent, and by 1988 it had reached 32.3 per cent. These figures are noteworthy given that 80 per cent of Ota's factories have fewer than ten employees. Many of the non-intro-ducers have no doubt decided not to introduce the machines, but earlier

---

[22] Numerical control technology was developed after the war, but it was not until the application of computers (CNC) in the late 1960s–early 1970s, which simplified the hardware, reduced costs, and improved reliability, that it became a viable investment for small firms. The subsequent development of machining centres, too, enabled several processes to be done on a single machine, easing space constraints in small factories.

[23] Whittaker (1990). For slow diffusion into small factories in the US, see Kelley and Brooks (1988). MITI's 1994 machine tool census showed a remarkable consistency in CNC possession across factory sizes in Japan; 18.8 per cent of machine tools in establishments with 50–99 employees (the smallest size category surveyed) were CNC, compared with 23.2 per cent in factories with 1,000+ employees (Tsusansho (ed.) 1995, 382–4).

introducers have also been busy purchasing additional and more sophisticated machine tools. The proportion with machining centres grew from 11 per cent in 1986 to 15 per cent in 1991, while those with robots increased from 5 per cent to 7 per cent over the same time. CNC laser cutters, costing ¥60 million or more and rare in large factories could be found in micro-factories by the end of the 1980s, in addition to less glamorous but equally expensive specialist machine tools.[24]

The machines are purchased for various reasons. In addition to technical requirements and versatility, substituting for labour in the face of labour shortages is one major reason. Owners also say they need the machines now to secure orders – if they do not have one or two they are likely to be considered backward by larger customers. This and a fad element – not wanting to be left behind – have resulted in some machines (10 per cent according to one Ward survey) being bought and seldom used. CNC also makes it easier for customers to cost work, and some owners reported a growing tendency for customers not to recognise programming time – which can be considerable for small-batch production – thus eroding profit margins necessary to cover the cost of the machines. The dangers of excessive capital investment, too, became apparent after the late 1980s investment boom, when recession-hit owners were struggling to repay the interest on their loans, let alone the principal. 'It's a debt hell. If the banks called in their loans, we'd all go down.' 'I know someone who bought a machine for ¥300 million. Three years on he can't even sell it for ¥15 million. He can't afford to close down.' 'With all this investment there's a lot more capacity, but no work.'

This is a far cry from the image of small firms as technological backwaters. It does not mean that they are all state-of-the art and bristling with new technology. Nor are they paragons of *kaizen*, TQC (total quality control), rational management, cleanliness, and tidiness. Such factories are more likely to be found outside the capital, or on its fringes, doing volume work for large assemblers. On entering a *machi koba*, one is likely to be confronted with a clutter of old machines, tools, and parts, changed only in the past decade by the accumulation of oil, modifications, and more tools. Only on closer inspection, hidden beyond a partition will you find the CNC machines or FMCs (flexible manufacturing cells, combining CNC with automatised loading or unloading), and sometimes CAD (computer aided design) in an adjacent room.

Most first generation founders are worker (craftsman)-managers, in that order. They have very detailed knowledge of the performance of machines which do their work, and often know exactly where in the world the best

[24] Ota ku (various years).

machines, tools, and materials are produced, more so it seems to me
than the vast majority of engineers in large companies, but they have
spent little time reading the latest literature on *kaizen* and TQC, let alone
on re-engineering or downsizing. Their approach to 'softer' types of
process innovation may therefore lack strategic planning or consistency. In
fact, this may characterise their overall approach to business; highly committed to production, and how to raise precision, reduce defects and tackle
new technical challenges, but failing to step back and take a detached look
at where they are heading. It may have sufficed in the past, but in the current
upheavals in Japanese industry, this last ability has become more important, as have general managerial skills.

Whether successors to the first generation founders will provide these
abilities is a critical issue. Before considering this, we might recall Florence's
contention, that the most important reason for *petit bourgeois* owners
wishing to 'cling to their own little business' is the 'feudal' desire to pass it
on to their children. This may be put more positively; the desire to pass on
a viable business to children provides an incentive to innovate. In fact it
might be the biggest incentive, more important than whether the firm is a
subcontractor or not, the background of the founder, or where the
company is located. In so many factories visited, the launch of a new
product or the presence of mechatronic machinery coincided with the presence of a successor. In some cases the innovation was carried out by the successor, but founders wishing to pass on a viable business also tended to be
open to new ideas. As an elderly owner who made a large investment in new
(non CNC) machines during the post 'bubble' recession commented: 'I
bought them with my retirement money. I wanted to be sure my sons are in
a sound position for the next ten years.'

Conversely, where there was no successor and the founder was nearing
retirement, there was much less incentive to innovate. These factories were
gradually contracting, and would close when the owner retired. Some
observers fear the loss of these factories as much as the overinvestors. In the
words of an SME advisor in Tokyo: 'There are a lot of tiny factories which
do terminal, unattractive work. They have no successor, and they haven't
kept up with technological innovation. But they have always fulfilled an
important role. Companies asked them do do work by tomorrow and they
did, cheaply. When they close, it will weaken the industrial base.'

Declining startups and succession

Forty three percent of Ota's top managers/owners were aged 60 or more in
1994. A further 35 per cent were in their 50s. Less than a quarter were under
50, and these figures presumably include factories in which a successor has

taken over. One quarter of Ota's factories were founded before 1955, half between 1955 and 1969, and a quarter since then, with declining frequency. Peak startup years were the 1960s.[25] Ota was once known as a ward for the young, but no longer. The aging of owners is not just a problem of Ota, however. It reflects a long-term decline in the number of startups in Japan, both in manufacturing and in the economy as a whole. From an annual startup rate of 6.0 per cent (of total manufacturing establishments) in the late 1960s, the figure had halved by the 1980s (figure 7.1. It is not clear at this stage whether the slight upturn in the 1990s represents a reversal of this trend).[26]

The decline in independent startups is even more dramatic. According to one set of estimates, 85.9 per cent of startups prior to 1979 were of this kind, with 8.5 per cent started as subsidiaries and 5.6 per cent through diversification. By 1991 the proportions had shifted to 47.4 per cent, 47.4 per cent and 5.3 per cent respectively.[27] And the dwindling ranks of independent startups show a marked change in profile, from middle school or high school-graduate, small firm blue-collar workers in their late 20s–30s, to managers, engineers, or salesmen, often with tertiary education, from somewhat larger companies, in their late 30s or 40s.[28] The proportion becoming independent without the help of their former company has also declined. The founder of J. Precision (eight employees) mentioned above personifies some of these trends. Although he received only high school education, he was the manufacturing director of a local ball screw company (40 employees) before it relocated in 1984. In his mid 40s, he used the opportunity to start his own grinding company (with some initial orders from his old company) and subsequently a second company (four employees) to do pre-grinding work. An obvious obstacle for blue-collar would-be founders is the sharp rise in startup costs, which more than doubled during the 1980s. Greater technical and managerial sophistication are necessary to gain orders as well. The bottom line is that starting out with a second hand lathe bought with severance money in small rented premises is no longer a realistic proposition.

In addition to rising barriers, there is the question of entrepreneurial drive. A popular perception is that new generations raised in affluence lack the drive – the 'hungry spirit' – needed to become independent and endure

---

[25] Ota ku (1995a, 32, 40).
[26] Six per cent may not seem particularly high; Storey (1994, 76) notes that 14 per cent of VAT-registered businesses in Britain in 1990 had been established in the past 12 months. If the Japanese figures were compiled on a yearly basis they would no doubt be higher too, since many firms disappear within one or two years of startup, and they may be missed in three-yearly calculations. The different time periods of evaluation may also alter the figures, but they provide the best estimates available.
[27] Chusho kigyo cho (ed.) (1992a, 169).
[28] Kokumin kin'yu koko (ed.) (1992, 63); Tokyoto shoko shidojo (1992, 72).

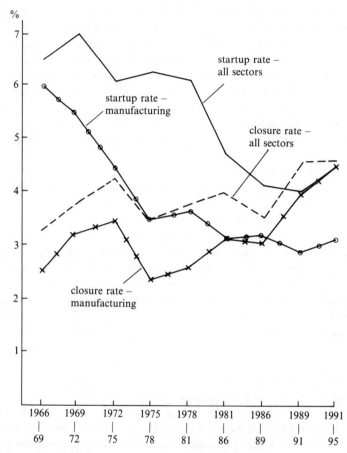

Figure 7.1 Startup and closure rates in Japan, 1966–1994
Note: Startup (closure) rates=

$$\frac{\text{no. of startups (closures) during period}}{\text{no of businesses at beginning of period}} \times \frac{1}{\text{years during period}} \times 100$$

Source: Chusho Kigyo cho (1995a, 126); Hori (1995, 30); originally Management and Coordination Agency, *Establishment Census of Japan* (various years).

adversity, or even to acquire the necessary skills in the first place. The following comments reflect owners' views on the situation:

'About 15 of our employees became independent in the past. They were usually good workers. None want to become independent now, though. The work is too specialised to learn easily. You need work scheduling and operations control, and to be able to do several things at the same time. The machines are complicated and expensive. You probably need ¥100 million for the machines alone.' (Mould maker. High wages in the industry might also serve as a disincentive for independence.)

'In this factory 70 per cent don't want to become independent, but 30 per cent do. There is less desire now, and it has become more difficult. Land and machines are too expensive. Owners have to help them to become independent.'

'Ours don't want to become independent. I wish a few more of them had the get-up-and-go spirit to do it.'

The dream of independence, to be their own boss, has been a powerful motivator for small firm employees, and is an important reason for the enormous number of small firms in Japan. But for many who have the inclination nowadays, it will remain a dream.[29]

The dynamic of rejuvenation through new startups has thus been curtailed, just as many postwar founders are approaching retirement. In the light of this reality, succession has become a critical issue: first, whether or not there is a successor, second, whether the process of succession is handled successfully, and, third, the attitudes and abilities of successors to run the company once they are in control. Let us look at these concerns in turn.

Many owners are pessimistic about their chances of finding someone to take over when they retire, with good reason. Only a third of factories in Ota (and Tokyo) with less than 20 employees have a definite successor, another third are hopeful, but the matter has not been settled, and a third have no successor, according to surveys. The smaller the factory, the less likely there is to be a successor.[30] Retirement without a successor is an important reason for the rising closure rates in both manufacturing and in the economy as a whole. Even where closures are obviously linked to other problems – 'parent' company closure or relocation, failure to secure orders, failure to recruit workers – the root cause may be the lack of a successor.

Part of the problem is that children are well aware of their parents' toil in maintaining their business through ups and downs over the years, and of the constant pressures brought to bear on them and their family through

---

[29] Less than 10 per cent of manufacturing companies in the Nihon rodo kenkyu kiko (1996) survey mentioned above had had employees become independent in the past five years.

[30] Tokyo shoko kaigisho, Ota shibu (1992); Jichiroren (1993); Tokyoto shoko shidojo (1992).

price cutting, tight delivery schedules, and demands for greater precision and fewer defects. This has undoubtedly contributed to the celebrated competitiveness of Japanese industry, but some of the stresses and tensions are being visited on the next generation in the form of disillusionment among children. Parents themselves are often ambivalent about wanting their children to take over: 'A survey in the Nikkei [newspaper] recently said 36 per cent of shop-floor workers at Toyota wouldn't want their children to do the same job. What would it be for *machi koba*? More like 100 per cent.' Children of owners are likely to go on to higher education, giving them access to jobs in large companies, and they may decide that, unlike their parents, even the workaholic 'salaryman' gets some time off for holidays.

On the other hand, they may decide that the traditional incentives for founding – making use of their talents, being their own boss, higher income, something worth devoting themselves to – apply to succession as well. This is indeed what one survey of successors found, with the added important reason of taking over the family business. Even this was not just a matter of filial piety, though; as many found the work as interesting and rewarding as their fathers. They could also put titles on their name cards like factory manager or managing director far earlier than their friends in large companies.[31]

Like recent founders, many of the successors have been to university and studied either economics or management or engineering. Then they often go to work for another company for a few years – a 'parent' company or the factory of a friend or acquaintance, but sometimes a company in a completely different line of business. Sometimes the succession is never in doubt, sometimes it comes after a change of heart by the successor. In other cases, especially where there are worker shortage problems, children – that is who successors generally are – begin working immediately after school or university. They may negotiate terms before taking the plunge. This may include a commitment to purchasing mechatronic equipment, for instance, which they are put in charge of. They may be given room to develop new business. As one said: 'You've got to make it interesting for yourself if you're going to be doing it for the rest of your life.'

At S. Machines (12 employees) the successor studied mechanical engineering at Tokyo Institute of Technology. His professors wanted him to go on to do postgraduate work, but his father opposed the idea. It would make him less likely to return. He then considered working for a major machine tool maker where his father had worked for many years, and went through the preliminary recruitment procedures and factory tour. He realised,

---

[31] Nihon shoko kaigisho (1984).

though, that he would only be working there for three or four years, gave up the idea and entered his father's company.

The successor at C. Manufacturing (13 employees) studied industrial management at Nihon University. He wanted to join a life insurance company, which his friends said would be a cushy job, but his father threatened not to let him marry if he did. Instead he went to work for another mould maker for two years before joining his father's company (and purchasing their first CNC machine).

As these examples suggest, parents are willing to let their children follow their interests, up to a point. There are advantages in them bringing back fresh ideas, but dangers of them being sidetracked. Parents are also aware of the conventional wisdom that businesses struggle in the second generation and collapse in the third. The transition, therefore, is taken very seriously, and handing over the reins takes several years. In addition to gaining the right management and technical skills, the successor must be accepted by customers and employees. Older workers in particular may feel ambivalent towards the 'gaffer's son', especially if he comes with grand and risky plans but no practical experience. Loyalty and deference has its limits.

For example, the founder of N. Machines (press machine maker with 40 employees, but only 12 at succession) was a first-rate draughtsman, but not a business manager. The company was faced with rising debts, and its future was thrown into doubt when he died suddenly. The bank was reluctant to extend new loans to the cousin who took over, and insisted that the founder's wife and/or son, who worked for IBM Japan, should be the principle owners. At first the son was simply an advisor, and he reluctantly increased his commitment at the urging of the factory manager. Although he was the son of the founder, some of the older craftsmen resisted being managed by a non-engineer, and someone whose commitment they questioned. Two or three left along with the cousin, and the son gave up his IBM job. He eventually put the company on a sound financial footing, changing it from a family business to a business enterprise.

This brings us to the third concern: successors' attitudes and abilities. Will successors be as committed to maintaining the businesses their parents built? When the going gets rough, will they really stick with it, or will they be prepared to sell the business and pursue other interests, as happened to the sons and grandsons of Victorian founders? Will they, in other words, conform to Veblin's prediction of a craft or handiwork-based economy giving way to a business era dominated by pecuniary principles?[32]

Founders themselves have mixed views on the 'junior problem'. Some fear the worst, others concede that 'juniors' might actually do a better job

[32] Veblin (1914, 216–17, 329).

in a challenging modern environment that calls for fresh ideas and vigour. Successors undoubtedly do belong to a new generation, with different views on management and business. A number of these differences have been noted: less reliance on traditional craft skills and a keen interest in mechatronic innovation, suggesting a technical approach to their work, a greater reluctance to borrow tools from 'parent' companies and become indebted to them, and a willingness to develop new business through on-line networks, suggesting a more 'businesslike' approach to management.

Some of these qualities are indeed demanded in the modern business environment in Japan. But also critical is whether the traditional strengths of the 'lord of the castle' and productionist orientations will be maintained or lost in the process. Where they are maintained, the old combined with the new, the prospects of survival in a fast-changing environment are rated by the founding generation as favourable. Where the traditional drive is diminished, however, and successors take a more instrumental approach to business, they may more readily sell or close down in the face of hardship.

Successors themselves still at least appear to harbour the 'feudal' desire to pass on their business to their own children: 'I'm lucky. My children can come and call me for lunch. They can see what life is about, what their daddy is doing. But if we just keep going on in the same old ways and don't make the place interesting, no-one will want to take over. That's what drives me on.' 'If my children see me sweating night and day and coming back home complaining all the time, they're hardly likely to want to take over, are they?' The spur to innovation this provides to the successor generation goes beyond purchasing new machines and rationalising production to rebuilding factories, finding new business, even changing lifestyles. They are forced to reduce excessive amounts of work, take holidays, and take a more measured approach to their business. Thus even traditional reasons may lead them in a more instrumental direction. It is a delicate balance.

Recalling Kiyonari's fourfold topology of employment – enterprise-type businesses, enterprise family-type businesses, livelihood family businesses, and side businesses, or household pieceworking – and the long-term trend towards the former type, it seems clear that succession will promote this evolution. It will also be promoted, however, by the closure of many small livelihood businesses with no successor, where there has been little invest-ment in new technology and where a changing and harsher environment will bring to an end the lifelong efforts of a generation to keep the flag flying over their little castles.

8   Employment, skills, and technology

Like management and innovation, employment in small firms tends to be attributed to external factors, such as exploitation or pressure from large firms. The latter can offer their employees job security and superior wages and conditions, while small firms can only offer insecurity and hard labour, with no collective protection. Small firm employees are by definition peripheral workers, since core workers are confined to the 'aristocracy' of regular employees in large firms. Once again, however, an appreciation of intrafirm dynamics – employment, skills and technology in this case – yields a different picture.

Since many small factory owners were once small factory workers, it is not surprising that the two groups have much in common. Just as owners were not typical 'salarymen', their workers are not typical 'company men'. Many are individualists of sorts; if this did not lead them to become independent, it traditionally led them to identify more with their craft skills than with the particular company they worked for. (Owners, too, gained their craft orientation from their 'apprenticeship' as employees.) In former times they moved from factory to factory in search of higher pay and/or more challenging work, but the craft orientation survived the transition to a more sedentary lifestyle.

Common backgrounds do not ensure harmonious employment relations. Owners tend to view their companies as their own personal property, not surprisingly, and their personnel practices are sometimes branded as premodern. More accurately, they might be described as a blend of familism and pragmatic adaptation. It is true that they have less scope than large firms to accommodate the needs and aspirations of their employees, but they will try hard to keep skilled workers, either in their employment, or as subcontractors if they become independent.

The problem is that many of these craftsmen are now middle aged or retiring, like the founders. There are problems not just in attracting younger workers, but in encouraging them to acquire skills as well. New technology has been used to fill the resultant skill gap and in attempts to attract young workers. It can only partially plug the gap though, and concern is mounting of a 'hollowing out' of the skills base.

This chapter begins with a brief overview of small firm employment and industrial relations. It then gives a sketch of personnel practices in selected factories in Ota, showing both diversity and common overarching concerns. Finally, it looks at the relation between skills and technology, the threat skill shortages pose to non-innovators, on the one hand, and the spur to innovators, on the other. The result is a reinforcement of trends identified in earlier chapters, a decline in the number of livelihood micro-businesses, and a more systematic approach to management elsewhere.

Peripheral workers and craftsmen

Around three quarters of Japanese manufacturing workers are employed in establishments with less than 300 employees, a quarter in establishments with less than 20 employees (table 1.1). If self-employed and family workers are included, the small firm share of employment is even more pronounced (table 2.2). The proportion increased in the 1970s, and has declined since the mid 1980s, but over the long term it has been remarkably stable. Given these statistics, a model of 'Japanese-style employment' could just as easily be based on small firms as on large firms, but it would be much harder to construct given the greater diversity of employment practices.

Employment in small firms has been the subject of debate in many countries. On the one hand, job spans tend to be wider than in large firms, where they may be broken down into discrete components performed by different workers. The 'personal touch' and lack of bureaucracy add a human dimension to the employment relationship. Small firm workers often score more highly than large firm workers in job satisfaction surveys. On the other hand, the human dimension is not always salutary. Owners can be dictatorial, and there is little recourse to collective support when disagreements occur. Working conditions, including health and safety, are often inferior.[1]

Of the contrasting views of small firm employment, there is no doubt as to which has predominated in Japan. In the Marxist view, small firms are the victims of exploitation by large firm monopoly capital. The position of small firm owners is somewhat ambiguous – they are sometimes placed in a separate category of exploited 'folk' capital – but the real victims are their workers, who have to do the dirty and dangerous jobs forced on to

---

[1] For a positive view of work in small firms in the UK, see Ingham (1970). For a contrasting view, see Rainnie (1989).

them by large companies, for low wages and with little welfare protection. Other ideological viewpoints support a negative view, too. The employer's federation Nikkeiren, for instance, points to problems within small firms themselves, such as low productivity, archaic 'one man' management, and 'premodern' employment practices.[2]

Such views have been challenged, notably by Koike, who argued that yawning wage differentials are misleading, not just because like is not compared with like, but because many blue-collar workers ultimately become independent (or white-collar workers), with earnings at least as high as their large firm counterparts. The majority of workers in small firms are as contented as workers in large firms; it is only older, blue-collar workers who really lose out. Since workers become independent or managers, low unionisation rates *per se* are not a problem either, and, besides, there is often an employee association which takes on some union functions.[3]

Declining startup rates undermine much of this argument. Wage differentials have doggedly persisted (cf. table 8.1). And, at the end of the day, job seekers with ability and academic qualifications prefer to work in larger companies. True, wages in Japan are strongly related to age, gender, education, years of employment, and employment status, in addition to company size, and when these are controlled for, and apples are compared with apples not pears, the wage gap shrinks considerably. But the fact is, there are many 'pears' in small firms. Pears here means a disproportionate number of older workers (where the wage gap is greatest; many are part of a 'downward drift' into smaller firms), a disproportionate number of women (particularly middle-aged women who have reentered the labour market after early child rearing, usually on a part time basis), workers with lower education levels (those with higher education seek employment in elite companies higher up the size scale) and fewer years of continuous employment (because of job changing, due to personal career development or job loss), and a higher proportion of non-regular employees.[4]

Statistics on non-regular employment are slippery, since a wide range of definitions is used, but figures for part timers in table 8.2 illustrate the last point.[5] Almost half of female part timers worked in firms with less than 30 employees in 1990. Working hours can be taken as an indicator of differences in conditions. Table 8.3 shows sharp differences, and if workers rather than firms covered is used as the basis of calculation, they are even greater. Large firms also offer more paid holidays, and a higher proportion of holiday entitlement is actually taken.

---

[2] Nikkeiren (1985). For an interesting, first-hand account of conditions of small firm workers in the construction sector, see L'Hénoret (1993).

[3] Koike (1981a).   [4] Cf. Chalmers (1989).

[5] Between 50 per cent and 60 per cent of non-regular employees are classified as part timers.

Table 8.1 *Wage and labour cost differentials by size of firm, 1991*

	Firm size (employees)			
	1,000–4,999	300–999	100–299	30–99
Cash earnings	100 (417,756)	90.8	81.2	73.6
Other labour costs	100 (82,934)	80.7	67.0	62.9
Of which: statutory welfare benefits	100 (41,174)	90.8	81.2	82.0
non-statutory welfare benefits	100 (14,470)	64.3	54.1	53.9
retirement/severance money	100 (20,818)	73.0	49.2	37.1
education and training	100 (2,635)	57.0	43.9	27.4
other	100 (3,837)	93.5	75.1	56.6

Note:
Size category 1,000–4,999 employees=100, other figures are relative to this.
Figures in ( )=average amount in ¥ per month.
Source: Rodosho (1992c), *Rodosha fukushi shisetsu seidoto chosa hokoku: Heisei 3 nen* (Survey Report on Systems of Worker Welfare Provision, 1991).

Table 8.2 *Part-time workers by firm size, 1992*

	Firm size (employees)					
	1,000+	300–999	100–299	30–99	5–29	Total
Proportion of employees who are part timers	6.8	12.8	13.5	13.7	15.4	12.4
Percentage composition	11.7	14.3	17.9	19.2	34.3	100

Note:
Part timers are defined as workers whose scheduled working hours per day or days per week are less than those of regular employees.
Source: Japan Institute of Labour (1995), *Japanese Working Life Profile*, p. 26; originally Rodosho, *Koyo doko chosa* (Survey on Labour Trends).

Table 8.3 *Extent of the five day working week*

	Firm size (employees)		
	1,000+	100–999	30–99
Five days	68.1	26.8	14.9
Five days, three times a month	16.8	23.8	11.6
Five days, alternate weeks	7.9	15.5	18.0
Five days, twice a month	3.0	14.4	14.8
Five days, once a month	2.0	10.2	23.3
Five and a half days	0.2	0.7	1.4
Six days	1.7	8.5	15.9
Other	0.3	0.2	0.2

Note:
Figures represent percentage of companies in each category.
Source: Japan Institute of Labour (1995), *Japanese Working Life Profile*, p. 45;
originally Rodosho, *Chingin rodo jikan seidoto sogo chosa* (General Survey on
Wages and Working Hours Systems).

It would be perverse, therefore, to romanticise work and working conditions in small firms in Japan, but there is more to the picture than these statistics suggest. For small firm owners, the use of cheap and non-regular
labour has to be weighed up against the need to secure essential skills. This
is especially so in metropolitan machining districts like Ota, where high
levels of machining skills are required for survival. Such districts have a low
proportion of non-regular employees – less than 10 per cent according to
one survey, compared with over a quarter in Japan as a whole. Only 17 per
cent of female workers were non-regular employees, compared with 40 per
cent. Striking, too, is the high proportion of male workers – almost three
quarters, compared with just under 60 per cent.[6]

The employment of foreign workers demonstrates the point. From the
mid 1980s there was a conspicuous rise in the number of foreigners entering Japan and working, often illegally. Economic conditions in home countries, dwindling employment opportunities in alternative destinations such
as the Middle East, the rise of the yen and Japan's international profile, as
well as labour shortages in Japan were all factors. By 1991–2 the number of
foreigners working illegally was estimated at several hundred thousand.

---

[6] Shinagawa rosei jimusho (1988). The statistics come from different surveys and are not
directly comparable, but they are suggestive.

Surveys showed around 10 per cent of factories to be employing foreign workers.[7]

Fears were voiced that illegal foreign workers would form a new reserve of exploitable labour, vulnerable because of their illegality, and that this would undermine conditions for other vulnerable Japanese workers. Owners in Ota had other preoccupations, however. Those interviewed gave as the main reason for employing foreign workers illegally severe difficulties in getting workers, *even part timers*. Their highest priority was to secure long-term employees. When they considered job assignment and employment status for their foreign workers, the main consideration was the likelihood of him or her staying. They would pay a premium for certain groups – Vietnamese refugees, for instance – because of this:

'I have Chinese and Vietnamese workers. The Chinese stay for two years, and you have to give them work appropriate for that span. The Vietnamese were introduced by the Refugee Centre. They have families here, and show promise. They've become regular employees, and members of the union' (casting factory).

'It's a real shame. One of our Vietnamese who has been with us for five years is going to quit and work as a translator at the Refugee Centre. He wants to go to university. If they stay they can learn the job and get promoted' (press factory. Another Vietnamese worker had been promoted to number two in the main machine shop).

'Look, I want workers, but I can't get them. People come here and work for three days then quit. I have a part timer in the office, but the factory work isn't really part-time work. I had a Bangla[deshi] working for me recently. He saw my light on one night and asked if I wanted help. He didn't stay long, either. But Y. Spray Painting gives housing and pays ¥300,000+ per month. They get good foreigners who stay.'[8]

Casting, press and spray painting are typical '3K' (*kitsui* – arduous, *kitanai* – dirty, *kiken* – dangerous) jobs, shunned by modern Japanese youth. It is in these factories that worker shortages are most acute, and foreign workers most likely to be employed. Even the foreign workers, though, often do not stay long.

Regardless of legal definitions, for owners in Ota a part-time worker tends to be someone whose main priorities lie elsewhere, and who cannot be expected to make the effort to acquire key skills, which is ideally the type of person they would like to recruit. Many employed no part timers, citing the nature of the work, especially where it was both skilled and heavy. As work became more specialised, as batch runs became shorter and toler-

[7] E.g.,Kokumin kin'yu koko (1992); Tokyo toritsu rodo kenkyujo (1991).
[8] From interviews in 1990. Such workers apparently kept their jobs in the subsequent recession, according to T. Koseki (personal communication, August 1995).

ances stricter, the weight of skilled setting and conceptual work had become greater. As a result, a number which used to employ part timers no longer did.

The key workers in *machi koba*, apart from the owners and their families, have traditionally been craftsmen, who represent a different line in the evolution of Japan's industrial structure than the well-known 'salaryman' or 'company man'. *Watari shokunin*, craftsmen who moved from company to company in search of challenging work and better pay, were a colourful feature of Japan's early industrialisation. Sometimes they worked in large factories, sometimes in small ones, and some like Aida Yokei (chapter 2) became independent and founded their own companies. The internalisation of career structures in large firms after World War I did not lead to their sudden disappearance, as is sometimes assumed. The ethos of 'not being a real craftsman until you've been fired three times' and 'tramping around until you're forty' was maintained by small factory workers, who relied on their own skills rather than a company career. Part of their pride was in their ability to get higher performance out of rudimentary machines. They carried their own tools and tinkered with – sometimes stripped down and rebuilt – the machine they were assigned to when they came to a new factory. They are said to have jealously guarded their key skill secrets, but young workers surreptitiously observed them, or got lessons in return for cigarettes. They thus acted as a vehicle for technology transfer in small factories.[9]

Just as 'tramping' died out in Britain in the nineteenth century, craftsmen in Japan became more sedentary as well. After changing jobs once or twice in their 20s, they settled down and often notched up long periods with the same employer.[10] Personnel methods changed, too. Seniority principles were superimposed on to traditional practices of offering higher pay for higher output, challenging jobs, and sometimes vague promises of assistance should workers eventually become independent. In spite of these developments, and rapidly changing technology which sometimes threatened prized skills, the craft ethos persisted, and craftsmen continued to identify with their skills rather than with their company.[11] They have been the skills base of many small engineering firms. Like the owners, though, these craftsmen are now middle aged, and many are approaching retirement. How to make up for their skills and recruit younger *regular* workers is the question that preoccupies many owners.

[9] Koseki (1984); also Gordon (1985).
[10] Gendai sogo kenkyu shudan (1994); also later in this chapter.
[11] Koseki (1984, 1986).

Labour unions and industrial relations

As part of their peripheral existence, small firm workers in Japan are seen to be weak and vulnerable because of a lack of collective representation. Enterprise unionism, which with lifetime (or long-term) employment and *nenko* (seniority plus merit) wages and promotion have formed the three pillars of 'Japanese-style employment' in large firms, left small firm workers isolated. Large firm workers appear to show little interest or solidarity with workers outside their enterprise, especially in small firms, and without their support and resources, organising small firm workers is a difficult process. Thus in 1991 almost 60 per cent of workers in firms with 1,000+ employees belonged to a labour union compared with less than 2 per cent in firms with fewer than 100 workers.[12]

Here, too, there is a complex picture behind the statistics. Given the independent outlook of craftsmen, and strongly held views by both parties in the employment relationship, it is not surprising that historically there has been quite a lot of conflict in small firms in industrial belts like Keihin. *Watari shokunin* featured in labour unrest as early as 1906–7, and were subsequently active in the growing labour movement before it was suppressed. After World War II the Occupation authorities legalised and initially encouraged labour unions. In 1948–9 the unionisation rate surged to over 50 per cent, with many small firm workers joining through the efforts of active organisers. In the subsequent rollback, enterprise unions became established in large firms. Federations of enterprise unions were formed within narrowly defined industries, such as automobiles, shipbuilding, and steel. By contrast, small firm sector organisation maintained many early postwar features, as well as a distinctive small firm sector logic. This is generally overlooked because of the dominance of the enterprise union model.

First, the unions or federations remained broadly based. The left-wing Sohyo affiliate Zenkoku Kinzoku and the right-wing breakaway Zenkin Domei organised workers across the metalworking industries instead of just the automobile, electrical machinery, or steel industry. In 1978–9, 44.1 per cent of members of Zenkoku Kinzoku worked in SMEs, compared with a mere 1.1 per cent of workers under Denkiroren (the electrical machinery workers' federation). Second, they often have a mixture of individual and enterprise union membership. These enterprise unions, moreover, differ from large firm enterprise unions in that a larger proportion of union dues are passed beyond the enterprise to support professional officials and organisers – 'orgs' – who are not concurrently enterprise employees.

[12] Rodosho (1992b, 19).

(Unlike in large firms, outside officials can play an important part in wage negotiations in small firms.) Third, regional and local organisation is important, particularly for the former Sohyo-affiliated organisations. Limited though it is, therefore, organisation of workers in the small firm sector is distinct from that of large firms.[13]

The Keihin Belt spawned many Zenkoku Kinzoku branch affiliates, which were known for their militancy.[14] One street in Ota was dubbed *Zenkin Ginza* and *Akahata Dori* (Red Flag Street) after the frequent, boisterous demonstrations organised by Zenkoku Kinzoku under red flags and banners in the early postwar years. Branches in large factories like Tokyo Keiki (Tokimec), Yamatake (Yamatake Honeywell), and Hokushin Electric (now part of Yokokawa Electric) were the 'locomotives' to advance the cause of labour, and spread their gains to smaller factories around them. Employers resisted, however, and many of the 'locomotives' were derailed by splits during the 1950s and 1960s. Local cohesion was further weakened with factory relocations, not just of the giants, but of medium-sized factories with 100–200 employees.[15] Some of the latter also declined or went bankrupt. Without the support of larger branches, and indeed under pressure from the management of these companies, union activities in small firms became much harder to sustain. The experiences of a postwar *watari shokunin* of sorts – veteran lathe operator and writer Koseki – show this vividly.

Koseki entered a factory with 25 workers in 1955, and tried to organise a union when he realised that pay and conditions were inferior to other comparable factories. The 'parent' company threatened to withhold work from the 'red flag' factory, and many thought the union would force the company to close. The owner organised a lockout, but secretly informed core workers they would be taken on again if Koseki left. He was made to feel responsible for their threatened livelihoods, left, and the union folded. Seven years later he tried to organise a union at another small factory, again unsuccessfully because of the classical free rider problem: 'It was our policy that any gains would be passed on to all, so then some said why should we pay our dues if we get the benefits? It was sad. In the end I was the only member.' Other factors contributed to declining union activity, too, such as improvements in living standards: 'People no longer had to go to the pawn shop to live.'[16]

[13] Tokyo toritsu rodo kenkyujo (1983).
[14] Hanshin, by contrast, had a greater proportion of Zenkin Domei affiliates. A large number of Keihin unions, too, joined the left-wing JMIU instead of being absorbed under the Rengo umbrella in 1989.
[15] Interview, K. Goto, Ota-ku rokyo, September 1993. Militancy in the Keihin Belt was a factor in some relocations. The introduction of new technology and working practices in the 1960s was smoother at greenfield sites; Inagami (1989b, 10).
[16] Personal communication, November 1992.

Although many unions disappeared – less than 2 per cent of Ota's factories are unionised today – they often left legacies. One was regular wage discussions in Koseki's second factory, and regular wage increases and minimum bonuses at his present factory. The interunion (public and private sector) coordination body Ota-ku rokyo organises various campaigns, and its leaflets passed out at train stations ensure that workers are aware of the wage settlements, holidays, no overtime days, etc., attained in other factories. For most employees, however, wages and conditions are not bargained over collectively, either by a union, or by employee associations, despite Koike's contention.[17] Nor are rates determined collectively on the employers' side. Asked about worker suspicions that the local industrialists' association conspired to keep down wages, one owner commented: 'The association doesn't discuss wages formally. The companies are different sizes. And wages are very secret. We only discuss them with close friends.'[18]

Collective agreements to prevent cut-throat competition and maintain standards are thus not a feature of industrial districts like Ota. Labour *markets* act as a more powerful constraint on owners. Unless they offer a certain level of wages and conditions, they have found it increasingly difficult to attract workers, especially younger workers. Neither younger workers nor the older craftsmen are easily replaced, moreover. Irrespective of whether they have a genuine paternalistic concern for their workers – many do – owners do not have a free hand in how they treat their workers.

Personnel management

Personal ties have traditionally been important in securing workers for small factories. Blood ties (*ketsu-en*) and hometown/prefecture links (*chi-en*) ensured that the employment relationship was more than a simple cash-for-labour exchange. Like interfirm relations, it was embedded in mutual expectations of goodwill and obligation. The 'gaffer' (*oyaji*) might have been expected to find a bride for male employees. He might have paid out of his own pocket for seasonal festival gear such as doll sets for employees' children. And he might have held out the prospect of assistance when

---

[17] One survey found that 61 per cent of SMEs in Tokyo with over 30 employees had an employee association, but only 14.3 per cent were involved in wage *discussions* (Tokyo toritsu rodo kenkyujo (1990)). Such associations are, of course, less common in Ota's tiny factories.

[18] According to another survey, local industrialists' associations, industrial associations, and cooperative associations serve as vehicles for information exchange, but few have been involved in formal industrial relations agreements or bargaining since the setting of minimum wages was delegated to deliberation councils in the 1960s; Tokyo toritsu rodo kenkyujo (1984).

workers finally took the step to independence. Such 'close' human relations were to some extent a substitute for better wages and conditions. They were paternalistic, even benevolent in the case of some employers, and exploitative in others.[19]

Not all employees were related by blood or territorial ties, of course, particularly after the mass hirings of the 1960s, but this type of relationship was extended to other workers as well. Labour shortages and changing worker attitudes have made it more difficult for paternalism to be used as a substitute for reasonable wages and conditions, but a certain amount is still expected. Many owners feel a strong sense of responsibility towards their employees. Asked why they did not sell up during the 'bubble' years, or, conversely, during the trough of recession, owners cited responsibility to employees *and* their families: 'I have twenty employees. That means eighty mouths depending on me.' This consideration was possibly as important as wanting to maintain their lifework.

This says something about the style of personnel management, but, at the end of the day, owners' strategies reflect the practical need to secure skills to get their work done. Let us look at concrete examples of small firms in Ota, bearing in mind the two key variables identified by one study of personnel management in SMEs: the degree of systematisation, and reliance on ready-made, externally recruited versus in-house trained labour.[20] Given that most of Ota's small factories are smaller than those of that study, it is not surprising that their personnel management is not very systematic, despite exhortation from administrative officials. They have to rely on a variety of workers, young and old, non-experienced and experienced, some recruited through acquaintances and relatives, others through the local employment agency, advertising or even the 'madam' at the local bar. Just how they can come up with systematic hiring, wage, and training policies is far from clear.

C. Manufacturing makes moulds to stringent specifications for precision instruments, electronic and medical goods. It often receives blueprints for the products, and has to reverse them for the moulds, so design work can take up to one third of total turnaround time. The company had 40 workers in the 1960s, 20 in 1985, and only 10 in 1994 in addition to the founder (aged 75, company chairman) and his son (45, company president), but output has increased through multi-machine and unmanned CNC operation. Much of the skilled work, however, cannot be fully computerised.

Profiles of the employees are given in table 8.4. There are two veteran

---

[19] See Kondo (1990), for an account of 'company as family' in a small confectionery factory in east Tokyo.   [20] Tokyo toritsu rodo kenkyujo (1989).

Table 8.4 *Employees of C. Manufacturing*

Age/sex	Years with company	Prior experience	Jobs
67 F	6	yes	formerly did office work at consumer coop, now in charge of office, opinion often sought by president, maternal figure for employees
55 M	40	yes	engineer/draughtsman>factory manager>director
51 M	36	no	engineer>factory manager (and director)
47 M	26	yes	3 years in another mould company, milling, section manager
49 M	19	no	lengthy hospitalisation, now milling, grinding, finishing work
40 M	9	yes	1 year mould course, 2 years in mould company, engineer, section manager
39 M	9	(yes)	car manufacturer 11 years, now spark erosion, wire cutting work
37 F	4	yes	formerly production management, child raising, currently CAM
35 M	2 (+5)	yes	joined company after school, left for family reasons, rejoined, now finishing work (grinding etc.)
34 M	2	yes	bookkeeping course, house builder, another mould company 10 years, now spark erosion, wire cutting, CAD/CAM

Note:
Prior experience refers to prior experience in the same type of work in another company. Family members not included.

workers who have been with the company all their working lives, who can use most of the machines, and who do most of the draughting work. 'We have three ¥30 million (CAD) computers, but they can't do curves accurately. We need the skills of those two. Take this gas mask here. They figured out how to make the mould in one piece instead of two. It saved a lot of money.' The other workers have a variety of backgrounds, but most had prior experience relevant to their current work. The more senior employees were involved in finishing, and the younger employees in CNC work, with one person operating two, sometimes three machines. (Some specialist jig boring and profile grinding work – 5 per cent of turnover – is subcontracted out to six companies, each with five or six employees.)

The principal motivational device is pay. Pay in the mould industry is relatively high, and C. Manufacturing pays competitive wages for its size within the industry. One basic reference is the yearly survey carried out by the Japan Die and Mould Industry Association, which gives a breakdown of pay by education, age, length of service, and job for both office and shop-floor workers. When deciding *increases*, the going increase in the steel industry is considered, and informal discussions are held with other cooperative association members:

We decide their pay based on these points of reference and on their effort. I think of pay on a yearly basis, which includes bonus and overtime [about 25 hours a month]. I think, this worker has done about this much. We have to guarantee two months bonus twice a year or the job agency won't introduce people to us. But one worker might get two months and another might get four. We don't tell them there's such a spread, but they probably know it, anyway. Hard workers work hard all the time.

As a rough benchmark, the president estimated the annual income of a 35-year-old in 1992 would be ¥5.5 million, and for a 45-year-old it would be about ¥6 million, but there would be considerable variation according to the particular person. Actual wages and bonuses are decided by the father, son, and factory manager. The decision is presented to the employees individually along with a chart showing the different components of the monthly salary (age, length of service, merit, various allowances) and bonus. This salary chart and the bonus calculation are similar to those used by larger firms, but are in fact a *post-hoc* breakdown of the annual figure.

Employees are formally interviewed prior to all this, and told what the company expects of them, and asked if they have any points they want to raise, any family problems or other things they want to talk about, and if they are satisfied with their present assignment. Regarding job assignments: 'I guess ideally workers should be rotated, but they become experts on their machines and when we move them, we lose efficiency. If they get bored we try to change them, or give them some variety.' There is no employee association. Social events such as bowling or dinner outings are arranged periodically, sometimes jointly with other members of the relocation association, as well as an annual weekend hot spring or sightseeing trip when profits permit. These are not considered major motivators, but are common amongst small firms, and show that the relationship is still more than a cash-for-work contract.

The main personnel problem is the lack of young workers. The average age is quite high, and the youngest worker is 34, meaning high labour costs. In the five years prior to early 1994 the company had had six young recruits, who had quit after only a few days. The president was teaching a course on moulds at Ota's Higher Vocational Training Centre in the hope of finding new workers, but without success. In 1994 an acquaintance had introduced a student soon to graduate from university who wanted to do something with his hands, but the president wondered whether he would actually turn up to start work. This problem was by no means confined to C. Manufacturing.

N. Precision both shares similarities and contrasts with C. Manufacturing. From doing lathe work for car and appliance makers, it moved to machining posts for a single mould component maker. Although this is to tolerances of several microns, batch runs are very large (thousands of parts per month), reducing the proportion of really skilled work. Nevertheless, there were no part timers. The overriding personnel concern was to secure a stable workforce, and prepare for future growth and diversification. It was still very much a family company, however, with four family directors (husband and wife, virtually retired father and uncle), and only four employees.

The employees' backgrounds are shown in table 8.5. Again, the key non-family employee had been with the company all his working life. Another long-serving employee (55 years old, 25 years of employment) had recently had a stroke and was forced to quit, following another older worker unable to commute when the factory moved in the late 1980s. Some rejuvenation had been achieved by recruiting former local truck drivers, two of them friends.

Wages had been raised to ensure that they did not leave. They were higher than in other factories on the same site, approaching those of C. Manufacturing in fact, but they included a lot more scheduled hours and a lot more overtime. To get his monthly ¥600,000–700,000 in 1992, for instance, the factory manager sometimes clocked up 100 hours or more per month in overtime (for which he was paid)! The workers were not paid a monthly salary: 'They are not ready for that yet.' They were on a daily rate paid monthly (*nikkyu gekkyu*) system, or more strictly, an hourly rate

Table 8.5 *Employees of N. Precision*

Age/sex	Years with company	Prior experience	Job
58 M	37	no	former carpenter, now factory manager, started out sweeping the floor
34 M	5	no	former driver, has mastered most machines, especially does CNC work
34 M	5	no	former driver, mostly lathe work
27 M	5	no	former driver, now does mostly CNC work

Note:
As for table 8.4.

(¥900–¥1,000), calculated daily and paid monthly. Since the bonus was practically fixed at four months wages, juggling to ensure an overall level was done within the wage under the guise of job-related or qualification supplements.

Employees were encouraged to go on outside courses to acquire qualifications, and internal training through rotation was practised – when they were not too busy – so that all employees could operate at least three different machines. 'I want them to be able to use all the machines. That's my personal philosophy, and also they get bored if they're always on the same machine.'

Like C. Manufacturing, several young workers had come and gone quickly in recent years. The president's wife, who was closely involved in personnel matters, commented; 'It's time nowadays as much as money. We've had Sundays and one Saturday off a month, but the job agency told us it's not good enough. From this year we're going to have every other Saturday off. The administrative guidance officials are advising a 44 [scheduled] hour week – we'll be down to 42!' She herself did not have Sunday off – that was when she went to labour law classes. She also knew that they would also have to do better than three days of paid summer holiday leave, both from the legal perspective, and for recruiting purposes, but her husband argued that changes could only be implemented slowly, or their solvency would be undermined.

K. Grinding responded to relentless price cutting pressures from customers by moving into high precision, high value added internal grinding and

Table 8.6 *Employees of K. Grinding*

Age/sex	Years with company	Prior experience	Job
53 M	13	yes	previously press work, now machining high precision parts
52 M	22	yes	12 years previous machining experience, now machining precision parts and gauges
32 M	15	no	precision parts, gauges
24 F	2	no	office work

Note:
As for table 8.4.

gauge work. The transition, plus the recession, had led to a halving of the number of employees in ten years. The owner's wife, too, was no longer involved in the company, but ran her own coffee shop. Until 1991 the company employed three women (and a student for a while) on a part time basis to do external cylindrical grinding work. They worked half-days to keep within public housing tenant income limitations. These women, plus two younger workers, were no longer with the company in 1994. The remaining employees are listed in table 8.6.

One of the employees joined the company soon after it was founded, and had as much machining experience as the owner. A second veteran had done press work before, and a third worker had been with the company ever since leaving school. A young woman had been recruited for office work (to the envy of some neighbouring owners, who saw the presence of young women as a precondition for attracting young men, though it does not appear to have been the primary motivation in this case).

Regarding wages: 'That's a tricky question. A 30-year-old with five years experience can get ¥350,000 to ¥400,000 [per month] in one company and only ¥250,000 in another. There can be a gap of ¥100,000 even in the same industry. It depends on profits, I guess, and ability, too. The large companies have their rules, but here a 30-year-old can get a 50-year old's wage.' Presumably his 32-year-old earned almost as much as the older workers, whose abilities, he implied, had peaked. His normative notion of age-related wages, as his words suggest, conflicted with his actual practice, which was based on ability and how badly he wanted to keep his workers. He was hopeful of keeping his current workforce, but pessimistic about recruiting young workers who would stay.

Having looked at three machining microfactories, let us look briefly at a larger, basic process factory. **K. Casting** is the sole remaining steel casting company in Tokyo, with 55 employees, down from 100 in the late 1960s. It casts tyre and automobile moulds for about 100 customers. Casting has been dubbed a '3K' industry, on top of which, wages are not attractive, or commensurate with the time needed to acquire the necessary skills. Skilled labour, however, cannot be easily substituted by advanced machinery.[21]

The company has been able to recruit workers from other casting factories closing down, but this has done nothing to lower the average employee age, which was in the mid 50s in 1992. Several craftsmen retire every year, and the company has trouble replacing them. Seven or eight are recruited, but typically only one remains. The company has tried recruiting foreign workers, but cannot retain many of them, either. The few workers who do stay, though, tend to stay until retirement.

The company has a union, which had a fearsome reputation amongst outsiders. The company president dismisses such talk: 'They give their demands, but they're not very aggressive.' He concedes that wages may be higher than they would otherwise be, but a 50-year-old with 17 years of experience would only have earned ¥300,000 a month excluding overtime in 1992.[22] This, however, was based on a seven hour working day, after which overtime was paid (a legacy, apparently, of productivity bargaining in the mid 1970s. Productivity has also been increased by non-replacement of workers.) 'Workers these days want shorter working hours, but they still want overtime.' He was renegotiating the agreement upwards to 7.5 hours in return for longer holidays.

The critical consideration at K. Casting is also yearly earnings, and for wage rises, references are going rates in the steel and casting industries. The wage system is another *nikkyu gekkyu* variant – 40 per cent hourly wage and 60 per cent salary. There is no planned job rotation. The owner cited the small size of the factory, and the fact that workers had their own specialities. Those who wanted more challenging work were given it, but moving workers unnecessarily created apprehension and decreased efficiency.

From these admittedly brief sketches of four factories in Ota, some salient issues are apparent. In addition to the skills of owners and their successors, there is a core of older, skilled workers, some with very long records of employment, promoted to positions like 'factory manager'. These are trusted employees, with whom key decisions are often discussed. Then there

---

[21] Cf. Ukai (1992); Tokyoto shoko shidojo (1993).
[22] Earnings in larger factories are usually cited without overtime earnings, while in small factories, everything is included.

is another group in the machining factories, but largely absent from the basic process '3K' factories. These are workers in their 30s, who have experience in other jobs, and who may settle down and acquire skills from the older workers before they retire, as well as CNC skills. Such workers are not numerous, and are found in stable or growing machining factories, but not in factories where there is no successor.

Conspicuous by their absence are young workers, who tend to come and go quickly. Owners say that they are not really interested in learning skills, and that they have to be handled with velvet gloves: 'Parents used to come around with heads bowed and ask us to teach their boys skills, and to belt them if they didn't learn. You can't do that now – they'd quit. They quit to drive rubbish trucks where they can get about as much without worrying about 1/5,000 or 1/10,000 tolerances. They don't think long-term any more.'

A number of factors lie behind this. Rationally speaking, the returns probably do not justify the investment in skill acquisition. Small firm owners cannot easily respond to market signals by raising wages because they cannot raise their prices. Indeed, the prices keep getting cut. Like the successor problem of the last chapter, knock-on effects of the extreme efficiency and competitiveness of the machine industries are evident in the next generation, which has a wider range of employment opportunities. Working conditions are equally if not more important. Young workers want an attractive working environment, reasonable working hours, and real holidays, and will shop around for a better combination. 'Close' human relations are no substitute. On top of this, there is an intractable image problem. For young people '3K' work is not confined to casting, painting and press work, but applies to blue-collar work in general.[23] Growth-oriented owners know that they need to attract younger workers and encourage them to acquire skills if they are to have a long-term future. The recession made it easier for medium-sized factories to recruit school leavers, graduates and other young workers, and growing small factories have been able to hire workers displaced by redundancy, but those hit hard by the recession had difficulty finding enough work to keep even their loyal core employees.

Skills and technology

Recent surveys confirm this picture. SMEs have trouble attracting young craft or engineering workers, and are even more pessimistic about their

---

[23] If the so-called 'new 3K' (*kyuryo ga yasui* – low wages – *kyuka ga sukunai* – little time off – *kakko warui* – unfashionable) is included, the total becomes '6K'. Owners curse the media for their part in popularising these images.

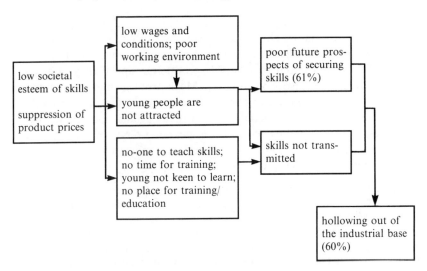

Figure 8.1 Craft skills and 'hollowing out'
Source: Rengo (1994), *Chusho kigyo no gino keisei ni kansuru chosa* (Survey of Skill Formation in Manufacturing SMEs), p. 4.

future prospects. They particularly seek workers who (can be trained to) have the knowledge and skills to improve the production process, and can become multi-skilled. In order to recruit/retain such people, they feel they must improve their wages and wage systems, improve opportunities to develop skills and recognition of these (many feel externally recognised qualifications would help), and improve working hours, holidays, and the working environment. It takes several years to train such workers – the period is longest in the basic process industries – and there is a limit to how much the training period can be shortened, or the extent to which skills can be replaced by machines. Owners are pessimistic about their future prospects and prospects for craft skills in general (figure 8.1).[24]

Obviously skills are linked with technology, but the relationship is more complex than might immediately be apparent, especially in small factories. During the 1980s many people studied the impact of new technology on skills. What was less often noticed was the impact skill considerations had on the introduction of new technology. Compensation for the loss of their craftsmens' skills as they retired, and difficulties in recruiting and training young workers, were often cited as factors in CNC purchase. Owners or their sons programmed and operated the machines initially. When young

[24] Nihon rodo kenkyu kiko (1996); Rengo (1994).

workers were recruited, they could be assigned to CNC with little experience on conventional machines, doing simple machine minding first and then programming, while the owner or son set up the machine. In a short period of time they could be relatively productive, and if they quit, they could be replaced reasonably quickly. Mechatronics thus offered some owners a stop-gap solution to their skill problem. In fact, it was used to entice young people, who would not work in a dark factory with old machines, but were willing to work on gleaming CNC machines, doing computer-related, technical tasks. There was much less of an image problem here. One owner put it like this:

There were two main reasons why I bought CNC. First, the average age of our operators was 45, and if we didn't get younger operators, we would go under in the end. The older operators were skilled and the young ones weren't, so we had to make up for that shortage of skills, and besides, we wouldn't have been able to attract younger workers without CNC. The second reason was that our machines were only running from 8:00 to 5:00. I wanted to get a few extra hours out of the machines after everyone had gone home and increase productivity.

Another put it even more bluntly: 'Look at primary school children these days. They're playing around with personal computers. If you don't give young workers something like that to do, if you keep them on filing, they'll quit. You've got to let them learn it like a game.'[25]

The result was, despite fears to the contrary, that older craftsmen continued to play an important role by doing non-replaceable (by new technology) tasks, and younger workers manned the mechatronic machines. Symbolising a change of generations as well as technology, there developed two distinct 'language' groups in small factories, the older, conventional 'machine language' speakers and the younger 'CNC language' speakers.[26] If the former asked the latter to go and 'lick a bit off' a part, the latter would want to know how many millimetres so they could programme their computer. Owners hoped they could hook young workers onto the technical challenges of CNC, and that they would gradually become interested in conventional 'machine language' as well, but more often the reality, at least in the 1980s, was that only a few people – owners or their sons, and one or two core workers – could speak both 'languages' fluently.

The issue of skills, and at an even more basic level, attracting and motivating younger workers, poses a critical challenge to small factories. To meet the challenge, owners must innovate, not just in terms of mechatronic machinery, but in terms of working conditions and improving the physical working environment. (One owner who was building a new factory had asked his younger workers to help design it to increase their enjoyment and

[25] Whittaker (1990, 107, 158).   [26] Koseki (1988).

commitment. The less it looked like a factory the greater the chance of attracting young workers.) It has also provided an incentive for interfirm cooperation, whereby owners cooperate because they cannot secure the skills in-house, or launch products and start new ventures which might attract young people. In some cases they spin off semi-independent companies as a motivational device akin to independence. Recession may have eased the immediate labour shortage, but the underlying challenge remains. Those who meet it will grow, but many micro and basic process factory owners are pessimistic about their long-term projects.

9   Policy and politics

One of the most contentious facets of the Japanese economy is the role of government regulation and promotion. Some – principally neoclassical economists – suggest that strong growth was related to relatively little direct government intervention, measured for instance by government expenditure as a proportion of GDP, or happened in spite of government intervention, not because of it. Others see government intervention as 'market conforming'. Yet others perceive a fundamentally different (from either textbook or Anglo-Saxon models) political economy, termed for instance the 'developmental state' model. Of the 'iron triangle' of big business, politicians, and bureaucrats, special emphasis is placed on the last, although the effectiveness – and desirability – of bureaucratic direction has declined, many would argue.

When it comes to small firms, which do not belong to the 'iron triangle', the situation is every bit as contentious. Did small firms prosper in spite of government neglect or hostility? Were they the beneficiaries of protective measures, prompted by the lobbying power of small firm organisations or their usefulness as potential mops for unemployment? Or were 'market-conforming', growth-promoting measures adopted here too? Research has been done on these issues, including the lobbying activities of small firm organisations and the concessions they have extracted because of their swing-vote, SME policy as industrial policy, and the significance of government financing and budgetary expenditure on SMEs, but most provides only a partial view of the proverbial elephant.[1]

I have touched on government policies in previous chapters, but here I will take a more systematic look in order to answer the above questions. I

---

[1] Friedman (1988) takes a dim view of government policy, while Calder (1988) perceives a politically motivated, positive small firm bias. Yokokura (1988) looks at SME policy as positive industrial policy, contrasting it with protective agricultural policy, while Vestal (1993), sees a dual industrial policy strategy in which the small firm sector cushioned the impact of rapid economic change.

will show, in brief, that government support for SMEs is significant, especially when viewed comparatively. In some cases it has been protective, but, on balance, in manufacturing at least it has been positive or promotional. Loans are extensive, for instance, outright subsidies are not. Many owners, though, do not make use of these loans, especially special measure loans. Other policies such as those affecting location (discussed in chapter 3) have been downright unhelpful as far as owners in Ota are concerned. As stressed in previous chapters, the primary reason for the survival and upgrading of small firms in Ota and in Japan has been their own efforts.

The first two sections consider the relationship between the state and small firms by sketching the historical development and current state of SME policy, showing how it has been shaped by politics as well as changing economic conditions and perceptions. Finance, a major policy implement, is discussed separately, focusing on the balance between public- and private-sector sources, and the views of owners. We then look at attempts by factory owners in Ota to create a favourable business environment through policy measures, and the serious obstacles they face, which compounds pessimism over the future viability of the district.

A historical overview[2]

'Italy's small business economy expanded and prospered because it had something its European counterparts lacked: a sympathetic state. While governments elsewhere celebrated its elimination, the Italians created a distinctive category of small capital and set about populating and replenishing it.' This is the conclusion of Weiss, who explored and rejected the notions that small firms in Italy expanded and prospered most when left to their own devices, that small firm policy was essentially an exercise in pacification, prevention, and protection, and that it was designed principally to gather votes or ward off unemployment. Such views, where they recognise a role for the state, see it as interrupting the normal course of development. On the contrary, Weiss argues that the state actively supported the most dynamic areas of the micro-economy based on its own ideological position.[3]

Japan shares with Italy the distinction of having the highest proportion of small firms amongst OECD countries, but whether the state can be given similar credit is debatable. In the past at least, policy makers were more likely to consider small firms a problem – 'too many, too small' – than an asset in Japan's quest for industrial advancement. But the 'problem' was

---

[2] Monetary, fiscal, trade, etc., policies all affect small firms, but for reasons of space I shall mainly discuss SME policies.   [3] Weiss (1988, 9, 26–30).

extensive, persistent, and had to be addressed, both for economic and political reasons. The cumulative result is a vast array of policies designed to protect and promote small firms. This has led Calder to argue that: 'One of the most striking features of recent Japanese public policy ... has been the fluctuating but generally pronounced bias shown toward the small, across a range of industrial, trade and credit-policy sectors, often at the expense of the large.'[4] Small firm owners who complain about a historical policy bias towards *large* firms do not see it this way, of course (though this very perception may encourage them to mobilise and lobby for the measures Calder talks of). Miwa, too, attributes the vast array of policies to the fact that it is 'easy to expand government organisation but difficult to reorganise it and almost impossible to shrink it'. The only lessons to be learned from Japan, he argues, are that 'some of the policies have proven to be ineffective and that none of the policies has proven to be effective'.[5]

A brief historical overview will put these contrasting views into perspective. Debates within the Japanese government over small firms and economic development surfaced in the early Meiji period, and as the exchanges between Maeda, a leading figure of the Ministry of Agriculture and Commerce, and Matsukata, the Finance Minister, in the early 1880s testify, they went to the heart of government policy. Trade deficits and ambitious infrastructure projects had led the government to issue paper notes which sparked inflation, prompting Matsukata to introduce sharp, deflationary policies. These were necessary, he insisted, to establish the basis for the growth of modern industry. Concerned about the impact on traditional and small-scale industry, Maeda advocated policies to strengthen and raise the productivity of these sectors, whose expanded output would reduce the trade deficit and boost tax revenues, which in turn could pay for infrastructure developments. Both proposed an industrial bank, but Matsukata's bank would raise funds in provincial Japan to be used for local infrastructure projects, in effect, in the short term at least, redistributing resources away from the small-scale sector, whereas Maeda's bank would have made funds available *to* it. Matsukata and the Finance Ministry prevailed and Maeda eventually left the MAC, but selected pieces of his programme were later adopted. As a private, 'one man MAC', too, Maeda continued to walk the country encouraging farmers, merchants, and small-scale producers to organise and cooperate to improve their performance.[6]

Encouraging small firm organisation to raise productivity, improve quality, and discourage price undercutting was the principal policy measure of the Meiji period. It reflected a mistrust of unfettered market forces by those in government, and cost relatively little. It has remained an

---

[4] Calder (1988, 312).   [5] Miwa (1995, 427, 426).   [6] Crawcour (1995).

important policy plank ever since. Small firms had to wait for financial support, however, and their disadvantageous access to capital was long a major source of grievance. Limited government loans at favourable interest rates were introduced in the 1920s, and in 1936, after several years of agitation, the Shoko Chukin Bank (Central Cooperative Bank for Commerce and Industry) was established with joint government and SME association capital.

Occupation reforms at the end of World War II, including the (partial) dissolution of the *zaibatsu*, were intended to reverse economic concentration and promote competition and economic democracy. Small firms stood to benefit, but reconstruction policies which channelled scarce resources into the favoured large-scale sectors of coal, electricity, and steel, had a deleterious impact. In reaction, numerous SME organisations sprang up, such as Zenchukyo, which campaigned for better access to raw materials and improved financing, as well as Minsho, which gained support from its campaigns against harsh taxes.[7]

Early postwar policies were thus influenced by Occupation economic reforms, prewar traditions, and political pressures. In 1947 the short-lived socialist government established the (forerunner of the) SME Agency, headed by an energetic campaigner for small firms (Ninagawa, later the governor of Kyoto for 28 years and a constant critic of conservative governments). Policy was far from systematic, however, and was compromised by overriding objectives. For instance, funds were made available briefly through the Reconstruction Finance Corporation, and the Peoples' Finance Corporation from 1949, but deflationary policies negated their effects.

The 1950s brought new problems for small firms, new campaigns for alleviation, and new compromise solutions by the government. In the slump following the initial procurements boom of the Korean War, large firms delayed or defaulted on subcontracting payments, and chain reaction bankruptcies resulted. Campaigners wanted a law with teeth; they belatedly got the Delayed Payment Law described in chapter 5. Although recession cartels were recognised from 1952, Chuseiren (the SME Political League, formed in 1956) campaigned for a new law to stop 'excessive competition', exempt small firms from certain provisions of the Antimonopoly Law, prohibit 'external interference' (from large firms), recognise the right of SME associations to bargain collectively (against large firms), and so on. They got a deliberation council, whose recommendations led to the 1957 SME Organisation Law.

This law was only partly protective, and SME policy was not just the

---

[7] Taxes have been a particular bone of contention, and a lightning rod for discontent about industrialisation policy and the distribution of its costs.

result of agitation. With the SME Agency under the jurisdiction of MITI, it took on the characteristics of industrial (or industrial structure) policy, promoting rationalisation, modernisation, and technological upgrading. Elimination of the dual structure meant, in effect, small firms becoming like large ones through mergers or joint activities and achieving scale economies through specialisation. These objectives were evident in the SME Basic Law of 1963 (again following agitation and a deliberation council), and the SME Modernisation Promotion Law of the same year. The former expressed the role of SME policy as 'upgrading the industrial structure, strengthening the international competitiveness of industry and achieving balanced growth of the economy'.[8]

Despite criticism that such laws primarily benefited medium-sized factories and encouraged overproduction and overinvestment, leading to 'modernisation bankruptcies', the structural upgrading thrust was maintained throughout the 1960s. By the early 1970s, however, the Agency's *rhetoric*, at least, was changing, recognising diversity amongst small firms, limits to the pursuits of scale economies, and advocating greater 'knowledge intensity'. Future policy should do less directing, and seek to provide a favourable environment for SMEs to develop under their own steam. But the industrial (structure) policy bent was not lost, while new difficulties for small firms resulting from trade friction, currency realignments, and then the first 'oil shock', as well as poor election results in 1972, encouraged the ruling Liberal Democratic Party (LDP) to come up with new relief measures.[9] Easy-term loans through government financing institutions rose conspicuously, and tax concessions were granted. Protection was offered to small retailers under the Large Retail Store Law of 1973, and laws were passed to assist small firms in depressed industries and regions, as well as to reduce the growing number of bankruptcies. Business support and advisory services through the Chambers of Commerce, and Industry and Commerce Associations, were also stepped up.

The worst doom and gloom scenarios for small firms in the 1970s did not materialise. In fact their performance was surprisingly robust, leading to a further change in official perceptions by the 1980s. Small firms were now seen as well suited to the new age, in view of changing market structures and social preferences. This did not mean that SME policy had become redundant, of course – for a bureaucrat to concede this would be stupid as

---

[8] At the same time, as a result of political pressure, it contained competition-limiting elements, calling, for instance, for 'appropriate business opportunities for SMEs by coordination with non SME parties' (i.e., keeping large firms off SME turf). Arita (1990, 68); Ito (1989, 157).

[9] The Communist Party had made inroads amongst small firms in the urban centres, which the LDP wanted to stem.

well as disloyal. SMEs still faced obstacles to realising their full potential, and to overcome these, new technology, foreign investment, and sub-contracting advisory services were launched. Organisation policy was given a new twist in the 'technology exchange plaza' and 'interindustry exchange' programmes (see chapter 7). Small firms were expected to create new technology as well as to use it. Once again, moreover, the post Plaza Accord (1985) yen appreciation highlighted the continued importance of emergency 'stabilisation' measures, as did the 'bubble burst' in 1991.

The 1990s have seen the emergence of new policies and measures (belatedly, perhaps) in response to the long-term and emerging problems of the small firm sector. These have ranged from encouraging SMEs to become more attractive places for workers, (re)vitalisation of small firm industrial districts (applied not only to traditional *jiba sangyo*, but to machining districts, including Ota City, Sakaki, and Higashi Osaka, but no district in Tokyo as of late 1995), and encouraging startups, diversification into new business fields, and 'creative' business activities. 'Venture business' has become the crusade of the 1990s, promoted not just by the SME Agency, but MITI and even the Finance Ministry. (We shall consider this crusade in the final chapter.)

Figure 9.1 gives an overview of current SME policy. The total budget for policy measures has been in the range of ¥200–300 billion in recent years.[10] This amounts to just 0.3 per cent of the total national budget, and is a modest figure by international standards.[11] However, budget figures do not include allocations under the Fiscal Investment and Loan Programme (sometimes called the 'second budget'), which channels post office savings and various insurance and pension funds into government financing institutions according to policy objectives. In 1989 some ¥4.2 trillion went into SME financing support under the FILP, 16 times the total budgetary allocation![12] In addition, SMEs benefit from general and policy measure-related tax concessions. The latter category alone is estimated to be worth some ¥200 billion per year.[13] In comparative policy and financial terms, small firms in Japan receive extensive government support.

Policy formation

The state–small firm relationship, as we have just seen, is less clearcut than that described by Weiss in Italy. Historically, policy has favoured big busi-

---

[10] There was a massive jump to ¥416 billion in 1993 as a result of the special economic stimulus package. As the special package unveiled in late 1995 finds its way into the budget, too, there will be another jump.

[11] According to figures supplied by Hughes (1992, 301), it is less than in Germany, but greater than the UK, but the figures for these countries include loans and credit guarantees, while the Japanese figures do not. Japanese budget figures are from Chusho kigyo cho (c), various years.   [12] MOF mimeo.   [13]   Chusho kigyo seisaku shingikai (1993, 35).

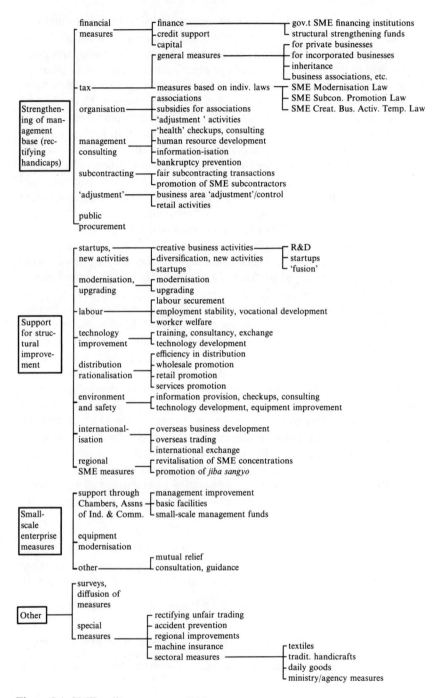

Figure 9.1 SME policy measures, 1995
Source: Chusho kigyo cho (ed.) (1995b, 1).

ness. Small firms were a structural problem, but they could not be ignored. Hence policies directed specifically at small firms date back over 100 years, and are now so extensive that *summaries* of policy measures run into hundreds of pages, and only the most intrepid specialists can claim to have read most of them. In part, though, this is related to bureaucratic budgetary politics. Bureaucrats need striking new policies to fight their corner with, and hopefully enlarge their budget, while old policies remain on their books.[14]

The policies themselves are both protective and promotional. *On balance*, one might say they are promotional in intent, as in Italy, although it is not always clear whose interests they are promoting. As Dore observed of the 1974 Textile Upgrading Law, which sought to encourage mergers and consequently did not find enough takers to use up the allocated budget: 'Vertical integration sounds like a splendid idea when you are thinking about the industry from Tokyo, but the natural tendency in most of the *sanchi* is in the quite contrary direction – towards fragmented specialisation.'[15]

This raises the question of how policies are formulated. Undoubtedly SME Agency and MITI bureaucrats have a major role in drawing them up, but do they also dream them up? In some instances perhaps they do, based on favoured economic theories and political and social considerations. Often, though, they are the formalisation of existing trends or regional initiatives. Osaka has been a particular source of inspiration, dating back to the organisation measures of the early 1880s. Other policies have been the result of pressure from SME organisations, or politicians' attempts to win the small firm vote. The pluralist model, though, only partially explains policy and policy formation.

Pempel and Tsunekawa see it as a corporatist process. They see small-scale business, like agriculture, as outside the main thrust of modernisation and industrialisation efforts in the Meiji period. As outsiders, these groups took to lobbying through political parties, and were eventually incorporated as junior partners into a system of 'corporatism without labour'. Peak organisations in this system had both top down – conduits for state policy – and bottom up functions, but the former were dominant.[16]

This model has weaknesses, but it does help in the understanding of policy formation today. Small firm organisations still mount campaigns occasionally, but since the 1970s, with the exception of left-wing organisations, they have gradually been 'incorporated' into the policy process. On the one hand, they meet with bureaucrats and politicians involved in policy on a regular basis and make annual policy requests/demands (*seisaku yobo*), and, on the other, they take part in the implementation of certain

---

[14] See Dore (1983b).   [15] Dore (1986, 232).   [16] Pempel and Tsunekawa (1979).

policies. Demands are tailored to bureaucratic policy frameworks and constraints, and aim for incremental gains. Bureaucrats may solicit demands (and surveys) to strengthen their case for policies they favour.

The 1995 *seisaku yobo* of the National Federation of Small Business Associations (Chuokai) included: economic policy which would benefit the economy as a whole (and incidentally their members, such as recession countermeasures and income tax reduction to revive the economy); budget expansion for a variety of current policies (expanded procurement, regional measures, small-scale retail support, working environment improvement, environmental measures, subcontracting adjustment, financing measures, and institutions); new promotional measures (making it easier to employ older or part-time workers, lowering the business inheritance tax); curbing measures detrimental to officials' or members' interests (no more deregulation of the Large-scale Retail Store Law, caution in the implementation of the Product Liability Law); markers for points under discussion (no uniform raising of the consumption tax in 1997); and of course more support for the Chuokai itself.[17] Progress checks by the Chuokai typically point to modest gains made in difficult circumstances, and some specific concessions, such as special status for SMEs under the Product Liability Law, and assurances that large firms will not be able to push responsibility on to subcontractors.[18]

This is all part and parcel of policy formation nowadays, but it is largely invisible and remote to most individual association members, who do not see their peak organisations as powerful lobbyists. To left-wing organisations on the outside it represents a sellout. These organisations exert some influence by mounting campaigns which force insiders to take up their demands, and bureaucrats to respond to them, in order not to undermine their claim of serving broad-based interests.

In addition, when it comes to broad policy directions and new laws, deliberation councils (*shingikai*) are used. There are four regular SME deliberation councils, for SME policy, modernisation, stability, and sectoral adjustment. The SME Policy Deliberation Council is the most visible, and is linked to the Prime Minister's Office. Its reports often follow those of the Industrial Structure Deliberation Council, and amplify their implications for SMEs. The stereotypical view of deliberation councils is as follows. A bureaucracy which wants to launch major policies will call for a delibera-

[17] Zenkoku chusho kigyo dantai chuokai (1994). SME organisations do not simply present their demands to bureaucrats and politicians, of course, but try to mobilise support from other organisations, including the predominantly large firm organisations Keidanren and Nikkeiren.

[18] Zenkoku chusho kigyo dantai chuokai (1995); also interview, I. Miura, Chuokai, September 1995.

tion council, which, with bureaucratic assistance, will come up with policy recommendations. These are then presented to the politicians, who order the bureaucrats to write the policy they originally envisaged. In this caricature, they are an instrument of bureaucratic manipulation. They are supposed to have representatives from industry, academia, mass media, labour, consumers, etc., but half of these are former bureaucrats, and others are bureaucrat friendly. Agenda are said to be set by bureaucrat supporting staff. On the other hand, some have argued that the economy is now too complex for bureaucrats who are tied to their desks and rotated frequently to come up with clear proposals and 'Visions', hence other parties are assuming a greater role.

In sum, policy making is shaped by pluralistic lobbying and political pressure, deliberation councils which supposedly solicit broad opinion but have traditionally had strong bureaucratic input, and 'corporatist' (or incorporated) peak organisation–state exchange. It is not surprising that policies embody different, sometimes contradictory, economic conceptions. They have not always been helpful to small firms, either, notably some of those linked to industrial (structure) policy in the 1960s and early 1970s.[19]

SME financing

Here we arrive at the key question. Granted that policy measures are extensive, how significant are they for small firms themselves? Do they, as one observer put it, merely water 'large flower pots with small sprinkling cans'?[20] How are we to describe the balance between public support and private initiative? In chapter 6 I looked at one of the main policy planks: organisation. Cartel associations are sometimes cited as evidence of protective or anti-competitive policy, but they play a very minor role today. Much more significant are cooperative and industry associations. Measures and funds are channelled through these to encourage small firms to work together. Ultimately, though, the effectiveness is dependent on the initiative of small firm owners themselves, and much cooperation also goes on independently of government support. The same may be said of the other two main planks, financing and technology and management support.[21] Here we will look at financing, which is the most visible policy plank.

---

[19] Friedman (1988) focuses his criticism on these policies. His depiction of MITI as single mindedly intent on forcing scale economies (versus sympathetic local government), though, is oversimplistic.

[20] A former Shoko Chukin Bank chairman, cited by Miwa (1995, 409).

[21] Technology and management support includes public testing facilities and technology consulting, various training facilities, information services, 'health' checkups, and so on.

As in other countries, a lot of SME finance comes from private sources, including retained earnings which are ploughed back into the business, savings, and loans from relatives. As far as external sources go, SMEs rely overwhelmingly on loans. At first glance, the government plays only a minor role here. According to table 9.1, its financing institutions provide less than 10 per cent of all SME loans. Upon closer inspection, though, the government's role is more significant.

First, its financing institutions – principally the Shoko Chukin Bank, which provides loans to associations, the Peoples' Finance Corporation (1949), which provides loans to very small businesses, and the Small Business Finance Corporation (1953), which provides loans to larger SMEs, as well as credit insurance (1950) and credit guarantee (1953) systems – were always intended to play a *supplementary* role to private-sector SME financing, which was encouraged through various controls, including interest rate and branch establishment regulations. Before the war mutual *mujin* companies, whose fund allocation was determined by lottery, and credit unions provided much of the external financing for small firms. In 1951 they were allowed to expand their activities. The former became mutual (*sogo*) banks, and most of the latter became credit banks (*shinkin*). The smallest remained as credit unions, which were heavily restricted in their dealings with non-members. Whereas in 1951 three quarters of SME loans came from 'ordinary' – city or regional – banks, 21 per cent from private-sector SME institutions, and 3.6 per cent from government sources, by 1955 the ratios were 61.0 per cent, 31.8 per cent, and 7.2 per cent respectively. These trends continued throughout the high growth period and into the 1970s, as table 9.1 suggests. While ordinary banks were funding the growth of larger companies, then, private-sector SME financing institutions, which were offered regulatory protection, stepped in to fund small firms. In 1980, just 12.2 per cent of outstanding loans from regional banks were to micro-firms (one to ten employees; the figure for city banks would have been lower still). For credit banks and unions the figures were 41.3 per cent and 62.3 per cent respectively.[22]

This stratified system of ordinary banks funding large companies and specialist institutions funding small companies began to break down as large firms scaled down their loans from ordinary banks, which then began to court SMEs. SME financial and informational needs, in turn, were becoming more sophisticated, which ordinary banks were better placed to meet. Faced with deregulation, contracting traditional customer bases, and more recently with enormous bad loans, private-sector SME financing institutions face an uncertain future, but they are still a significant source of SME loans.

[22] Peoples' Finance Corporation (1989, 57).

Table 9.1 *SME loan sources*

		1960	1970	1980	1988	1995
City banks [11]*		26.9%	18.5%	22.0%	29.6%	30.8%
Regional banks [64]		26.0	22.2	20.0	20.0	21.0
Long-term credit banks [3]		1.2	2.8	3.8	5.0	5.5
Trust banks [7]		0.8	0.4	0.8	3.4	3.2
Trust accounts		1.0	1.0	3.1	4.1	2.9
	Subtotal	55.7	44.9	49.9	62.1	63.4
Sogo banks [65]		18.8	18.0	15.1	11.3	9.2
Shinkin banks [422]		13.2	20.5	17.4	13.5	13.5
Credit unions [376]		3.1	6.2	5.9	4.7	5.2
	Subtotal	35.1	44.7	38.4	29.5	27.9
Shoko Chukin Bank		3.5	4.2	4.5	3.8	3.2
Small Business Finance Corp.		3.3	3.3	3.5	2.2	2.4
Peoples' Finance Corporation		2.3	2.4	3.1	2.2	2.5
Environmental Sanitation Business						
Finance Corp.		–	0.4	0.6	0.2	0.6
	Subtotal	9.1	10.3	11.7	8.4	8.7
Total		100	100	100	100	100

Note:
*[Figures] show numbers as of 1995. Sogo banks had by this time become a second tier of regional banks.
Source: People's Finance Corporation (ed.) (1989), *Small and Medium Enterprises in Japan and Financing Available to Them*, Tokyo, p. 77; *Shoko kinyu*, July, 1995. (orig. BOJ Monthly Economic Statistics).

Second, government financing institutions provide different types of loans from the private sector. They tend to be long term; in 1986–7, 82.3 per cent of PFC loans and 97.9 per cent of SBFC loans were for periods of more than three years compared with around 30 per cent for city and regional banks, even though the proportions of operating and investment funds were similar.[23] Many of the loans, particularly from the PFC, are for small amounts. The average PFC loan is ¥3 million, one seventh that of credit banks, which in turn is a quarter that of city banks. Further, many of the loans – 80 per cent for the PFC in 1986–7 – are not secured, although guarantors are normally required. This is because the loans themselves are small, but also because borrowers have already offered what security they

---

[23] Peoples' Finance Corporation (1989, 60–2). For the Shoko Chukin, the figure was 65 per cent in 1991.

have to private institutions for loans. Government institutions have also been willing to loan to new and restructuring companies which find it difficult to borrow from private sources. In recessions, when private-sector financing dries up, government loans help tide vulnerable firms over. In 1989 the SBFC made ¥2.33 trillion in new loans to SMEs and the PFC made ¥3.22 trillion, while the Shoko Chukin made ¥561 billion in net loans (new loans minus repayments). In 1991 the figures rocketed to ¥7.76 trillion, ¥7.12 trillion and ¥732 billion respectively.[24] Thus government loans fill gaps which might otherwise not be filled by the private sector.

Third, indirect support is given through the credit guarantee scheme. The amount of loans from public and private sources guaranteed under this scheme doubled between 1987 and 1993 to reach ¥15.1 trillion.[25] The Small Business Credit Insurance Corporation also deposits funds in financial institutions and authorises them to lend up to five times that amount in guaranteed loans. In 1991, ¥358 billion was loaned in this way.

Fourth, in addition to general loans, special loans tied to policy measures are available. The equipment modernisation programme, listed under small-scale enterprise measures in figure 9.1, is an example of such *seido yushi*. The programme was launched in 1956 and has been revised several times, with leasing added as well as a separate 'high tech.' leasing system. It is summarised in table 9.2. The programme is administered at the prefectural level, and, for the loan system, prefectures must match central government funds (¥1.5 billion each in 1995, together with ¥46 billion in repayments; the leasing systems are more complex, but a combined total of ¥51.3 billion was available in 1995). Because of repayments, this programme is much more extensive than its budgetary allocation figures alone would suggest.

Finally, regional and local authorities have financing programmes of their own. Ota's policy guide lists 17 run by the Tokyo government, and ten local ones, although some of the latter are hardly used. Most are variations of national programmes, with progressively lower ceilings, and progressively smaller customers. The bulk of Ota's recent funding – ¥6.7 billion in 1993 and ¥4.4 billion in 1994 – has come under the category of 'business management funds', at least half of which has been emergency recession loans with a ceiling of ¥5 million.[26]

---

[24] Chusho kigyo cho (ed.) (1990c, 110; 1992c, 83). Other contributing factors include tumbling interest rates, and loans renegotiated at the lower rates would have inflated the figures. In the new climate of caution and retrenchment, however, banks nudged SMEs towards public financing, and to make greater use of credit guarantees.

[25] Chusho kigyo cho (ed.) (1990c, 158; 1992c, 115; 1994c, 28).

[26] These loans are not provided directly, but funds are deposited with private institutions which provide approved small emergency loans totalling up to four times the amount deposited, multiplying the total amount available.

Table 9.2 *Equipment modernisation programme*

	Equipment modernisation loan system	Equipment leasing system		
		Equipment leasing (instalment)		Equip. leasing
		general equipment	high-tech. information processing equipment	high-tech. information processing equipment
Main recipients	SMEs with 100 employees or less	SMEs with 20 employees or less	SMEs with 80 employees or less	SMEs with 80 employees or less
Maximum loan or leased equipment value	half of funds required, up to ¥40 million	equipment worth up to ¥35 million	equipment worth up to ¥60 million	equipment worth up to ¥60 million
Interest or charge	interest free	10% guarantee plus 3.25% annual charge	10% guarantee plus 3.25% annual charge	c6% p.a. (including tax and insurance)
Period	5 years (12 yrs for anti-pollution equipment)	4 yrs 6 mths (11 yrs 6 mths for anti-pollution equipment)	6 yrs 6 mths (11 yrs 6 mths for anti-pollution equipment)	up to 7 years

Source: Chusho kigyo cho (ed.) (1995b, 353).

What do small firm owners make of this array of programmes and financing? On the one hand there is the following view:

I'm not good at borrowing money. I've been helped by the Shoko Chukin, and so I feel I should borrow some money from them, and for tax purposes, but mostly I rely on retained earnings. As you say, there are all these programmes and facilities, but who can understand them? They were about a year late with the emergency funds, and a lot of people had already borrowed up to their limit . . . Frankly, I would rather see lower taxes. Then prices would come down and we could start competing again.

This owner had a basic mistrust of government, but felt he was repaying a favour by borrowing from the Shoko Chukin. One or two other owners were also opposed to government programmes in principle, but not to its financing institutions. Others had practical reasons to avoid special loans; when the officials came around for the 'health checkup' they might discover things they should not. Red tape associated with special loans was a common source of discontent: 'It takes a month, sometimes three, and there are a lot of forms. I prefer to go to a bank and get the money right away.' Many medium-sized factory owners felt they had 'graduated' from government funds, although some returned for more during the recession.

On the other hand, a few habitually used them:

Once you have used the upgrading programme, it's easy to keep on getting loans. If I want new machinery I go straight to the Tokyo government offices and talk to them. I've used the equipment modernisation programme twice, although I didn't use it last time because I was in a hurry . . . Our industry will be designated for structural improvement from next year, so we will be eligible for special depreciation and other measures. And I've just been to an explanation of the new business activity law. We might be able to get something from that.

Some owners were apologetic, guilty even, about being able to get funds so easily (but at the same time hoped the government would grant them an interest holiday on their loans because of the recession). The majority of owners, it would be safe to say, would go to their local credit union or bank first when they wanted to borrow money or receive financial advice. The government financing institutions were seen as reasonably accessible (all have branches in Ota Ward), but the majority of owners either didn't know about government programmes (despite readily available information), or considered them difficult to use. Those most likely to use them were members of cooperative or relocation associations.

In conclusion, direct and indirect government support has enabled many small firms to secure long-term funds more cheaply than they could otherwise have done. Loans from government institutions may also encourage private banks to offer loans and exercise interest rate restraint. Small firm owners grumble about special programmes being hard to use, loan insurances being set too high and emergency fund limits being set too low, but many British counterparts during the early 1990s recession would gladly have put up with these inconveniences for funds to tide them over. The fact that government loans are not significantly below the market rate and constitute less than 10 per cent of total loans, therefore, does not make them unimportant. But they are screened loans, not handouts. The intent is supplementary financing, not protective subsidy. They may give some small firms a better chance, but do not keep them artificially alive; annual closure rates have ranged between 3–5 per cent since the 1960s. The key element in the survival and upgrading of remaining firms is their own efforts.

Local policy and politics

Small firms in Ota try to influence local policy and politics, through for instance four district-based organisations, and association federations on Jonan and Keihin Islands. Some of these organisations are very active, more so than the umbrella coordinating body, Ota koren, which has a small office and a staff of two in the Industry Hall. On the same floor of the Hall, the Ota branch of the Tokyo Chamber of Commerce has a staff of 14.[27]

Similar in some ways to the national arrangement, the main vehicle through which policy objectives are elaborated is the Industry Promotion Measures Committee (IPMC), organised by the Industry Promotion Section of the Ward Office. It has around 50 members, most of whom are SME owners, as well as three ward councillors, plus two ward officers and the head of the local Chamber of Commerce branch. Reports from the IPMC to the mayor stress the importance of Ota's 'national technopolis' for the nation's economy, the challenges it faces – encroaching housing, aging factories, disappearance of rental factories, and steep startup costs – and positive policy responses it sees as necessary. Policy measures must be made simpler to understand and use, financing improved, and collateral criteria broadened. More support must be given for technology use, development, training of young workers, and so on.[28]

Minsho and its supporters view the IPMC as a talking shop for larger, conservative, house-trained SME owners. It was Minsho agitation, they suggest, that pushed the IPMC into demanding emergency relief in 1992.

[27] Chamber consulting and small loan services are supported by the government, hence the large staff. It was through such support that the government sought to counter the appeal of the Communist Party and its affiliate Minsho (Peoples' Chamber of Commerce).

[28] The Chamber also makes policy demands to the mayor and council head every year on issues such as use of land vacated by relocating factories, industry–resident co-existence, zoning issues and relaxation of the factory laws, and measures to attract and train workers.

What they got was limited funds that were difficult to obtain. The factory apartments, which it had advocated, too, ended up too big and expensive for its members to use. Minsho may prompt insiders into action, then, but the outcome from its point of view is always less than satisfactory, reinforcing its outsider role.

The biggest party in the Ward Council in 1993 was the LDP conservatives, followed by the (Buddhist) Komei Party and then the Communist Party. The communists have a reputation for being well organised and maximising their votes, and standing up for the most vulnerable, but suffer from their former subversive image and fear of their ideology on the part of many owners. The LDP–Komei–DSP block which dominated the ward's politics did not have a reputation for actively fighting for local industry, but benefited from the pro-business image of their national parties and their links with them. In fact, only three councillors out of more than 50 were really considered industry representatives.

There are formidable obstacles to the realisation of even insiders' objectives due to politics within the ward, and Ota's location in Tokyo, the capital city. First, in Ota's urban setting, interests of residents are diverse, and not necessarily sympathetic to local industry, since many residents work outside the ward. Owners would like to see big improvements in the road and transport infrastructure, for instance, but many residents are against this. Achieving a balance between the mayor's 'three pillars' of industry, residence and culture is no easy task, and requires tradeoffs. Logically speaking, there are structural reasons to favour residents, since business taxes are collected by the Tokyo government and disbursed on a *per capita* basis. Ward bureaucrats deny that this influences policy decisions, but there is no compelling reason to favour industrialists locally.

Hence the central planning and coordinating branches of the local administration do not appear to have been very sympathetic to the voice of industry. Zoning is a good example. The Industry Promotion Section would like an end to what it sees as creeping zoning restrictions, especially the zone which restricts rebuilding over 150 m², but the powerful Urban Planning Department dismisses their pleas. Retorted one representative: 'We don't hear the factory owners complaining. It's only them over in the Industry Promotion Section. Our zoning decisions basically reflect the status quo.' In fact, the 150 m² restriction was lifted from one area after a campaign by the local industrial association with support from residents. Where industry and resident solidarity has been weaker, this buffer zone between industry and shops and housing has remained or expanded.

Another major issue has been the use of some 200 ha of land which will be made available when Haneda Airport is moved further out into Tokyo

Bay.[29] Local industrialists submitted requests for a technology development centre, factory apartments, and a major aircraft repair facility with links to local industry. The Urban Planning Department incorporated some of these views into its plan, which featured park space, civic forum space, a museum, art gallery, etc. for the residents. Industrialists would like to see vacated factory land adjacent to the airport as the site for a futuristic industry and housing development, but the Urban Planning Department favours commercial and shopping amenities.

There are, admittedly, signs that industrial promotion is beginning to assume greater importance in ward planning. Yet even if the ward becomes more active in promoting industry, the Haneda saga points to the second difficulty, Ota's location in the capital city. The national government, as we have seen, has long pursued industrial dispersion policies. The Tokyo government, too, has not been very sympathetic to industry, and its Labour and Economic Bureau faces the same types of problems as Ota's Industry/Economy Department and its Industry Promotion Section. The national and Tokyo governments have their own plans for Haneda, of course. Both envisage parks and airport-related facilities. The Ministry of Transport naturally sees the land as a chance to solve some of its transportation problems; an interchange would be a likely feature. The Tokyo government would like facilities for Tokyo residents, including a hospital, condominiums, and office space. In the end there will be some compromise, but the ultimate authority and purse strings are held by the Tokyo and central governments.

Small firms in Ota thus have problems in creating a favourable business environment. The fact that they have survived for so long is a testimony to their tenacity, and the countervailing benefits of their industrial district. Compared with small provincial, geographically contained concentrations of one or two clearly defined industries, their needs are much more difficult to articulate and press for. The power of politicians to intervene on their behalf is strictly limited. The 'national technopolis' declaration described in chapter 4 was intended to create an image for local industry and a greater awareness of its needs, and the widely publicised plight of local firms during the recession sowed the seeds of awareness amongst policy makers that something needs to be done. But in Tokyo's complex, bureaucratic environment, it takes a long time before such seeds actually bear fruit. While surveys are carried out, plans are debated and pronouncements made – or not made – the rapid decline in factory numbers (over a quarter of Tokyo's factories between 1983 and 1993) will continue.

---

[29] Originally scheduled to open in 1995, the new airport has been delayed by several years due to slow settling of the reclaimed land, and planning and financial problems.

10 A comparative view: small factories in Birmingham

Birmingham in the West Midlands of Britain, and Ota/south Tokyo in the Keihin Belt have much in common. Both are home to exceptional concentrations of manufacturing, especially machine industries, and have given birth to myriads of small workshops as well as household-name companies. Both have shared the reputation that 'if it can be made anywhere, it can be made in Birmingham/Ota', a reputation which long acted as a magnet for work and workers. In both cases this resulted in congestion, and official attempts to disperse industry. They have suffered contrasting fates, however. Ota's industry survived the exodus of large firms in the 1960s and 70s, and even strengthened its position in the national economy. Birmingham's fall, by contrast, has been spectacular. From its leading position in Britain's employment and earnings 'league tables', it has been beset by factory closures and redundancies; Britain's industrial heartland has been in danger of becoming an industrial wasteland.

What lies behind this contrast? Is it largely attributable to contrasting performances by large firms in the respective countries, or are there other reasons? Could it be related to small firms – a decline in the spirit of independence and constructive cooperation in Birmingham, for instance, and their persistence in Ota? Does the recent drop in small firm numbers suggest that Ota will ultimately share Birmingham's fate, anyway, at least in terms of manufacturing prowess? Can attempts to revive industry in Birmingham provide lessons for Ota in stemming the decline of manufacturing industry and small firms there?

A comparative view of industry in Birmingham prompts such questions, which will be addressed in the final two chapters. Chapter 10 begins with a historical overview of industry in Birmingham, of factors contributing to its rise, and factors attributed to its decline. Small firms, and their role in the process, are then considered, based both on published materials and the views of (surviving) small firm owners. Finally, we look at attempts to revive industry, and Birmingham's industrial community. Industrial districts such as Birmingham and Ota may have been formed largely spontaneously, but in a 'de-industrialising' economy, they must be rejuvenated by design. It is, however, an uphill battle.

The rise and fall of industry in Birmingham

Sixteenth-century observers found the market town of Birmingham 'ringing with the noise of anvils', a description later echoed by Alexis de Tocqueville and Charles Dickens (and later still, by observers of Ota).[1] They attributed this to the cheap cost of smith's tools, and the availability of iron and coal from nearby Staffordshire. Expansion of the metal trades in the seventeenth and eighteenth centuries was further aided by a lack of regulation restricting the growth of new industry and labour markets:

The past pressed less heavily on Birmingham than on the older towns of the neighbourhood, such as Coventry and Walsall, and the men of enterprise in the early years of modern industrialism viewed it as a haven of economic freedom. It was, therefore, the resort of the new type of manufacturer who was appearing at the end of the eighteenth century, and, indeed, of all who were in conflict with the conservative tendencies of the time.[2]

Birmingham's openness, and its broad base in the metal trades, enabled it to survive and prosper as old industries declined and new ones took their place. As the buckle trade declined, metal button manufacture expanded, along with brass wares, pins – which so inspired Adam Smith – silver, tin and pewter wares, japanned and enamelled goods, and then metal pens. It was long known for its swords and guns. Its population increased from 187,000 in 1801 to 819,000 in 1861, and by the middle of the nineteenth century it was known as the 'city of a thousand trades'.

Birmingham's contribution to British manufacturing was not limited to the finishing trades. James Watt made his steam engines in Matthew Boulton's giant Soho Manufactory, for instance. Nevertheless, just as Tokyo could not match Osaka's heavy industry and textile concentration during Japan's early industrialisation, textiles in Britain flourished further north, and with its heavy industrial and shipbuilding base, Glasgow's industrialists 'could look down on their great rival Birmingham, land-locked, with its range of miscellaneous small-scale trades, sharing with Glasgow the manipulation of metal, but providing the world with no such grand products.'[3] In both cases, the emergence of the machine industries, especially vehicles and electric machines, turned the tide. The 1875–6 depression, the raising of tariffs abroad, increased international

---

[1] Chinn (1994, 4, 20).   [2] Allen (1929, 26).   [3] Checkland (1976, 11).

competition and the depletion of close-by natural resources hit Birmingham's established industries extremely hard, prompting demands for protectionist measures. But far from decline, it was set for a new transformation and new prominence.

The Birmingham Small Arms Company symbolises the transformation (and later, the decline). In mid century, several small arms manufacturers banded together to compete with Springfield manufacturers in the US (or more precisely, with Britain's Enfield factory, established to compete with Springfield). Their factory was the first in Birmingham to adopt mass production methods.[4] In 1880, shortly before the 'safety cycle' boom, BSA began to make bicycles. In 1908 it began to make cars, and the following year motorcycles, which is what most people associate the name with nowadays.

In the new machine industries Britain had lost its earlier industrial supremacy, but in the quarter century prior to World War I they flourished in Birmingham, and enabled it to grow during the difficult interwar years. Employment in the electric machine industry almost trebled between 1911 and 1921, and in the cycle, motor, and accessories industries it doubled, to comprise one third of the national total.[5] The following year Herbert Austin exhibited his famous Austin Seven, which propelled his company into the leading ranks of car manufacturers. After the Depression, domestic demand recovered, and foreign competition eased with the decline of international trade. The Empire provided an enormous market for Birmingham's goods. World War II brought a surge in weapons production, although bombing caused substantial damage as well. Finally, the postwar reconstruction boom, and a continued respite from serious international competition, contributed to two decades of unparalleled prosperity. Unemployment seldom rose above 1 per cent. Average earnings outstripped even London. The West Midlands produced the highest number of cars and trucks outside the US, contributing up to 40 per cent of total UK exports.[6]

The employment and earnings league tables plot its subsequent decline, however. In 1966 unemployment in the West Midlands stood at just 0.8 per cent; by 1973 it had edged up to 2.2 per cent and by 1976 it was 5.4 per cent, above the national average of 5.2 per cent. In the early Thatcher years of 1979–81 it more than doubled, and went on to a peak of 19.1 per cent (in Birmingham) in 1993. Though it fell in the subsequent recovery, some of the inner wards continued to record unemployment rates of around 30 per cent. In terms of earnings, London usurped the West Midlands' top income

---

[4] Allen (1929, 191).   [5] Allen (1929, 399–403).
[6] West Midlands Enterprise Board (ed.) (1992, 12).

position in the early 1970s, and by the 1980s the West Midlands had fallen well down the regional league tables. The very industries on which Birmingham's prosperity was founded led the decline. Employment in manufacturing halved between 1971 and 1991, from 50 per cent to around 25 per cent of the labour force. Half of all machine industry jobs were lost between 1978 and 1991, although they still comprise the bulk of manufacturing employment and proportionately are almost double the national average.

Declining manufacturing employment may be expected as a result of productivity gains and structural changes. It has been evident in Ota as well. But whereas output continued to rise in Ota, it plummeted in Birmingham in the late 1970s, and thereafter remained relatively flat. Rises in service sector employment have been less than increases in unemployment. This has not been a case of 'positive de-industrialisation'.[7]

The obvious trigger for the decline was intensifying international competition in the 1960s, following the Kennedy Round of tariff reductions and the elimination of preferential Commonwealth trading, but this is only part of the picture, and the root causes go back much further. Most accounts point a finger at Birmingham's giant companies and concentration through mergers and acquisitions. Birmingham's bloated giants built up managerial inefficiencies, and did not respond decisively enough to increasing competition. At the same time, they became multi-nationals, and, when they restructured in the late 1970s–early 1980s, they dramatically cut employment in their home bases. In 1976, 43 per cent of Birmingham's workforce was employed by just ten companies, and 39 per cent in just 30 establishments. Between 1978 and 1982 these companies trimmed a quarter of their workforces. Almost all of this was in their home bases; overseas employment actually rose during this time.[8]

Concentration began in the last decades of the nineteenth century, and is personified in the career of Dudley Docker, who in 1902 arranged the merger of five rolling stock companies into the giant Metropolitan Amalgamated Carriage and Wagon Company. Docker sought a further merger with Guest Keen and Nettlefold (GKN – itself formed by a merger in 1902) during World War I, but eventually amalgamated the company with Westinghouse and Vickers from Sheffield. A leading director of BSA from 1906 to 1912, Docker was also associated with many of that company's acquisitions, such as Eadie in 1907 and Daimler of Coventry in 1910. His son Bernard continued the merger tradition as chairman after World War II. In the view of Docker's biographer, only the first rolling

---

[7] Rowthorn and Wells (1987). The statistics are mainly from BEIC mimeos.
[8] Gaffikin and Nickson (1984); Marshall (1987).

stock merger made sense, and the eventual collapse of BSA in 1973 was foreshadowed by 70 years of managerial trouble.[9]

Thus the widely noted increasing size of manufacturing operations was not just a product of mechanisation and modern factory production, but changing attitudes which encouraged amalgamation. Although they were justified on the grounds of efficiency gains, many of the mergers and acquisitions were ill-conceived, poorly executed, and failed to achieve such gains.[10] Accumulated inefficiencies were exposed by international competition from the late 1960s.

Labour and investment problems are also commonly cited. The West Midlands was traditionally associated with weak trade unions, due to the predominance of small workshops, craft divisions, and the rural backgrounds of factory recruits. With low levels of unemployment and organisation of (semi-skilled) workers in large plants, however, unions were in a position to resist management attempts from the 1950s to change working practices, gain greater control over the production process, and raise productivity. High wage costs, labour friction, and low productivity provided employers with an incentive to relocate, and allegedly discouraged investment, which lagged behind national levels, and far behind international levels.[11] A common image of Birmingham's industry during this time is of increasingly obsolete plant and equipment, with companies living off past investments.

Government policy is implicated, too, including unsympathetic macro-economic policy, 'stop–go' demand management – BSA claimed that the squeeze of 1959–60 cut its sales by one third, and that the policy was the tenth change in eight years, allowing foreign competitors into the market during upturns whilst making planning virtually impossible – and merger promotion.[12] Regional policy – especially the reluctance to issue Industrial Development Certificates for upgrading and expansion within Birmingham – also impeded investment and encouraged relocations. Between 1956–66, 17 per cent of plant in the old core industrial areas of Birmingham was lost through relocation.[13]

Undoubtedly successive governments had a worse record of producing a

---

[9] Davenport-Hines (1984, 325). According to Davenport-Hines, 'Docker was a self-consciously modern capitalist who, by early middle age, had rejected many traditional attitudes of Victorian England as epitomised by the writings of Samuel Smiles . . . One observer commented in 1890, "The future Smiles will write *The Lives of the Market Riggers* or *The History of Trusts, Syndicates and Corners*"' (p. .24).

[10] Bennett (1981).   [11] Spencer *et al.* (1986, 28, 79).

[12] Regarding stop–go demand management and its effects on the motor industry, see Spencer *et al.* (1986); Dunnett (1980).

[13] Spencer *et al.* (1986, 124–6). Just how much this was due to IDCs, though, is the subject of debate.

stable pro-manufacturing environment than in Japan, but this must be put alongside weaknesses within industry itself when accounting for the fall of industry in Birmingham. The picture given so far is incomplete, moreover, since it has not considered the role of small firms. The effects of concentration and restructuring could at least partially have been offset by a dynamic small firm sector, evident a hundred years earlier. What happened to the vitality of Birmingham's small firms, for which it was once so famous?

Small firms and economic vitality

Boulton's giant Soho Manufactory was exceptional in early industrial Birmingham. As Joseph Chamberlain (later the city's mayor) noted in 1866, fifty years earlier there were very few large factories. Most businesses were carried on in small premises attached to residences. He predicted, however, that such businesses would decline because of the introduction of machinery and steam power, which required a lot of capital. He welcomed this prospect and the arrival of large factories, since they would result not only in lower prices, but better working conditions and wages. (He himself was a partner of the large screw-maker Nettlefold and Chamberlain; the former subsequently became part of GKN).[14]

Such predictions did not come to pass. The factory system co-existed with small-scale manufacture, at least initially. Independent workers often rented space, power, and lighting in factories under the coordination of a factor or merchant. And the number of small factories increased. In a description which could easily have been made of south Tokyo a few decades later, a French visitor described a typical factory with 10–20 employees in 1895 as follows:

The manufacturer had begun life as a worker himself . . . and he had become prosperous as a result of his own self help and perseverance. He was proud of his independence. He would work alongside his men in a fifty five hour week, from seven in the morning until seven in the evening, and since his workshop and home were in the same building, he could put in overtime without difficulty, whenever it was necessary. In his spare time he still pursued his mechanical interests, and . . . had built himself a bicycle. His son, aged fifteen, was employed in the works.[15]

As late as 1914 Neville Chamberlain noted: 'The majority of masters in Birmingham are probably still "small men", and it will take more than a generation for the old order to pass.'[16]

Allen, too, predicted the demise of the 'old order'. In the mass produc-

[14] Chinn (1994, 41).
[15] P. de Rousiers, cited in Briggs (1952, 56). Self help and perseverance, of course, were Smiles' favourite words.   [16] Cited in Briggs (1952, 48).

tion factories set up around the turn of the century labour was employed directly, and processes like plating and casting were brought in house, making the factories largely self-contained. By 1914: 'there was a marked contrast between the large up-to-date factories of the suburbs and the small, dark shops in the older parts of Birmingham'.[17] And yet, reflected Florence just after World War II: '(Allen) points repeatedly to the growing size of the typical plant, and the tendency to specialise in product. Nevertheless, much "vertical" specialisation, process by process, continues to be carried on by relatively small- or medium-sized plants. Different firms take on different processes in the transformation of raw material into finished goods.'[18] Beesley, too, maintained that in Birmingham in the interwar and immediate postwar years, a virtuous cycle was at work, in which small firm dynamism created new opportunities for more small firms. A 'complex of juxtaposed and interdependent processes' created a favourable environment for experimentation with new parts and products, which attracted new startups and branch establishments, absorbing resources which had fallen into disuse elsewhere. Thus 'areas like Birmingham may still be setting the pace for new enterprise, in spite of the official policy of restrictions'.[19]

A contrasting view may be gleaned from these same two authors, however. Florence was puzzled that many of Birmingham's factories were medium-sized rather than small. His explanation was Birmingham's large population and growth through economies gained by specialisation. This is not entirely convincing, since we would expect similar developments in Ota, but it does suggest that the number of workshops and very small factories had already declined significantly by the end of World War II. Beesley's own 'exit' figures actually exceed his 'entry' figures for almost all the interwar years. Birmingham was probably not an exception to the national trend of declining small firm numbers, after all.[20]

Further, the background to Florence's comment on the 'feudal' mentality of small firm owners was not a celebration of individualism, but criticism at their slow response to rationalisation and innovation, which Allen hinted at. This may have been linked to changing generations, as Marshall suggests, whereby the success of Victorian founders 'engendered easy-going habits of life and work among many of the sons and grandsons', who were less dedicated to family enterprise.[21] Independence and the idea of handing on a family business intact meant less to them, and growing opportunities to liquidate their assets presented an attractive alternative. Even if they wanted to remain in business, mergers reduced personal risk and offered finance and marketing advantages.

---

[17] Allen (1929, 324).   [18] Florence (1948, 54–5).   [19] Beesley (1955, 47–8, 61).
[20] Prais (1976/1981, 11).   [21] Marshall (1923, 579, 581).

This cultural change was not universal. The preference of small firm owners for independent co-ordination through associations rather than amalgamation persisted into the twentieth century, even into the interwar years.[22] But mergers and acquisitions of small or medium-sized firms became more common, and they sometimes followed the breakdown of looser forms of co-ordination, in effect substituting for them, and reducing competition. Again, Birmingham was probably not an exception to the national trend.[23] Managers in merged companies and wholly owned subsidiaries, moreover, often had limited discretion and were unenterprising. And businesses were kept alive which would have failed had they remained independent.[24] These 'quasi firms', then, were quite different from Ota's 'quasi firm' subcontractors.

Given that small firms appear to be better incubators than large firms, a decline in their numbers probably had a snowball effect.[25] All of this served to undermine Birmingham's Marshallian industrial district strengths based on Victorian individualism, specialisation, and interfirm cooperation. This in turn would undermine Birmingham's ability to adapt to changes in markets and technology in the 1970s, in contrast to its transformation a century earlier.

Despite its fall, Birmingham today still has a very large concentration of manufacturing establishments, half of which are in the machine industries (table 10.1). The vast majority are small; three quarters employ fewer than 20 workers (table 10.2). As a result of restructuring, less than a third of workers are now employed in the largest 32 establishments, with over 500 employees. The concentration of small machine industry factories is not as pronounced as in Ota, and, in terms of employees, the differences are striking, but it is a remarkable concentration nonetheless.

Small firm sketches

Survivors are by definition a select group, and interviews with a small number cannot give a representative picture of small firms in Birmingham, but they can shed light on similarities and differences with small firms in south Tokyo. Four SMEs from the Aston–Newtown area of Birmingham

---

[22] Briggs cites the example of Birmingham Registered Gunmakers, registered as a company in 1919 (1952, 50–1, 284). Allen cites the Birmingham Association of Machine Tool Makers, founded in 1916, which encouraged specialisation of member companies (1929, 417).

[23] The Bolton Report (1971), cites a survey in which over half of small firms leaving the sample did so because they were taken over. Of these, a quarter mentioned succession problems and 14 per cent estate duty payments, one third cited financial failure, and 14 per cent competition reduction (p. 10). See also Prais (1976/81); Hannah (1983).

[24] Bennett (1981, 16–17).   [25] Johnson and Cathcart (1979).

Table 10.1 *Machine industries in Birmingham and Ota Ward*

	Birmingham		Ota Ward	
	est.	employees	est.	employees
Metal products	24.6%	21.6%	23.2%	16.4%
Machinery & equip.	12.4	11.8	31.3	25.0
Transportation equip.	3.1	20.4	4.6	5.5
Electrical machinery	} 9.4	} 10.1	13.3	18.9
Precision equip.			3.8	3.6
Machine industry total	49.6	63.9	76.2	69.3
Total manufacturing	100	100	100	100
(*N*)	(4,552)	(130,795)	(7,160)	(69,003)

Sources: Birmingham Municipal Database; Ota ku (ed.) (1995b, 22–6).

are looked at here, with some additional references to other small firms. We begin with a brief profile of each and then look at attitudes towards business, interfirm relations, and the business environment.[26]

Attitudes towards business

S. Dies and Stamping was founded in 1862, before Japan's Meiji Restoration. As was common in Birmingham, and later Tokyo, the founder was the youngest son of a large family who came to the city to seek his fortune. He started work as a die sinker, and the company still does this work today. Succeeding generations of sons have served apprenticeships, usually with outside machine tool makers, before returning to take control of the company. The current owner believes the company has survived five generations because of flexibility in the work it will take on. It makes its own machine tools for its die and stamping work, and takes orders for them as well. It does mould work, once in a separate factory, but this has been brought back in house. In the 1970s it set up another factory to make trophies. In 1993 the main factory had 48 employees, and the trophy factory 56.

T. Hydraulics is descended from Birmingham's tradition for invention. In the reception is a drawing of a steam engine invented by an ancestor in the eighteenth century. The present company began in 1903 by making marine steam engines, but this work soon became unprofitable, and the owner turned to subcontracting for the emerging automobile industry,

[26] Based on interviews in August–September 1993, and September 1995.

Table 10.2 *Small firms in Birmingham and Ota Ward*

Size (employees)	Birmingham		Ota Ward	
	est.	employees	est.	employees
1–4*	37.5%	3.2%	47.2%	10.2%
5–9*	20.3	4.6	33.7	20.0
10–19	17.6	7.9	10.1	14.3
20–49	14.5	14.6	6.8	20.1
50–99	5.6	12.7	1.3	8.8
100–199	2.7	12.3	0.6	8.0
200–499	1.2	12.1	0.3	8.1
500+	0.7	32.8	0.1	10.4
total	100	100	100	100
(*N*)	(4,555)	(130,818)	(7,160)	(69,003)

Note:
* Ota figures are for 1–3 and 4–9 employees respectively.
Sources: As for table 10.1.

before relaunching a product in the 1930s – a hydraulic pump used for air-craft. Subcontracting still provided two thirds of income, however, until the 1970s, when the grandson took over and decided that the future lay in their own product line – hydraulic pumps and equipment. There were 55 employ-ees in 1993.

F. Press started as a wood turning company in 1935, but began to sub-contract for Lucas during World War II, making components for tanks and gun turrets. The relationship with Lucas has continued ever since. When the son took over in 1960, he decided not to move out of subcontracting, but from lathe turning to specialised press work, on the grounds that higher entry barriers would reduce cut-throat competition. He was encouraged by Lucas to set up a sister company (cf. S. Ltd in chapter 4) doing rist, cable, and harness work, and still does almost half his work for Lucas or de-merged Lucas companies as a 'bought out supplier' (meaning the custom-ers no longer do the work in house). The company had 172 employees.

These factories are all closer to the 'new key' factories in Ota rather than the micro-factories which specialise in machining work, which are harder to find, although table 10.2 suggests there are a lot of them. Y. Gauge (ten employees) which makes gauges, tools, and does precision machining work, is one example. It was started in a small backstreet workshop in 1959 by three partners who wanted to be their own boss. Two of the partners left, leaving the third with sole ownership. The son joined in 1979 with no background in engineering. Like the successor of N. Machines (chapter 7), he faced initial suspicion from the older craftsmen because of this, and because he tried to systematise management to create a sounder financial basis.

All four are family enterprises, and share many characteristics of SMEs in Ota. There are differences, however. Unlike many of Ota's owners, or 'small men' in nineteenth century Birmingham, none of the owners live above or adjacent to their factory. 'It amazes me that anyone would want to live above a factory. No-one around here does,' commented the successor at Y. Gauge. (His father had two ambitions in life – to be his own boss, and to own a nice house in the suburbs.) Thus there is a greater separation of living or family and work spheres, and a subtle difference in attitudes towards work: 'We work hard when we have to, like when we are founding the company or taking it over, or moving into a new line of business. But once it's established, we expect to be able to take things a bit easier.' Since owners do not live locally, it may also weaken the community aspects of the district, information exchange, *sessa takuma*, and socialisation of new generations into the industrial community.

The successor at Y Gauge suggested that many of his company's former competitors (the number had fallen from over 30 in the mid 1960s to four or five) were run by 'live to work' owners, for whom hard work and craft skills were a substitute for efficient management. 'I bought the customer list of a company four years ago which boasted of being the cheapest gauge company. The guy took no money out of it – he actually put his own in – and he worked 70–80 hours a week. He didn't know what he was paying his staff. There was no order.' Thus, the craft skills of 'live to work' owners may no longer be a sufficient basis on which to build a viable business.

Systematic management – certified by BS5750 or ISO 9000 qualifications sometimes – is necessary nowadays to gain orders from large companies. The same increasingly applies to Japan. But the 'gentlemanly' business may also be insufficiently 'hands on', and be sold when it fails to meet the objectives of its owner. The sale of companies was commonplace. One owner waved a sale letter from an accountancy firm: 'I get letters like this all the time. Usually there's something wrong with them, of course, but it may be worth buying the work.' As we have seen, the same trend has been predicted for Japan, but it will have to wait for a new generation, if it happens at all.

Interfirm relations

'Birmingham was subcontracting country in the 1940s and 1950s,' according to the owner of F. Press. Like his company, many small firms were forced into subcontracting during the war, but, unlike his company, many attempted to escape from it soon after.[27] The incentive to do so was no doubt stronger than in Japan. The basic in-house policy of large companies has been mentioned. According to this, overflow – and sometimes rush or specialist – orders were subcontracted out. Given wide fluctuations in demand, sometimes blamed on government 'Stop–Go' demand management, subcontracting was almost guaranteed to be a precarious, stressful, and short-term oriented activity. Sometimes there was too much work, sometimes none. In addition, the *style* of subcontracting traditionally emphasised price, with customers switching suppliers if they offered a more competitive rate, and sometimes playing suppliers off against each other. This and frequent changes in orders increased uncertainty. One way to reduce this was by mergers (vertical and horizontal), another was by quitting subcontracting. Thus the following comments:

'We do do a little bit of work for the automobile industry, but it's always up and down. And they are bad payers, so we never wanted to become too dependent on them.' (S. Dies and Stamping).

'There used to be lots of other suppliers, and customers would screw you for prices, and drop you the minute you messed them around' (Y. Gauge). 'Subcontracting was too uncertain. We had to get out of it.' (T. Hydraulics.)

From the *customer's* point of viewpoint, there were problems as well: 'We get our bar-turned parts from the US. I've looked around here, but I'm just unable to find competitive vendors. There are companies with 15–40 employees that can do the work, but they're 200–300 per cent more expensive. It's not as if they're doing it on different machines, either – I've looked at that. Even with a markup and transportation costs, it's cheaper to get them abroad.' On the other hand, F. Press shows that long-term trust-based subcontracting relationships are possible. In this case 'taking control of their own destiny' meant becoming a bought out supplier, a process which took twenty years.

Instability of subcontracting would mitigate against a high degree of specialisation by small workshops. In addition, horizontal interfirm relations, informal and formal, are less extensive than in Ota. This might be related to the fact that owners do not live locally. In addition, though, there was a striking difference in the number of times the word 'competitor' was mentioned. It was almost never mentioned spontaneously in Ota, but frequently in Birmingham. This does not mean that interfirm competition is fiercer in Birmingham, but it does appear to loom larger in the minds of

---

[27] Wartime institutional innovations and arrangements have been less durable in Britain than in other countries. For industrial relations, see Fulcher (1991), and Fox (1984). On Japan, see for instance Okazaki (1994), and chapter 2.

owners. Trade association membership is common, but, even here, one owner said: 'I don't get involved very much because they are competitors, after all.'

Horizontal interfirm relations appear to have been more extensive in the nineteenth century. In addition to cultural and residential change, their decline may be related to the subcontracting practices just described. Where orders are volatile, there is the real possibility of suddenly losing orders to a competitor. Volatility may have impeded the establishment of reciprocating norms. Quality and delivery problems were also seen as impediments to confrere trading: 'We used to subcontract out quite a lot of work, but there were quality problems. You lose control over it, and, besides, you don't make any money' (Y. Gauge). Thus the dynamic interplay of specialisation, *sessa takuma* and interfirm cooperation appears to have been weaker than in Ota. I did not come across counterparts of M. Precision, for instance, whose owner was constantly thinking up new products that could be made by his network of owner friends, with development expenses shared.

Attitudes towards helping employees become independent are telling: 'We don't help those who might compete against us.' 'We haven't been rich in entrepreneurial offspring.' Some employers did help workers become independent, but drew the line at similar types of work (the definition of which was quite broad) which might foster competition: 'We've started a few companies in the past, such as for washing boxes, and a training company. I say to them we'll give you orders for two years, then it's up to you. We subcontract out tool work to former employees, too, and when we got out of parts turning, we sold it to an employee. But they haven't been in our core line of business – we have enough competition already.' The end result must surely be a less fertile incubation mechanism and fewer micro-factories.

There have been changes in recent years. Local business groups have been formed with the aim of improving the business environment and stemming industrial decline. Owners involved in these groups have become used to discussing common problems and pursuing cooperative solutions. They may begin to bring these attitudes back into their daily business. There have been changes in subcontracting, too: 'If you show a commitment to change they [customers] will work with you now. They'll say you have to cut your costs, but let's work at it together, and send their expertise in if necessary. It's only if you really refuse to change that they'll drop you' (Y. Gauge, speaking of large customers in the car industry). A manager at Lucas, where the proportion of turnover bought in has increased markedly in recent years, agreed: 'Now we have fewer subcontractors, and relationships are long-term partnerships where we try to engineer costs out of the system.

This is driven by the car manufacturers, who only want to deal with first tier suppliers, but they expect us to follow the same pattern.'[28] Greater stability is unlikely to encourage fine interfirm specialisation, though, given the emphasis on limiting suppliers and the contracting customer base. On the other hand, the trend towards fewer, larger suppliers is also evident in Ota, where it is imparting a new urgency for small subcontractors to 'take control of their own destiny' by quitting subcontracting, at least for volume assemblers.

Business environment

Like their counterparts in Ota, owners had some complaints about the local infrastructure and government, but generally saw their location in Birmingham as an asset, mainly because of the concentration of customers and, to a lesser extent, of suppliers. When faced with refusal for an Industrial Development Certificate in 1970 – to turn his warehouse into a factory – the owner of F. Press argued that he would be forced to move, but all his work would come back into the city, anyway, since all his customers were there. (He got his IDC in the end.)

They were, however, much more critical of the central government: 'Mrs Thatcher did some good things. The attitudes of working people needed sorting out. But manufacturing will never recover from the damage she did.' (This owner was a Conservative Party member.) 'I'm not looking for handouts, but there ought to be more understanding. If they'd moved Parliament to Birmingham a hundred years ago, things would be a lot better today.' Taxation was a particular bone of contention, and changes were deemed necessary to improve incentives for manufacturers: 'The returns are so low already. Unless there are tax advantages, why go into it?' Low interest rates and the cost of capital in competitor countries – Japan and Germany – were viewed with envy.

This relates to another aspect of the London–Birmingham gulf, the City–industry divide. Birmingham's history has remarkable instances of industrialists ploughing their wealth back into local industry, such as Lloyds Bank in its early days. The Midland Bank was established in Birmingham, too, and Barclays and National Westminster both have historical links to the city. Today's owners derive little comfort from this: 'Their small business corners are a front. They're only interested in squeezing money out of you.' 'We had dreadful problems with financing when we

---

[28] These changes are sometimes called 'Japanisation', and Lucas is held to be a prime example. But, as this manager pointed out: 'The changes are driven by getting the sales/employee ratio right', or the financial demands of the City. In motivation, conception, and outcome, they are not simply mimics of Japanese practices.

were trying to expand. We bought property and within nine months the price had dropped to 65 per cent. The bank raised interest rates, and started demanding a repayment charge to balance out the collateral.'

Owners in Ota had their complaints too, of course, but their criticisms of the national government were more likely to centre on its slow response during recessions or its favouritism towards big business rather than a blanket lack of sympathy for manufacturing. Banks are seen as fair weather friends, but refrain from exacting their pound of flesh during recessions. In owners' perceptions, and most probably in reality, the business environment for small firms was much less favourable for small firms in Birmingham.

Birmingham revival?

Mrs Thatcher came to power determined to recreate an 'enterprise culture' in Britain. Small firms came to be seen as a key to this revolution, and the range of small firm support programmes, initiated in the 1970s, was expanded. Startup support through the Enterprise Allowance Scheme, for instance, was given particular emphasis (not incidentally, this took the unemployed off the politically sensitive unemployment registers).

At the same time as this 'revolution', initiated by the central government, various organisations and initiatives have been launched in Birmingham in the past two decades to halt the city's industrial decline. Most significant are a number of public–private sector 'partnerships' which seek to ensure a coordinated approach to regeneration. They bid for central government (and European) funds, and try to minimise duplication and confusion resulting from the proliferation and frequent changes of central government policy. The strategic objectives they have developed may even conflict with those of the government: 'The Thatcher idea was to set businesses up and the whole problem, culture as well, would be solved. But there's much more to it than that. Take the Enterprise Allowance Scheme – half the start-ups failed and then the people had lost their savings as well . . .'

The core partnerships have been formed by the Birmingham City Council, the Birmingham Chamber of Commerce, and the Birmingham Training and Enterprise Council (TEC).[29] Together they launched the Birmingham Marketing Partnership for promoting inward investment, tourism, conferences, exhibitions and sporting events, and 'marketing

---

[29] TECs were launched in 1989–90 to manage a range of government training, education, and enterprise programmes locally in tune with local needs. Their boards must have a 2/3–1/3 private–public sector (including community groups) weighting. Information here comes from interviews of representatives in May–June 1993 and September 1995, as well as mimeos and brochures.

Birmingham to the people of Birmingham', as well as the Economic Development Forum, which is consulted in the drawing up of the City Council's Economic Development Strategy. And, most significantly, they have created Business Links Birmingham (BLB), which is not just a 'one stop shop' for co-ordinating 250 business services, but a key tool for implementing the Economic Development Strategy at the mico-level.

Strategic priorities for economic regeneration include:

strengthening existing businesses, particularly in the vehicle and components industry (but also, for instance, in the growing garment industry, with many Asian owners and workers). Joint customer–supplier seminars and a local sourcing initiative are part of a strategy to build not only a competitive supplier base for local assemblers, but for the whole of Europe. This involves raising awareness of competitiveness requirements, encouraging total quality management, and developing human resources: 'The biggest obstacle is the attitudes of owner-managers to change. That is what we have to work on, but in a supportive way.'[30]

nurturing new, high growth and high technology industries. Birmingham has lagged in new industries, despite being home to some well-known companies, like Apricot Computers (which built its production facility in Scotland in 1983). Projects like Aston Science Park (ASP), founded on an old Delta site in 1983 by the partnership of the City Council, Aston University, and Lloyds Bank, are important initiatives in this respect. ASP's twin objectives are bringing new technology to existing businesses and developing new technology businesses, and at the centre of the park there is an incubation centre. In 1995 there were some 90 companies on the site with 1,200 employees.

skills and education levels. Many of the unemployed are classified as low- or semi-skilled, employers have been reluctant to offer training, and there has been an outward migration of highly educated young people. Various initiatives have been launched to tackle these problems.[31]

inward investment, for which the West Midlands Development Agency was established in 1984. Between 1988–94 foreign investment of some £2.5 billion was attracted to the region, creating 22,000 jobs, bringing the output share of foreign-owned companies to an estimated 20 per cent.[32]

creating a more appealing urban environment, to attract potential entrepreneurs. Keeble and others have identified an urban–rural shift

---

[30] Alun Dow, Director BLB (Interview, September 1995).
[31] These include TEC-funded courses, coordinated efforts to meet National Vocational Qualification targets, and encouraging employers to sign up for the Investors in People scheme. Events are sponsored to promote the local employment – mainly in SMEs – of local graduates.   [32] *Financial Times*, 7 November 1994.

in entrepreneurial activities in Britain, but the partners hope to counteract this through better theatres, restaurants, galleries, transportation and housing, and green areas.[33] There is also an attempt to change culture in a different sense by promoting business and manufacturing awareness in schools.

In sum, a strategic response to Birmingham's industrial decline has evolved in recent years. A coordinated infrastructure has been put in place to implement it, and to offer business support unparalleled in Birmingham's history. But will these efforts succeed? It is easy to be skeptical. Birmingham still lags in key labour market and economic indicators. And, while the number of VAT-registered businesses in Britain increased by 33 per cent between 1979 and 1990, in Birmingham they only increased by 9 per cent.[34] If there *is* to be a revival, it will probably require the supporting structures and initiatives that have been forged in recent years. Industrial districts and their communities may have been formed largely as a result of historical circumstance, but in a de-industrialising economy, they can perhaps only be resuscitated through conscious long-term effort, which is regionally and locally based. But it will be difficult to rejuvenate them, given corporate globalisation and the internationalisation of supply chains, weak local linkages of many high tech. firms, the urban–rural shift in entrepreneurial activity, and prevailing attitudes towards industry.[35] If these efforts do succeed, it will be a remarkable turnaround indeed.

[33] E.g., Keeble (1990, 1993).   [34] Birmingham Economic Information Centre (1994).
[35] Cf. Curran and Blackburn (1994); Massey *et al.* (1992).

11   Sunrise or sunset for Japan's small firms?

The 1990s recession has had a major impact on the Japanese economy and perceptions of it. The spectre of 'hollowing out' or de-industrialisation, initially raised in the mid 1980s, resurfaced with a vengeance as the yen appreciated still further, undermining price competitiveness and forcing exporters to move production abroad. At the same time, large firms saw profits from overseas production fall, and falling prices at home and rising R&D costs further ate into profits. Established markets offered few opportunities for growth, and large firms' strengths were less decisive in the new industries they were moving into. As the recession dragged on, a growing number of voices claimed that nothing less than a fundamental overhaul of the 'Japanese system' would suffice to rejuvenate the economy. The medicine they would prescribe is drastic deregulation. Relatedly, a 'paradigm shift' school argues that the leading role of large companies is – should be – giving way to a more fluid, open system with entrepreneurial firms, quick to adapt to new or fragmented markets and technology shifts, assuming the mantle of economic leadership.[1]

The 'paradigm shift' school draws much of its inspiration from abroad, in addition to the domestic re-evaluation of small firms in the 1980s. There is little doubt, though, that for many small firms in Japan any 'new age' will be one of unprecedented tribulation. Price-cutting pressures, depressed capital investment, the transfer of production overseas, increasing competition from imports . . . all give grounds for pessimism. Good workers are still hard to recruit, and many postwar founders face the prospect of retiring with no successor. 'Paradigm shift' supporters agree that there will be a significant reduction in the number of 'old type' SMEs tied into mass production networks dominated by large assemblers – or benefiting from

---

[1] Deregulation proponents include academics like I. Nakatani, and even former bureaucrats like T. Sakaiya. A random list of 'paradigm shift' literature includes Makino and Tsukio (1994), and relating to SMEs, Nakamura (1994), Sato *et al.* (1994) and Chusho kigyo sogo kenkyu kiko (1995).

regulatory protection which has outlived its usefulness, and unable to adjust to an increasingly volatile and competitive environment. But they insist that the buds of new enterprise are emerging, and these must be allowed to flourish through a combination of positive support and deregulation. Optimists and pessimists about the prospects of small firms agree that changes are necessary in industrial and SME policy, and more broadly in social support for entrepreneurship, to ensure that small firms can fulfil their vital economic role.

The final chapter looks first at the future prospects of small firms in Ota Ward, the bedrock of Japanese manufacturing industry. Will they survive, or even lead, the current transition, or will Ota suffer the same fate as Birmingham? It then goes on to consider the prospects of SMEs in general, and the question of a 'paradigm shift', both in its descriptive/analytical and its prescriptive guises. The new orthodoxy, identified in chapter 2, paints a much more positive picture of small firms than the old dual structure orthodoxy. In the paradigm shift concept, however, it becomes a kind of reverse dual structure; large firms are by definition sick, the new age is for small firms. This new view of large firms – and small – is as partial as the old view of small firms, and evidence for a fundamental shift is flimsy at best. In the concluding comments we will consider the decline in the small firm share of the Japanese economy in relation to the resurgence of small firms widely noted in other countries. Is Japan really an exception to this trend?

The future of industry in Ota

Ota's industry has so far withstood the tests of time. It appears much better placed than Birmingham (or other districts within Japan for that matter) to adapt to the restructuring that is currently under way in the Japanese economy. There is a higher percentage of small firms, and these are less reliant on a small number of local giants. There is a high proportion in general machinery and equipment factories, which coupled with related processes, constitutes a promising base for new product development. The dense concentration of workshops and factories doing low volume work provides a fertile seedbed for experimentation, and Ota's location in Tokyo, and in Japan's industrial structure, allows for the rapid absorption of new ideas.

On the other hand, threats to the continued vitality of Ota's industry have been hinted at in various chapters. These include:

intensified interregional/district competition which undercuts the premium Ota's factories could once demand for their skilled work (chapter 3);

locational problems such as encroaching housing, cramped sites and
limited possibilities for expansion or rebuilding (chapter 4);
reduced work from 'parent' companies and shrinking profit margins of
remaining work (chapter 5);
an alleged diminution in value placed on horizontal cooperation, especially by stronger association members, and difficulties in sustaining
cooperation during prolonged recession (chapter 6);
retirement of the founding generation, often without a successor, and a
conspicuous decline in startups, especially independent startups
(chapter 7);
retirement of the older generation of craft workers and difficulties in
recruiting youth and passing on skills (chapter 8);
limitations on creating a favourable business environment through policy
measures (chapter 9).

In the words of Seki, once an enthusiastic 'national technopolis' propo-
nent: 'Having followed Ota Ward's industry for some time, I sense that I am
seeing the end of an era. The major factories will move out and the small
shops will decline in number. One day, the vitality that was Ota Ward's
industry will be only a memory.'[2] This vitality was evident not only in
factory output or mushrooming factories, but in the streets as well. Ota was
once known as a town of youth, but no longer. The aging population is symbolic of its industry.

Between 1983 and 1993 the number of factories in Ota Ward declined by
a quarter (table 11.1), and the trend is set to continue. The question is not
whether this downward trend will be stopped or even reversed, but how far
factory numbers will fall, and what type of industry will be left. These questions have concerned local industrial promotion authorities, of course, who
recently commissioned a survey and a 'Vision' to guide their attempts to
stem the decline. It is worth taking a brief look at these in turn, with supplementary background information added where necessary.[3]

Factories with 30 or more employees declined by a third between 1983
and 1993, mainly as a result of relocation or shrinkage. Those which are
left, according to the survey report, have responded positively to the changing environment, and owners want to expand their business. Succession has
taken place in most, and they own their own land and factories (though
they often live elsewhere). Many have branch factories elsewhere in Japan
or overseas as well, and they gain orders from throughout Japan and
abroad. Factories with 10–29 employees are a transition category, the other
end of which is micro-factories (figure 11–1), which account for three quar-

[2] Seki (1994, 80–1).
[3] Ota ku (1995a); Ota ku sangyo bijion iinkai (1995). The 'Vision' committee was chaired by
H. Nakamura, of leading medium-sized enterprise theory (*chuken kigyo ron*) fame.

Table 11.1 *Decline in factory numbers in Ota, 1983–1993*

| | Year | | |
Size (employees)	1983	1988	1993
1–3	4,070	3,676	3,377
4–9	3,365	2,868	2,416
10–19	919	830	724
20–29	394	387	348
30–49	216	194	138
50–99	138	130	91
100–299	65	48	52
300+	23	18	14
Total	9,190	8,151	7,160

Source: Tsusansho (ed.) (respective years), *Kogyo tokei hyo* (Census of Manufactures).

ters of closures. Micro-factories have been finding it particularly hard to adjust. Assemblers are looking for suppliers which can design and manufacture prototypes or parts as well as mass produce them, which few micro-factories have the capacity to do. Order volumes have been reduced, and they have been squeezed, but they have not developed sales, development or systematic management expertise, which might help them to get new work. Many rent their premises, which they also live on. As many as 70 per cent with 1–3 employees have no successor. They are the 'terminal' factories on which larger factories rely for specialised or speedy machining work, contributing to the organic flexibility of the district, but many are in terminal decline.

The diffusion of mechatronic machinery is eroding much of the skill advantage formerly enjoyed by Ota, the report claims, and it will further erode as older workers retire. With on-line technology, too, the advantages of factory concentrations may diminish. Subcontractors can no longer rely on 'invisible roads of work' to bring orders in. They must become more active and outward-looking to survive, but many are failing to do this. The weakening of direct links with assemblers' volume networks will thus continue. Subcontractors will try to gain orders from smaller product makers, which are themselves attempting to diversify into new areas such as environmental technology, medical equipment, and education equipment as well as to find new markets overseas. Others will try to become product

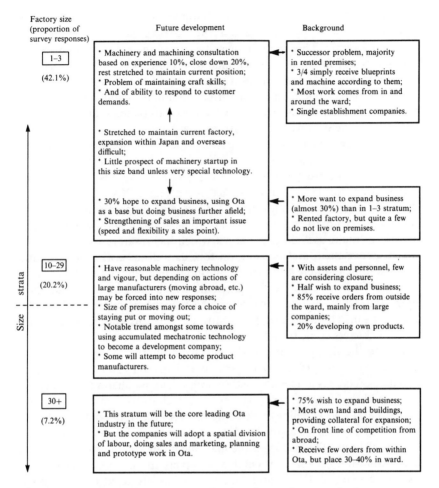

Figure 11.1 Management responses to the changing environment in Ota
Note: Survey *N*=2,024 companies.
Source: Ota ku (1995a, 113).

makers, too, either by themselves, or with other small firms. Ota must move beyond being a 'national technopolis' to become a 'new industry creativity core' (*shin sangyo sozo koa*). This core would be based on the ward's traditional manufacturing strengths, and the nurturing of new manufacturing technology, skills, and products.

Although Ota is home to electronic game makers Sega Enterprises and Namco, and to some software and system houses like Hitachi Systems Engineering, the centre of the software industry is outside the ward, currently in the belt between Shibuya-Shinjuku and Yokohama. Ota should draw on the strengths of neighbouring districts, again becoming more outward looking. This is not an easy task, and the report recognises that the number of factories will continue to decline. Some of the basic processes may be lost, or relocated to other parts of Japan or Asia. This may be unavoidable, but a 'manufacturing minimum' campaign should be launched to ensure that processes which need to be maintained locally to support the 'new industry creativity core' are not lost.

Recognition that a strategic response rather than piecemeal measures is necessary to arrest the decline of Ota's industry led to the establishment of the Ota Ward Industry Vision Committee in 1993. The 'Vision' it produced imagines a pilot development district in the year 20XX which achieves a dynamic integration of industry, residence and shopping. For shopping, there is an 'eco-mall', consisting of fashionable shops and boutiques set in a park, a 'multi-use' shopping street which has restaurants above shops, offices above them and housing on top, as well as workshop-boutiques which stimulate interest in producing things, or manufacture. There is an information centre, and a machine mall, which links industry and shopping, and expresses Ota's character as a machine industry world leader. People using Haneda Airport are attracted to this shopping area, and machine buyers come from far and wide.

Behind the shopping area is the industrial quarter. New factories with glass faces invite passers by to peer in and marvel at machines making machines. There is a 'techno-condominium' – an incubator for young factories with housing on top – as well as a 'techno base camp', which has support and R&D facilities, also bringing in people from far and wide. The base camp also serves as the headquarters for the industry open museum, which celebrates the history of the machine industries in Ota and beyond. The exhibition on this particular day depicts the history of technology exchange between China and Japan, and has attracted a good crowd. Finally, on the other side of the shopping area is residential space, which features co-generational housing and an 'urban spa'. Cosmopolitan trainee accommodation encourages information exchange and friendship.

Ota Ward in this 'Vision' has become an '*international* technopolis', based on three core strategies:

O – open mind: open to and doing business with the world;[4]

T – techno front: a world leading machine industry technology concentration;

[4] The O strategy envisages Ota as a pivotal district within Asia, reflecting the spread of Japan's machine industries and regional economic integration. Young workers will come from throughout Asia for training in advanced machining techniques and technology. (This will simultaneously provide young workers.) The first significant step in this direction was Ota's hosting of a symposium on SMEs and industrial development following the APEC summit in Osaka in November 1995.

A – 'amenity stock': a place which draws people to work, study and live in.

Many of the underlying perceptions of what needs to be done in Ota and Birmingham are similar. Existing industry must be upgraded, closer links forged with educational establishments (a new college of industry is proposed for Ota), and new industry nurtured. Most important, a holistic approach must be adopted which addresses living and culture. The dowdy image of manufacturing must be replaced. The actual approaches, however, offer a sharp contrast. Birmingham has produced an evolutionary, step-by step approach; Ota has produced a Vision. It must next map out a path towards its realisation. This will be tortuous.

An informal 'Vision' study group cutting across departmental boundaries within the ward's administration has been set up, but the Industry Promotion Section must gain the active support of the rest of the ward's administration, particularly the Urban Planning Department, and then the Ward Council.[5] As the mayor's introduction to the Vision hints, this will not be easy, not least because of its budgetary implications. The process must be repeated at the Tokyo level, since the metropolitan authority's support will be vital. Public-private sector partnership is also necessary. The Ota Ward Industry Promotion Association was formed in October 1995 for this purpose, but how effective it will be remains to be seen.[6]

There is, in addition, the question of whether Ota is an appropriate unit for this initiative. Ota is just one of Tokyo's 23 wards, and is not clearly delineated geographically. A more appropriate unit might be south Tokyo – Jonan – which encompasses Ota, Shinagawa, and Meguro Wards. The Tokyo government has adopted this approach. Since the mid 1980s its planning documents have mentioned Jonan as Tokyo's 'Mechatro Centre'. As a concrete step, it has established a Tokyo SME Promotion Corporation branch office and a Technology Development Centre in Ota's newly opened Industry Plaza complex to service the Jonan area. Joint initiatives might also be developed with the Kanagawa portion of the Keihin Belt, into which quite a few of Ota's factories have relocated.[7]

---

[5] The transition from planning to economic development in Birmingham can be traced through the 1980s, originally to the West Midlands County Council (abolished in 1985–6). Only recently are there signs that economic development is being seriously considered within the planning framework in Ota.

[6] The Association's board is chaired by a director of Nissan, and also includes a director of Ricoh, but it may not be easy to gain the active cooperation of Ota's multi-national corporations.

[7] In Birmingham such alliances have been created, mainly to attract inward investment. The same applies to Stuttgart in Germany. Baden-Württemberg's response to concern over its industrial future lies between that of Birmingham and Ota. A Future Economy 2000 Commission was set up in 1992. Its report – 'Departure from the Crisis' – also emphasises a double strategy of improved competitiveness in existing industries and a concerted thrust into new, emerging fields (Zukunftskommission Wirtschaft 2000 (1993)).

Crisis lends urgency to producing concrete measures and creating alliances. Part of the problem industry promoters in Ota – and Tokyo – face is that their perceptions of crisis are not necessarily shared by others. Output has declined only since 1991, but it may pick up again. Many of the factories which have closed are small and the owner has retired. Unemployment is still relatively low. Even the industry promoters have barely begun to contemplate inward investment, one of Birmingham's five key strategies. The number of factories will decline a lot further, therefore, before a really concerted response is put in place.

Ota is still a formidable industrial district, of course, and the mass of small factories both supports and is supported by energetic small product makers. Despite the *seizo banare* (manufacturing desertion) trend, these product makers are able to recruit workers, even young workers. If indeed a 'manufacturing minimum' can be maintained in and around the district, there may be a relatively smooth transition, and at least some of Ota's 'Vision' will be realised. There is no guarantee of this, however. Seki claims that giants such as Hitachi, Toshiba, NEC, and Canon, fearful that such a minimum will not be maintained and that fundamental technologies will be lost through the closure of *machi koba*, are taking steps to nurture these technologies in house. The potential for a vicious circle is evident:

In 1992, newspaper reports that Canon would invest ¥7.5 billion to build a plating plant in Ibaraki Prefecture sent a shock wave through the small plating companies of the Tokyo-Yokohama area, who were concerned about their ability to continue business. Canon, understandably, was acting in its own best interest in response to fears about future supplies. The small- and medium-sized firms of the Tokyo-Yokohama area, though, interpreted Canon's action as yet a further loss of confidence in them. Events like this are causing these companies to lose what will they have to stay in business, adding impetus to the wearing away of the industrial base of the once-crucial Tokyo-Yokohama area.[8]

If the slack could be taken up with orders from new product makers through 'skill concentration' networks, the outlook would be less alarming, but Seki also claims that few if any product makers have emerged since the mid 1980s, supporting his claim of declining vitality. Again, there is the potential for another vicious circle here. This, then, is the spectre of 'hollowing out from below'.

A new age for small firms?

Japan has lost its traditional small firm 'problem' – too many, too small – only to be confronted by another, namely how to nurture dynamic, new

---

[8] Seki (1994, 136).

small firms. Given what was said in the last section, and in spite of the decline in startups, restructuring and rising closures, which give ample grounds for pessimism, it may be surprising to know that there is a more optimistic school which sees the mantle of economic leadership passing from large to small firms, or vigorous SMEs and LMEs. The school accepts that there will be many small firm casualties, such as amongst Ota's *machi koba*, as there will be large firm casualties, but argues that such a 'paradigm shift' is the key to Japan's economic future. This section looks at the prospects for resolving Japan's new SME problem, indeed for a 'paradigm shift'. In order to do this we shall need to broaden the scope beyond traditional manufacturing.

Talk of a 'new age' of small firms is both (selectively) descriptive/ analytical and prescriptive. The descriptive/analytical stream draws inspiration from developments both prior to and after the 'bubble' burst in 1991. As we have seen, Nakamura and Kiyonari consistently pointed to dynamic smaller businesses in their attack on dual structure orthodoxy. They coined the term 'venture business' in 1970 to refer to the sprouting of knowledge-intensive and innovative small businesses in what has now become known as the first venture business boom. This fizzled shortly afterwards, during the turbulence of the early 1970s, but a second boom occurred in the early 1980s. Concurrent with this second boom was the mushrooming of innovative new businesses which were not technology-oriented, but exploited structural changes in the economy, and offered a new product or service or new way of delivering these. They were dubbed 'new business' and 'new service' enterprises. A small but growing proportion were started by women and/or for women as womens' social and economic roles changed.[9]

At the same time, small firms were becoming more independent from large firms. With accumulated technological and managerial resources, a growing number of subcontractors developed their own design and R&D sections (37.6 per cent and 26.4 per cent of manufacturing suppliers respectively, according to a 1989 survey), and even their own products (24.1 per cent).[10] 'Servicisation', '2.5-isation' (the fusion of manufacturing and services), 'information-isation', and market changes such as fragmentation, fusion and new niches were working in their favour, as was the micro-electronics revolution on balance. Thus:

[I]n the changing industrial structure and corporate restructuring responses to it, the breakdown of industrial divisions (*yugoka*) makes diversified patterns of economic behaviour by individual actors indispensable. This will be achieved by

---

[9] The proportion of incorporated companies with a woman president doubled from 2.4 per cent to 4.7 per cent in the 1980s, and had reached 5.2 per cent by 1994. About a quarter of sole proprietorships are led by women; Kasumi (1995, 42).

[10] Chusho kigyo cho (1990a, 160); see Whittaker (1994).

independent, positive companies loosely coupled with others to reinforce each other and positively use external resources to bring about economic efficiency. We can see the beginning of the transformation of Japan's industrial organisation, which is quite different from the pyramid type symbolised by large peak firms and their keiretsu subcontractor systems.[11]

When the 'bubble' burst, companies in most sectors of the domestic economy were hit hard, but the giants failed to rebound. While they were busy investing abroad, they began to rationalise their domestic operations. Their attempts at diversification, spinning off new companies and encouraging 'intrapreneurship' were only partially successful. In Kiyonari's view: '[T]he lack of entrepreneurial skill made most such attempts unsuccessful. Because of this experience, by 1993 large corporations became generally hesitant to make new business attempts and instead shifted their focus to merely trimming their workforces.'[12]

Large firm doldrums were symbolised by number one profit maker Toyota, which saw its profits decline steadily from ¥734 billion in fiscal year 1991 to around ¥286 billion in 1994 (and further shrink in 1995). By contrast, midget Nintendo, with less than a thousand employees and a fraction of the assets and turnover, saw its profits rise from ¥140 billion in 1991 to ¥164 billion in 1993, before dropping to ¥115 billion in 1994, still easily enough to make it the highest profit per share earner. Recurring profits of over-the-counter (OTC) companies increased by almost 20 per cent in 1993, while they declined by 14 per cent in first and second section-listed companies. Profit to sales ratios were almost four times higher, and profit to capital twice as high.[13] JAFCO, a venture capital company, has been one of the top performers, symbolic of the vitality of this sector. Thus: 'Many fund managers maintained that the OTC market was the place to be as Japan exited an era of growth built on government protection of selected export-oriented industries and entered an economy driven by new services and consumer demand.'[14]

But would this turn out to be yet another venture boom and bust cycle, a 'venture bubble'? The venture boom of the 1980s was marred by a high incidence of closures and takeovers of star performers. Would the same happen in the 1990s, or did the boom mark a definitive transition in the Japanese economy towards venture business, LMEs, and dynamic small firms, similar to the US, which is allegedly experiencing a 'dramatic transformation from a corporate-bureaucratic to an entrepreneurial-driven

---

[11] Nakamura (1990, 57).   [12] Kiyonari (1994, 6).

[13] Nikko risarchi senta, respective years; Kiyonari (1994, 4). Aggregate pre-tax profits of OTC companies were expected to grow by 30 per cent in fiscal 1995, more than double those of listed companies; *Nikkei Weekly*, 30 October 1995.

[14] A. Ishibashi in *Nikkei Weekly*, 30 October 1995.

economy'?[15] The short answer is, not without significant reforms. There were almost nine times as many NASDAQ listings in the US than OTC listings in Japan between 1983 and 1992.[16] Companies like Intel, Apple, Microsoft, and Novell became listed within two to five years; in Japan it takes an average OTC company 29 years to be listed, and even star performers take ten years. Tortoises might succeed where the hare falters, but the hares seem to be running off with all the prizes.[17] Where are Japan's Microsofts? What is stopping them?

Software is actually very germane to these questions. Despite being a high growth industry of the 1980s, it seemed to fall victim to the rigidities of the 'old paradigm'. Eight of the top ten information services companies are spinoffs from large manufacturers or users, which have dominated the industry. Three quarters of orders are customised – software products are underdeveloped – and these flow from large manufacturers through large system vendors or integrators to software design houses and finally to software production houses. This hierarchical structure has obvious parallels with the machine industries, but it is more often likened to the construction industry, where conditions are even more precarious for small subcontractors.[18] In the words of the chairman of UBA, an association of around 100 SME software companies formed to oppose the (computer) manufacturer-centred industry structure and industrial policy: 'MITI's policy of thinking that if they nurtured computer makers, software would automatically develop was a mistake. There's no doubt that the large makers have excellent human resources, but there's no place for them to really display their creativity in large companies.'[19]

There is a growing belief in Japan that industrial policy has become on balance counterproductive. The medicine prescribed is deregulation. Sweep away the regulations, allow the winds of competition to blow, and the seeds of new enterprise will sprout. The bureaucrats do not see things this way, of course, and are not eager to promote deregulation which undermines

[15] The citation is from Kasarda (1992, 1).

[16] The difference after closure rates are taken into account is only two and a half times. This statistic is usually ignored; Abo (1994, 182–3).

[17] Or, as the MD of the Venture Enterprise Centre argues, competitiveness in growth industries depends on speed and the ability to attract resources quickly and set *de facto* standards; Hata (1995, 10).

[18] Spatial characteristics are also similar to manufacturing; Imano and Sato (1990). See Cusumano (1991), for a detailed account of Japan's 'software factories' at the apex of this division of labour.

[19] Half of UBA's members formed a group – 'Hurricane' – in 1993 to compete directly with large companies for public contracts, hitherto awarded exclusively to manufacturer-linked companies. They would be doing most of the development work anyway. At first they had little success, not even from the SME Agency, but a change of official policy was announced in 1995 (Nikkei sangyo shinbun (ed.), 1995, 12–16).

their position. They have come up with a number of initiatives which seek to address the decline in startups, restructuring, and de-industrialisation, as well as to encourage venture business.

The Temporary Law for Smooth Movement of SMEs Into New Business Areas (1993, revised and expanded in 1995) targets firms in or moving into manufacturing, printing, software, and information processing which have been affected by the high yen or structural changes in the economy, as well as startups in these industries. Successful applicants are eligible for a wide range of finance, tax and consulting benefits. The Law to Promote Creative SME Activities (1995) targets potential startups, SMEs, or associations which have been founded for less than five years, or which spend more than 3 per cent of turnover on R&D. Successful applicants are likewise eligible for a wide range of finance, tax, and consulting benefits.[20] The package of economic measures unveiled in September 1995 offered further support for startups and venture business, and proposals to recognise intellectual property for collateral purposes, which is of particular relevance to software.

MITI carried out a shakeup of its affiliate Venture Enterprise Centre in 1994, placing it under a key bureau (Industrial Policy), increasing the number of experts, the number of times they meet, the range of areas they can cover (e.g. software development), and, as a result, the number of loans guaranteed. VEC's capital base has been increased, financial institutions outside the capital are being encouraged to act as agents, and it is improving its information, seminar, and training services. MITI has also negotiated with the Fair Trade Commission to relax Antimonopoly Law guidelines so that venture capital companies can place directors on the boards of venture companies, and it negotiated with the Ministry of Finance over relaxation of OTC listing requirements.[21] This led to major reforms in 1995, including the opening of a second OTC market for high tech. ventures with stricter disclosure but less strict asset and profit requirements.

In addition, a business incubator boom has been gathering momentum. Regional and local authorities have set up about 20 incubators, in addition to 12 MITI-approved 'research core' projects (which must have an incubator as well as an open testing and experimental facility, training, and exchange facilities), and a dozen local public–private initiatives which receive funds from the Small Business Corporation. To give two examples, Kanagawa Science Park (KSP) was the first of the 'research core' projects, opened in 1989 on a former Ikegai site. It was backed by Kanagawa Prefecture, Kawasaki City, and the developer Tobishima, and is an impor-

---

[20] Recipients of the former law numbered 1,600 by the end of August 1995, including 103 in software, and 267 developing business overseas; Chusho kigyo cho mimeos.
[21] Nikkei sangyo shinbun (ed.) (1995, 128–37).

tant initiative in Kanagawa's bid to become a world-class industrial R&D centre. Most of its 37 incubation rooms are occupied by recent startups.[22] A more low-key but very successful initiative is Toyama's High Tech. Mini Enterprise Estate, with 43 incubation rooms, launched in 1986 by a large local car parts maker (who started out with a single lathe) who persuaded Toyama City to back the project.

The conservative nature of financing has been an impediment to venture business in Japan, but there are signs of change here, too. Faced with a serious slump in lending, looser ties with large firms, and seeing a surge in OTC investment, banks have been busy gathering company names, training screening and consultant personnel and making networks of venture and 'new business' companies, offering not just loans, but equity participation as well. They hope that this will cover any increase in loan defaults. Life insurance companies are getting in on the act, and venture capital companies are moving away from spreading their money thinly across a wide range of sectors and companies to concentrating on targeted markets, and training or recruiting experts – analysts and consultants – so that they can identify and fund winners more quickly. Equity partnerships are on the rise, some former venture companies themselves have been setting up venture funds, and even 'business angels', though still rare, are appearing.[23]

Another bottleneck has been human resources, or the preference of talented researchers to seek jobs in large companies and stay with them rather than joining potentially risky startups. The government's economic package of September 1995 included a 'limited stock option system' to attract such people to venture businesses. Under this system they will receive equity that they can cash in when the firm is listed. 'Large firm malaise' (*daikigyobyo*) also means fewer jobs for bright graduates in large companies, and the erosion of lifetime employment, which will further serve to free up human resources. In sum: 'A social system to facilitate rapid growth of venture business, already found in the US today, will be established in Japan by early next century.'[24]

Whether large firms are really so sick, and the future is so bright for venture business, is of course debatable. The demise of large firms has been predicted since the early 1970s.[25] For dinosaurs, they have proved remarkably adaptable to climatic change, in the process providing global models for 'lean production', *kaizen*, and so on. According to the SME Agency's calculations, the number of large establishments actually *rose* between 1991 and 1994, while the number of small and medium-sized establishments dropped. The former gained half a million workers, the latter lost a million.

[22] KSP brochures, interview with T. Kubo, President, Y. Agata, Executive Director, November 1992.   [23] Nikkei sangyo shinbun (ed.) (1995, 128–37).
[24] Kiyonari (1994, 6); cf. also Momose (1985).   [25] E.g., Nakamura (1970).

Production indices of large firms, too, have risen more than indices for small firms in recent years.[26]

Large firms and their spinoffs occupy commanding positions in a great range of new, high tech. fields. Many spinoffs have not been notably successful, but others have grown into large firms themselves, and closure rates for spinoffs are lower than for independent startups. For better or for worse, large companies and their offspring will remain key players in Japan's economy in the foreseeable future, even if their contribution to economic growth is muted. Rather than wishing them away, an important question will be what types of relationships can small, entrepreneurial firms forge with them. The latter frequently face problems in production, marketing, and follow-up products. They enter into relationships with large firms as equals at first, but soon find they cannot keep up with commercial application and expansion, and end up losing control over their venture.[27] More flexible types of arrangements need to be explored and supported, both with large firms, and with other small firms, such as the examples given by Nikkei Industrial Newspaper of small firms creating joint development associations and using large companies to manufacture or market the products.[28]

For better of for worse, too, the majority of 'venture business' enterprises, like Ota's 'new key' product makers, will continue to be established, diversifying SMEs. Half of those surveyed annually by VEC were founded before 1965, a much greater proportion than in the overall company population. Around 40 per cent are run by second or third generation or other family members, and less than half are still founder run.[29] Such businesses have established a competent technological base, a core workforce, income revenue, and a track record with banks, customers, and job seekers, which are all important for doing business in Japan and probably will continue to be. There may be greater fluidity in labour markets in the future, and courses on how to become an entepreneur are booming, but the majority of talented graduates will still seek jobs in established companies, and their ideas will be developed for and funded by those companies, rather than them hiving off and obtaining the backing of venture capital. There may be increasing diversity and individuality if not individualism in Japanese society, as 'paradigm shift' supporters suggest, but this does not automatically equate with entrepreneurship.

[26] Chusho kigyo cho (ed.) (1995a, 136, 142).
[27] A VEC consultant described his main job as trying to stop venture firms from being swallowed up (which was often impossible because they started consultation too late); interview, I. Iwata, December 1992.   [28] Nikkei sangyo shinbun (ed.) (1995, 16–19).
[29] Nihon kaihatsugata kigyo ikusei senta (1995, 30, 45; 1992, 5, 13). Nintendo is the epitome of this tendency – it was founded in 1889!

That is not to deny that centrifugal, individualistic, or entrepreneurial forces exist in Japan; this whole book has been about them. Craft or productionist entrepreneurship has been a very important source of Japan's industrial vigour. It is ironic that this culture, which flourished with limited official recognition and support, is waning with the retirement of many small firm owners, just as its need has become obvious and support mechanisms put in place to encourage it. It is thus less a matter of whether a new entrepreneurial culture can be created in Japan *ex nihilo* as whether the flame of the old culture can be rekindled in a new environment, and spread to more diverse segments of the population, across a broad range of industries.

Final comments: Japan as an exceptional case?

Small firms appear to be experiencing a resurgence in many industrialised economies. The extent of this resurgence and the reasons for it are hotly debated, and cannot be reviewed in any detail here. At the risk of oversimplification, countries start on the road to industrialisation with a high proportion of small firms and the self-employed. These normally decrease as factory production takes root, but eventually begin to increase again as a result of sectoral shifts such as the rise of tertiary sector employment, changes in patterns of demand, technology, rationalisation by large firms, and so on. In Britain's case the upswing in the U-shaped curve started from the late 1960s.[30]

Japan does not fit neatly into this pattern. It has *always* had a high proportion of small firms, the reasons for which are complex, but must include the outlook and efforts of small firm owners themselves. On the other hand, large firms have also demonstrated resilience in the face of great change in the past twenty years. The vitality of both contributed to rising employment in manufacturing right up to the early 1990s, although manufacturing's share of total employment levelled off and began to decline from the mid 1980s. Unmistakable signs of 'de-industrialisation' have appeared in the 1990s, however. Absolute and relative employment in manufacturing have fallen. Victims of their own success to some extent, large firms have been forced to move production abroad, and are moving along the painful road of restructuring within Japan.

Yet instead of a surge, the number of small firms has been declining visibly, with closure rates exceeding startup rates in many sectors, including manufacturing. The proportion in self employment and employed in small firms has also dropped (table 2.2). How is this apparent oddity to be

[30] Storey (1994), provides a good review of the debates, and evidence from Britain.

explained? Perhaps as follows: Rapid postwar economic growth coupled with the willingness of owners to work extremely long hours for modest reward, common to first generation migrants from the countryside, meant small firms survived in large numbers later into industrialisation than in countries like Britain. With founders' eventual retirement, Japan is experiencing a belated decline, or 'delayed modernisation'.[31] The decline of the industrialising generation of small firms is therefore overwhelming the growth of a new generation of small firms associated with 'mature' industrial economies, assuming there is such a growth, at least for the time being. The continued vitality of large firms, and the fact that they were already lean (or their delayed and muted efforts at restructuring, as some would suggest now) also muted the potential for an upswing.

A transformation is undoubtedly taking place *within* Japan's small firm sector. The owners who played an important though invisible role in Japan's industrialisation, with limited formal education but a strong sense of wanting to be their own boss and build their own castle, are retiring. Their place is being taken by a new generation of highly educated, urban successors and founders. They are more open to systematic planning and management concepts, information technology, and networking, but their vitality and prospects for any real small firm resurgence in Japan in the future will partly depend on their inheritance of Japan's traditional small firm strengths.

[31] 'Delayed modernisation' was suggested to me by R. Rowthorn.

Bibliography

Abo, K. (1994), *Bencha bijinesu kapitaru saisei no michi* (Road to Regeneration of Venture Business Capital), Tokyo: Dobunkan.

Acs, Z. and D. Audretsch (eds.) (1993), *Small Firms and Entrepreneurship*, Cambridge: Cambridge University Press.

Allen, G. (1929), *The Industrial Development of Birmingham and the Black Country: 1860–1927*, London: Frank Cass.

(1940), 'Japanese Industry: Its Organization and Development to 1937' in E. Schumpeter (ed.), *The Industrialization of Japan and Manchukuo: 1930–1940*, New York: Macmillan.

(1983), *Appointment in Japan*, London: Athlone.

Aoki, M. (1988), *Information, Incentives and Bargaining in the Japanese Economy*, Cambridge: Cambridge University Press.

Arisawa, H. (1937), *Nihon kogyo tosei ron* (On the Control of Japanese Industry), Tokyo: Yuhikaku.

Arita, T. (1990), *Sengo nihon no chusho kigyo seisaku* (Japanese Postwar SME Policy), Tokyo: Nihon hyoronsha.

Asahi shinbun (various dates).

Asanuma, B. (1989), 'Manufacturer–Supplier Relationships in Japan and the Concept of Relationship-Specific Skill' *Journal of the Japanese and International Economies*, No. 3.

(1990), 'Nihon ni okeru meka to sapuraiya to no kankei' (Maker–Supplier Relations in Japan) in M. Tsuchiya and Y. Miwa (eds.), *Nihon no chusho kigyo* (Japanese SMEs), Tokyo: Tokyo daigaku shuppankai.

Beesley, M. (1955), 'The Birth and Death of Industrial Establishments: Experience in the West Midlands Conurbation' *Journal of Industrial Economics*, 4/1.

Bellah, R. (1957), *Religion in Tokugawa Japan*, Cambridge MA: Harvard University Press.

Bennett, A. (1981), 'An Economic Prospect for the West Midlands' Report to Williams and Glyn's Bank Ltd.

Best, M. (1990), *The New Competition: Institutions of Industrial Restructuring*, Cambridge: Polity Press.

Birmingham City Council (1992), 'Report of the Director of Economic Development, Economic Development Subcommittee' Birmingham.

(1994), *Economic Development Strategy for Birmingham, 1994–97*, Birmingham.

Birmingham Economic Information Centre (1994), *The Birmingham Economy: Review and Prospects*, Birmingham.

Bolton Committee (1971), *Report of the Committee of Inquiry on Small Firms*, London: HMSO.

Briggs, A. (1952), *History of Birmingham, Volume II, 1865–1938*, Oxford: Oxford University Press.

Calder, K. (1988), *Crisis and Compensation: Public Policy and Political Stability in Japan, 1949–86*, Princeton: Princeton University Press.

Capecchi, V. (1990), 'A History of Flexible Specialization and Industrial Districts in Emilia-Romagna' in Pyke, Becattini, and Sengenberger (eds.), *Industrial Districts and Interfirm Co-operation in Italy*, Geneva: International Institute for Labour Studies.

Chalmers, N. (1989), *Industrial Relations in Japan: The Peripheral Workforce*, London: Routledge.

Checkland, S. (1976), *The Upas Tree: Glasgow 1875–1975*, Glasgow: University of Glasgow Press.

Chiiki shinko seibi kodan (1978), *Ota ku ni okeru kojo ritchi no tenkai* (Developments in Factory Location in Ota Ward), Tokyo.

Chinn, C. (1994), *Birmingham: The Great Working City*, Birmingham: Birmingham City Council.

Chuo daigaku keizai kenkyujo (1976), *Chusho kigyo no kaiso kozo: Hitachi seisakujo shitauke kigyo kozo no jittai bunseki* (The Stratified Structure of SMEs: Empirical Analysis of the Subcontractor Structure of Hitachi Ltd), Tokyo: Chuo daigaku shuppanbu.

Chusho kigyo cho (ed.) (various years, followed by letter a), *Chusho kigyo hakusho* (SME White Paper), Tokyo: Okurasho insatsu kyoku.

(various years, followed by letter b), *Chusho kigyo shisaku no aramashi* (Outline of Measures for SMEs), Tokyo: Chusho kigyo chosa kyokai.

(various years, followed by letter c), *Chusho kigyo yoran* (Outline of SMEs), Tokyo: Chusho kigyo sogo kenkyu kiko.

(1990d), *90 nendai no chusho kigyo bijion* (Vision for SMEs in the 1990s), Tokyo: Tsusan sangyo chosakai.

(1990e), *Dai nana kai kogyo jittai kihon chosa hokokusho* (7th Basic Survey Report on the State of Industry), Tokyo: Tsusan tokei kyokai.

(1992d), *Shitauke torihiki handobukku* (Subcontracting Transaction Handbook), Tokyo: Tsusan shiryo chosakai.

Chusho kigyo jigyodan (1989), *Chusho kigyo no kigyokan joho netowaku ni kakaru jirei to chosa kenkyu* (Case Studies and Survey Research on SME Interfirm Information Networks), Tokyo.

Chusho kigyo kenkyujo (ed.) (1985), *Nihon no chusho kigyo kenkyu* (SME Research in Japan) Vols. I–III, Tokyo: Yuhikaku.

(1987a), *Waga kuni keizai no hatten katei ni oite chusho kigyo ga hatashita yakuwari ni kansuru kenkyu* (Research into the Role of SMEs in the Development of Japan's Economy), Tokyo.

(1987b), *Gijutsu kakushin to chusho kigyo no taio ni kansuru kenkyu* (Research into Technological Innovation and the Response of SMEs), Tokyo.

(1992), *Nihon no chusho kigyo kenkyu* (SME Research in Japan) Vols. I–III, Tokyo: Doyukan.

(1993), *Chusho kigyo no M&A senryaku* (SME M and A Strategies), Tokyo: Doyukan.

Chusho kigyo seisaku shingikai (1993), *Chusho kigyo seisaku no kadai to kongo no hoko* (Issues and Future Directions in SME Policy: Interim Report), Tokyo.

Chusho kigyo sogo kenkyu kiko (1995), *Chusho kigyoka seishin* (The Spirit of SME Entrepreneurs), Tokyo: Chuo keizaisha.

Clark, R. (1987), *Venture Capital in Britain, America and Japan*, London: Croom Helm.

Coase, R. (1937), 'The Nature of the Firm' *Economica*, November.

(1988), *The Firm, the Market, and the Law*, Chicago: University of Chicago Press.

Crawcour, S. (1988), 'Industrialization and Technological Change, 1885–1920' in P. Duus (ed.), *The Cambridge History of Japan, Vol. VI*, Cambridge: Cambridge University Press.

(1995), 'Kogyo Iken: Maeda Masana and his View of Meiji Economic Development' Oxford University, Nissan Occasional Papers Series No. 23.

Curran, J. and R. Blackburn (1994), *Small Firms and Local Economic Networks: The Death of the Local Economy?*, London: Paul Chapman.

Cusumano, M. (1991), *Japan's Software Factories*, New York: Oxford University Press.

Davenport-Hines, R. (1984), *Dudley Docker: The Life and Times of a Corporate Warrior*, Cambridge: Cambridge University Press.

Dore, R. (1958), *City Life in Japan*, Berkeley: University of California Press.

(1983a), *A Case Study in Technology Forecasting: The Japanese Next Generation Base Technologies Programme*, London: Technical Change Centre.

(1983b), 'Goodwill and the Spirit of Market Capitalism' *The British Journal of Sociology*, 34/3.

(1986), *Flexible Rigidities: Industrial Policy and Structural Adjustment in the Japanese Economy, 1970–80*, London: Athlone.

(1987), *Taking Japan Seriously*, London: Athlone.

Dore, R. and M. Sako (1987), *How the Japanese Learn to Work*, London: Routledge.

Dore, R. and D.H. Whittaker (1994), 'Introduction' in K. Imai and R. Komiya eds. *Business Enterprise in Japan*, Cambridge MA, MIT Press.

Dunnett, P. (1980), *The Decline of the British Motor Industry: The Effects of Government Policy, 1945–79*, London: Croom Helm.

Elliott, D. and M. Marshall, 'Sector Strategy in the West Midlands' in P. Hirst and J. Zeitlin (eds.), *Reversing Industrial Decline?*, Oxford: Berg Publishers.

Evans, D. (1995), 'Japanese Small and Medium-Sized Enterprises in Japan and East Asia' unpublished paper.

Florence, S. (1948), *Investment, Location and Size of Plant,* Cambridge: Cambridge University Press.

Foreman-Peck, J. (1985), 'Seedcorn of Chaff: New Firm Formation and the Performance of the Interwar Economy' *Economic History Review*, August.

Fox, A. (1984), *History and Heritage*, London: Allen and Unwin.

Francks, P. (1992), *Japanese Economic Development: Theory and Practice*, London: Routledge.

Friedman, D. (1988), *The Misunderstood Miracle*, Ithaca: Cornell University Press.

Fujita, K. (1965), *Nihon sangyo kozo to chusho kigyo* (Japan's Industrial Structure and SMEs), Tokyo: Iwanami shoten.

Fujita, K. (ed.) (1943), *Shitaukesei kogyo* (Subcontracting System in Industry), Tokyo: Yuhikaku.

Fujitani, F. (1993), *Toyota igai wa minna kieru* (All Will Disappear Except Toyota), Tokyo: Yell Books.

Fukada, Y. and R. Dore (1993), *Nihongata shihon shugi nakushite nan no Nihon ka* (What is Japan Without Japanese Style Capitalism?), Tokyo: Kobunsha.

Fukushima, H. (1991), 'Chusho kigyo no kaigai shinshutsu to kokusaiteki shitauke seisan shisutemu' (The Movement of SMEs Abroad and the International Subcontracting Production System) in M. Watanabe, K. Nakayama, and H. Fukushima (eds.), *90 nendai no chusho kigyo mondai* (SME Problem in the 1990s), Tokyo: Shinhyoron.

(1993), 'Kokusaika no shinten to chusho reisai kigyo' (The Advance of Internationalisation and SMEs/Microfirms) in *Keizai*, March.

Fukutake, T. (1989), *The Japanese Social Structure*, 2nd edition, Tokyo: University of Tokyo Press.

Fulcher, J. (1991), *Labour Movements, Employers and the State*, New York: Oxford University Press.

Furukawa, K. (1985), 'Chusho kigyo to chiiki keizai, shakai' (SMEs and Local Economies, Society) in Chusho kigyo kenkyujo (ed.), *Nihon no chusho kigyo kenkyu* (Japanese SME Research) Vol. I, Tokyo: Yuhikaku.

Furuki M. (1981), *Wagasha no gijutsushi: Tokyo Keiki 64 nen gijutsu no ayumi* (The Technical History of Our Company: The 64-Year Technical History of Tokyo Precision Instruments), Tokyo: Tokyo keiki OB kai.

Gaffikin, F. and A. Nickson (1984), *Jobs Crisis and the Multinationals – the Case of the West Midlands*, Birmingham: TURC.

Gendai sogo kenkyu shudan (1994), *Teinen, shigoto soshite kurashi parto II: Chusho kigyo koreisha no raifu desain* (Retirement Age, Work and Living, Part II: Life Design of Older Workers in SMEs), Tokyo.

Gordon, A. (1985), *The Evolution of Labor Relations in Japan: Heavy Industry, 1853–1955*, Cambridge MA, Harvard University Press.

Grabher, G. (ed.) (1993), *The Embedded Firm*, London: Routledge.

Hannah, L. (1983), *The Rise of the Corporate Economy*, 2nd edition, London: Methuen.

Hashimoto, T. (1989), 'Keizai, sangyo kozo no tenkan' (Changes in the Economy and Industrial Structure) in Kokumin kin'yu koko (ed.), *Gendai shitauke kigyoron* (Perspectives on Modern Subcontracting Firms), Tokyo: Chusho kigyo risarchi senta.

Hata, K. (1995), 'Venturing Out' *Look Japan*, December.

Heim, C. (1983), 'Industrial Organization and Regional Development in Interwar Britain' *Journal of Economic History*, 43/4.

Hondai, S. (1992), *Daikigyo to chusho kigyo no doji seicho* (The Simultaneous

Growth of Large Firms and SMEs), Tokyo: Dobunkan.

Hopwood, B. (1981), *Whatever Happened to the British Motorcycle Industry?*, Yeovil: Hanes.

Hori, H. (1995), 'Chusho kigyo o yukizuke, shinko o saseru tame no seisaku' (Policies to Encourage and Promote SMEs) in *Shoko kin'yu*, December.

Hughes, A. (1989), 'Small Firms' Merger Activity and Competition Policy' in J. Barber, J. Metcalfe, and M. Porteous (eds.), *Barriers to Growth in Small Firms*, London: Routledge.

(1992), 'Big Business, Small Business and the Enterprise Culture' in J. Mitchie (ed.), *The Economic Legacy, 1979–1992*, London: Academic Press.

(1993), 'Industrial Concentration and the Small Business Sector in the UK: The 1980s in Historical Perspective' in Z. Acs and D. Audretsch (eds.), *Small Firms and Entrepreneurship*, Cambridge: Cambridge University Press.

Hwang, W. (1993), *Nihon toshi chusho kogyo shi* (History of Japanese Urban Small- and Medium-Scale Industry), Tokyo: Rinsen shoten.

Ide, S., A. Takeuchi, and H. Sawada (1977), *Keizai chiiki no kenkyu: keihin chiiki no kogyo to nogyo* (Research on Economic Districts: Industry and Agriculture of the Keihin district), Tokyo: Bunka shobo hakubun sha.

Imai, K. (1986), 'Netowaku soshiki: tenbo' (Network Organisation: Prospects) in *Soshiki kagaku* (Organisation Science), 20/3.

Imano, K. and H. Sato (1990), *Sofutouea sangyo to keiei* (The Software Industry and Management), Tokyo: Toyo keizai shinposha.

Inagami, T. (1989a) *Tenkanki no rodo sekai* (World of Labour in Transition), Tokyo: Yushindo.

(1989b), 'On Postwar Japanese Sociology: Prospects and Retrospect' mimeo.

(1992), 'Gastarbeiter in Japanese Small Firms' in *Japan Institute of Labour Bulletin*, 31/3, March.

Inagami, T., Y. Kuwahara, and Kokumin kin'yu koko sogo kenkyujo (1992), *Gaikokujin rodosha o senryokuka suru chusho kigyo* (SMEs Using Foreign Workers as a Strategic Force), Tokyo: Chusho kigyo risarchi senta.

Ingham, G. (1970), *Size of Industrial Organization and Worker Behaviour*, Cambridge: Cambridge University Press.

Itakura, K. (1988), *Nihon kogyo no chiiki shisutemu* (The Regional System of Japanese Industry), Tokyo: Taimeido.

Itakura, K., S. Ide, and A. Takeuchi (1973), *Daitoshi reisai kogyo no kozo* (The Structure of Microindustry in Large Cities), Tokyo: Shinhyoron.

Ito, M. (1989), *Sangyo to chiiki no keizai seisaku* (Economic Policy of Industry and Regions), Tokyo: Gakubunsha.

Iwauchi, R. (1989), *Nihon no kogyoka to jukuren keisei* (Industrialisation and Skill Formation in Japan), Tokyo: Nihon hyoron sha.

Japan Institute of Labour (1993 and 1994), *Japanese Working Life Profile*, Tokyo.

Jichiroren (1993), *Fukyoka no machi koba no keiei jittai ni tsuite* (Management Situation of Small Urban Factories Under Recession), Tokyo.

Johnson, C. (1982), *MITI and the Japanese Miracle*, Stanford: Stanford University Press.

Johnson, P. and D. Cathcart (1979), 'The Founders of New Manufacturing Firms:

A Note on the Size of Their "Incubator" Plants' *The Journal of Industrial Economics*, 28/2.

Kagaku gijutsu cho (ed.) (1993), *Chiiki ni okeru kagaku gijutsu shinko* (Regional Science and Technology Promotion) Tokyo: Okurasho insatsu kyoku.

Kakinuma, S. (1988), 'Johoka, kokusaika no naka no Tokyo no sangyo keizai' (Tokyo's Industrial Economy in the Context of Information-isation and Internationalisation) in K. Murata (ed.), *Sangyo botoshi Tokyo* (Tokyo, Industrial Base City), Tokyo: Toyo keizai shinpo sha.

Kamata, S. (1995), 'Chusho kigyo no sogyo to koyo mondai' (SME Startups and Employment Problems) in *Nihon Rodo Kenkyu Zasshi*, No. 425, August.

Kameyama, N. (1985), *Gijutsu kakushinka no chusho kigyo* (SMEs Under Technological Innovation), Tokyo: Nihon rodo kyokai.

(1990), 'Komento' (Comments) in M. Tsuchiya and Y. Miwa (eds.), *Nihon no chusho kigyo* (Japanese SMEs), Tokyo: Tokyo daigaku shuppankai.

Kanagawa ken chusho kigyo shien zaidan (1993), *Kanagawa kennai jidosha kanren shitauke kigyo no doko chosa hokokusho* (Survey Report on Trends in Automobile Subcontractors in Kanagawa Prefecture), Yokohama.

Kasarda, J. (1992), 'Introduction' in D. Sexton and J. Kasarda (eds.), *The State of the Art of Entrepreneurship*, Boston: PWS-Kent.

Kasumi, T. (1995), 'Nihon ni okeru josei kigyoka no kaigyo doki' (The Motivation for Female Entrepreneurs in Japan) in *Shoko kin'yu*, December.

Keeble, D. (1990), 'Small Firms, New Firms and Uneven Regional Development in the United Kingdom' *Area*, 22/3.

(1993), 'Small Firm Creation, Innovation and Growth and the Urban–Rural Shift' in J. Curren and D. Storey (eds.), *Small Firms in Urban and Rural Locations*, London: Routledge.

Keizai kikakucho (EPA) (ed.) (1990), *Keizai hakusho* (White Paper on the Economy), Tokyo: Okurasho insatsu kyoku.

Keizai koho senta (1994), *Japan: An International Comparison*, Tokyo.

Kelley, M. and H. Brooks (1988), 'The State of Computerized Automation in US Manufacturing' Harvard University, Kennedy School of Government report.

Kenkyu kaihatsugata kigyo ikusei senta (1992 and 1995), *Bencha bijinesu doko chosa hokoku* (Survey Report on Trends in Venture Business), Tokyo.

Kinmonth, E. (1981), *The Self-Made Man in Meiji Japanese Thought*, Berkeley: University of California Press.

Kiyonari, T. (1972), *Gendai chusho kigyo no shin tenkai* (New Developments of Modern SMEs), Tokyo: Nihon keizai shinbunsha.

(1975), *Chiiki no henkaku to chusho kigyo* (Local Change and SMEs), Tokyo: Nihon keizai hyoron sha.

(1986), *Chiiki sangyo seisaku* (Regional Industrial Policy), Tokyo: Tokyo daigaku shuppankai.

(1990), *Chusho kigyo tokuhon* (SME Reader), 2nd edition, Tokyo: Toyo keizai shinposha.

(1994), 'High Tech. Venture Business and Venture Capital Trends in Japan' *VEC Annual Report, 1993*.

Kiyonari, T., T. Inagami, Y. Abe, and M. Yamamoto (1982), *Toshigata chusho kigyo no shintenkai* (New Developments in Urban SMEs), Tokyo: Nihon keizai shinbunsha.

Kiyonari, T., H. Nakamura, and K. Hirao (1971), *Bencha bijinesu* (Venture Business), Tokyo: Nihon keizai shinbunsha.

Koike, K. (1981a), *Chusho kigyo no jukuren* (Skills in SMEs), Tokyo: Dobunkan.

(1981b), *Nihon no jukuren: sugureta jinzai keisei shisutemu* (Skills in Japan: A Superior Skill Formation System), Tokyo: Yuhikaku.

(1983), 'Workers in Small Firms and Women in Industry' in T. Shirai (ed.), *Contemporary Industrial Relations in Japan*, Madison: University of Wisconsin Press.

Kokudo cho (1990), *Chiiki sangyo kodoka to igyoshu koryu* (Regional Industrial Upgrading and Exchange Across Industries), Tokyo: Okurasho insatsu kyoku.

Kokumin kin'yu koko (ed.) (1989a), *Nihon no chusho kikai kogyo* (Japanese SME Machine Industry), Tokyo: Chusho kigyo risarchi senta.

(1989b), *Gendai shitauke kigyoron* (Perspectives on Modern Subcontracting Firms), Tokyo: Chusho kigyo risarchi senta.

See also Peoples' Finance Corporation.

(1992 and 1995), *Shinki kaigyo hakusho* (White Paper on New Startups), Tokyo: Chusho kigyo risarchi senta.

Komiyama, T. (1941), *Nihon chusho kogyo kenkyu* (Research on Japanese Small- and Medium-Scale Industry), Tokyo: Chuo koron.

Kondo, D. (1990), *Crafting Selves*, Chicago: University of Chicago Press.

Kosei torihiki iinkai (ed.) (1992), *Kosei torihiki iinkai nenji hokoku* (Fair Trade Commission Annual Report), Tokyo: Kosei torihiki kyokai.

(1995), 'Endakato ni yoru shitauke torihiki no henka ni kansuru chosa hokokusho' (Survey Report on Changes in Subcontracting Transactions Due to the High Yen, etc.), Tokyo.

Kosei torihiki iinkai and Chusho kigyo cho (1992), *Shitauke torihiki tekiseika suishin koshukai tekisuto* (Text for Workshop on the Promotion of Rationalisation of Subcontracting Transactions), Tokyo.

Koseki, T. (1984), *Omori kaiwai shokunin orai* (Craftsmen's Paths Around Omori), Tokyo: Asahi shinbunsha.

(1986), *Machi koba no jikai* (The Magnetic World of the Machi Koba), Tokyo: Gendai shokan.

(1988), 'MEka ga susumu koba no genba kara' (From Shop Floors Where Microelectronics Technology Has Been Introduced) in Koyo sokushin jigyodan (ed.), *Gino to gijutsu* (Craft and Technology), November.

Koshiro, K. (1986), 'The Labour Market of Small Business in Japan', mimeo, Yokohama National University.

(1990), 'Japan' in W. Sengenberger, G. Loveman, and M. Piore (eds.), *The Re-emergence of Small Enterprises*, Geneva: International Institute for Labour Studies.

Koyo joho senta (1991), 'Machi koba kara umareru haiteku kako gijutsu' (High Tech. Processing Technology From Small Urban Factories) in *Enpuroi* (Employ), month unknown.

Kuramochi, Y. (1981), *Sengo chusho kigyo sogishi* (A History of Postwar SME Disputes), Tokyo: Rodo kyoiku senta.

Lane, C. (1991), 'Industrial Reorganization in Europe: Patterns of Convergence and Divergence in Germany, France and Britain' Cambridge University SBRC Working Papers No.11.

Leibenstein, H. (1966), 'Allocative Efficiency Versus X-Efficiency' *American Economic Review*, June.

L'Hénoret, A. (1993), *Le Clou qui Dépasse: Récit du Japon d'en bas*, Paris: Éditions La Décourverte.

Lockwood, W. (1954), *The Economic Development of Japan*, Princeton: Princeton University Press.

Makino, N. and Y. Tsukio (1994), *Nihon o kaeru shin seicho sangyo* (New Growth Industries to Change Japan), Tokyo: PHP.

Marshall, A. (1923), *Industry and Trade: A Study of Industrial Technique and Business Organization*, London: Macmillan.

   (1947), *Principles of Economics*, London: Macmillan.

Marshall, M. (1987), *Long Waves of Regional Development,* London: Macmillan.

Massey, D. (1979), 'In What Sense a Regional Problem?' *Regional Studies*, 13/2.

   (1984), *Spatial Divisions of Labour*, London: Macmillan.

Massey, D., P. Quintas, and D. Wield (1992), *High-Tech Fantasies: Science Parks in Society, Science and Space*, London: Routledge.

Millward, A. (1989), 'The Cycle Industry in Birmingham, 1890–1920' in B. Tilson (ed.), *Made in Birmingham: Design and Industry, 1889–1989*, Studley: Brewin Books.

Minami, R. and Y. Kiyokawa (eds.) (1987), *Nihon no kogyoka to gijutsu hatten* (Industrialisation and Technological Development of Japan), Tokyo: Toyo keizai shinposha.

Ministry of International Trade and Industry (MITI) (ed.) (1989), 'Outline and Present Status of the Technopolis Project' Tokyo, mimeo.
   See also Tsusansho.

Minoguchi, T. (1936), 'Chusho kogyo sonzoku no konkyo ni tsuite' (On the Basis of the Continued Existence of Small- and Medium-Scale Industry), Tokyo: Tokyo shoka diagaku, Hitotsubashikai.

Misoue, Y. (1993), *Jidosha buhin gaisha go tairyo tosan suru hi* (The Day of Mass Bankruptcies Among Automobile Parts Companies), Tokyo: Appuru.

Mitsui, I. (1985), 'Reisai kigyo' (Micro-firms) in Chusho kigyo kenkyujo (ed.), *Nihon no chusho kigyo kenkyu* (Japanese SME Research) Vol.I, Tokyo: Yuhikaku.

Miura, K. (1991), 'Chusho kigyo no soshikika' (The Organisation of SMEs) in S. Momose and M. Ito (eds.), *Chusho kigyoron* (Theories of SMEs), Tokyo: Hakuto shobo.

Miwa, Y. (1990), *Nihon no kigyo to sangyo soshiki* (Japan's Enterprises and Industrial Organisation), Tokyo: Tokyo daigaku shuppankai.

   (1994), 'Subcontracting Relationships: The Automobile Industry' in K. Imai and R. Komiya (eds.), *Business Enterprise in Japan*, Cambridge MA: MIT Press.

(1995), 'Policies for Small Business in Japan' in H. Kim, M. Muramatsu, T. Pempel, and K. Yamamura (eds.), *The Japanese Civil Service and Economic Development*, Oxford: Oxford University Press.

Miyanaga, K. (1991) *The Creative Edge*, New Brunswick: Transaction Publishers.

Momose, S. (1985), *Nihon no bencha bijinesu* (Japan's Venture Business), Tokyo: Hakuto shobo.

(1989), *Chusho kigyo kumiai no rinen to kasseika* (Principles of SME Associations and Revitalising Them), Tokyo: Hakuto shobo.

(1991), 'Kisei kanwa no mondaisei to chusho kigyo kumiai' (SME Associations and the Problems of Deregulation) in S. Momose and M. Ito (eds.), *Chusho kigyoron* (Theories of SMEs), Tokyo: Hakuto shobo.

Mori, K. (1981), *Machi koba: mo hitotsu no kindai* (Small Urban Factories: A Different Type of Modernity), Tokyo: Asahi shinbunsha.

(1982), *Machi koba no roboto kakumei* (The Robot Revolution in Small Urban Factories), Tokyo: Daiyamondo sha.

(1991a), *Nihon wa chusho kigyo kuni dakara tsuyoi* (Japan is Strong Because it is an SME Country), Tokyo: Daiyamondo sha.

(1991b), 'Chusho kigyo wa abunai' (SMEs in Danger) in *Shukan daiymondo*, 16, November.

Murakoso, T. (1992), *Asia to no seisan, gijutsu kanren no shinten to daitoshi chusho kigyo no taio* (Production and Technical Links With Asia and the Response of SMEs in Large Cities) in *Shakai kagaku*, No.50, September.

Murata, K. (1988), *Sangyo botoshi Tokyo* (Tokyo, Industrial Base City), Tokyo: Toyo keizai shinposha.

Murata, K. (ed.) (1980), *An Industrial Geography of Japan,* London: Bell and Hyman.

Nakaguma, Y. (1988), *Igyoshu koryu no susumekata* (How to Develop Interindustry Exchange), Tokyo: Nihon keizai shinbunsha.

Nakamura, H. (1964), *Chuken kigyo ron* (LME Theory), Tokyo: Toyo keizai shinpo sha.

(1970), *Daikibo jidai no owari* (End of the Age of Large Scale), Tokyo: Daiyamondo sha.

(1990), *Shin chuken kigyo ron* (New LME Theory), Tokyo: Toyo keizai shinposha.

(1992), *21 sekigata chusho kigyo* (21st Century-Type SMEs), Tokyo: Iwanami shoten.

(1994), 'Daikibo jidai no owari' (End of the Age of Large Scale) in *Mita Hyoron*, July.

Nakamura, H., S. Akiya, T. Kiyonari, M. Yamazaki, and T Bando (1981), *Gendai chusho kigyo shi* (History of Modern SMEs), Tokyo: Nihon Keizai Shinbunsha.

Nakaoka, T. (1994), 'The Learning Process and the Market: The Japanese Capital Goods Sector in the Early Twentieth Century' LSE STICERD Discussion Paper No.JS/94/271.

Nihon kaihatsugata kigyo ikusei senta (1995, 1992), *Bencha bijinesu doko chosa hokoku* (Survey Report on Trends in Venture Business), Tokyo.

Nihon keikaku gyosei gakkai (ed.) (1987), *Toshi kogyo no ritchi kankyo seibi keikaku*

(Restructuring Plan of the Spacial Environment for Urban Industry), Tokyo: Gakuyo shobo.

Nihon keizai shinbun (various dates).

Nihon kogyo shinbunsha (1988), *Nihon kogyo nenkan* (Japan Industrial Yearbook), Tokyo.

Nihon kosaku kikai kogyokai (1988), 'Showa 62 nen NC kosaku kikai seisan jisseki to chosa' (1987 Machine Tool Production Results Survey), Tokyo.

Nihon ritchi senta (1993), *Chusho, chuken kigyo no kaigai tenkai to chiikikan bungyo ni kansuru chosa* (Survey on the Overseas Development of SMEs and LMEs, and Inter-District Division of Labour).

Nihon rodo kenkyu kiko (1996), *Chusho seizogyo no gijutsu, gino shuseki ni kansuru chosa* (Survey on SME Manufacturing Technology/Craft Concentrations), Tokyo.

Nihon shoko kaigisho (1984), *Shokibo jigyosha wakate kokeisha ikusei mondai kenkyu chosa hokokusho* (Survey Report on Issues Relating to Raising Young Small Firm Successors), Tokyo.

Nikkei BP sha (1989), *Nikkei benchiya* (Nikkei Venture), No.53, February, Tokyo.

Nikkei sangyo shinbun (ed.) (1995), *Bencha shin jidai* (New Age of Venture), Tokyo: Nihon keizai shinbunsha.

Nikkei Business (various dates).

Nikkei shinbuni (various dates).

Nikkei Weekly (30 October 1995).

Nikkeiren (1985), *Chusho kigyo no seisansei, chingin, roshi kankei* (Productivity, Wages and Industrial Relations in SMEs), Tokyo.

Nikko risarchi senta (various years), *Toshika no tame no gyokai bunseki* (Industry Analysis for Investors), Tokyo: Keirin shobo.

Nishiguchi, T. (1992), *Strategic Industrial Sourcing*, New York: Oxford University Press.

Nomura sogo kenkyujo (1987), Chuken kigyo shin jidai (A New Age of LMEs), in *Zaikai kansoku* (Business World Observation), November.

Odaka, K. (ed.) (1956), *Imono no machi: sangyo shakaigakuteki kenkyu* (Casting Town: from an Industrial Sociology Perspective), Tokyo: Yuhikaku.

OECD (1977), *The Development of Industrial Relations Systems: Some Implications of the Japanese Experience*, Paris.

Ogawa, M. (1990), 'Chusho kigyo no netowaku katsudo ni miru kigyo no joho kodo' (Corporate Information Behaviour seen in SME Network Activities) in Tokyo shoko shidojo (ed.), *Shoko shido*, No.441.

 (1993a), *Kigyo no joho kodo* (Corporate Information Activities), Tokyo: Dobunkan.

 (1993b) 'Soshiki kozo kara mita chusho kigyo seicho no joken' (Conditions for Growth in SMEs from the Perspective of Organisation Structure) in Tokyo shoko shidojo (ed.), *Shoko shido*, No. 454.

Ohama, T. (1989), 'Den'en toshi no riso to genjitsu' (Ideals and Reality of Pastoral Cities' in Ota ku (ed.), *Shi shi* (History Journal), 31, Tokyo.

Ohkawa, K. and H. Rosovsky (1973), *Japanese Economic Growth*, Stanford: Stanford University Press.

Okazaki, T. (1994), 'The Japanese Firm Under the Wartime Planned Economy' in M. Aoki and R. Dore (eds.), *The Japanese Firm*, Oxford: Oxford University Press.

Okimoto, D. and G. Saxonhouse (1987), 'Technology and the Future of the Economy' in K. Yamamura and Y. Yasuba (eds.) *The Political Economy of Japan, Volume I: The Domestic Transformation*, Stanford: Stanford University Press.

Okumura, H. (1990), 'Seitoka dekinai *keiretsu* no gorisei' (Keiretsu Rationality Can't be Justified) in *Ekonomisto*, 10 July.

Omori ku (ed.) (1939), *Omori ku shi* (History of Omori Ward), Tokyo.

Osaka furitsu sangyo kaihatsu kenkyujo/Osaka shoko kaigisho (1991a), *Osaka – Asia seisan rinkeju ni kansuru chosa* (Survey on Osaka – Asian Production Linkages).

(1991b), *Asia nikkei kigyo no seisan rinkeju* (Production Linkages of Japanese Firms in Asia).

(1991c), Chiiki keizai kankyo henka to Osaka kogyo no taio ni kansuru chosa (Survey on Responses of Osaka Industry to Changes in the Regional Economic Environment).

Ota ku (1986), *Ota ku ni okeru kodo kogyo shuseki no kadai* (Issues in Ota Ward's High Level Industrial Concentration), Tokyo.

(1989), *Ota ku kogyo no kozo henka to shorai tenbo: Showa 63 nendo* (Structural Change and Future Prospects for Ota Ward Industry, 1988), Tokyo.

(1992, 1993), *View: Ota ku sangyo joho shirizu* (View: Ota Ward Industry Information Series), Tokyo.

(1994), *Ota ku sangyo dantai meibo* (List of Industrial Organisations in Ota Ward), Tokyo.

(1995a), *Ota ku kogyo no kozo henka ni kansuru chosa hokokusho* (Survey Report on Changes in the Structure of Ota Ward's Industry), Tokyo.

(1995b), *Ota ku no kogyo* (Industry in Ota Ward), Tokyo.

Ota ku (ed.) (1951), *Ota ku shi* (History of Ota Ward), Tokyo.

(1964), *Ota ku kikai kinzoku kogyo no jittai chosasho* (Survey Report on Metal/Machine Industries in Ota Ward),Tokyo.

Ota ku sangyo bijion iinkai (1995), *Ota ku sangyo bijion* (Industry Vision for Ota Ward), Tokyo: Ota ku.

Ota kuritsu kyodo hakubutsukan (1994), *Koba machi no tanken gaido* (Explorative Guide Book: The History and Development of Ota Industry), Tokyo.

Patrick, H. and T. Rohlen (1987), 'Small-Scale Family Enterprises' in K. Yamamura and Y. Yasuba (eds.), *The Political Economy of Japan*, Vol.I, Stanford: Stanford University Press.

Pempel, T. and K. Tsunekawa (1979), 'Corporatism Without Labour? The Japanese Anomaly' in P. Schmitter and G. Lehmbruch (eds.), *Trends Towards Corporatist Intermediation*, London: Sage.

Penrose, E. (1959), *The Theory of the Growth of the Firm*, Oxford: Basil Blackwell.

Peoples' Finance Corporation (1994), *Trends in the Formation of Business Openings*, Tokyo.

(1989), *Small and Medium Enterprises in Japan and Financing Available to Them*, Tokyo.

See also Kokumin kin'yu koko.

Piore, M. and C. Sabel (1984), *The Second Industrial Divide*, New York: Basic Books.

Prais, S. (1976, 1981), *The Evolution of Giant Firms in Britain*, Cambridge: Cambridge University Press.

Pratten, C. (1991), *The Competitiveness of Small Firms*, Cambridge: Cambridge University Press.

Pyke, F., G. Becattini, and W. Sengenberger (eds.) (1990), *Industrial Districts and Interfirm Co-operation in Italy*, Geneva: International Institute for Labour Studies.

Pyke, F. and W. Sengenberger (eds.) (1992), *Industrial Districts and Local Economic Regeneration*, Geneva, International Institute for Labour Studies.

Rainnie, A. (1989), *Industrial Relations in Small Firms*, London: Routledge.

Rengo (1994), *Chusho kigyo no gino keisei ni kansuru chosa* (Survey of Skill Formation Manufacturing in SMEs), Tokyo.

Reubens, E. (1947), 'Small Scale Industry in Japan' *Quarterly Journal of Economics*, 61, August.

Rodosho (ed.) (1992a), *Rodo tokei yoran* (Handbook of Labour Statistics), Tokyo: Okurasho insatsu kyoku.

(1992b), *Nihon no rodo kumiai no genjo* (Current State of Labour Unions in Japan), Tokyo: Okurasho insatsu kyoku.

(1992c), *Rodosha fukushi shisetsu seidoto chosa hokoku: Heisei 3 nen* (Survey Report on Systems of Worker Welfare Provision, 1991), Tokyo.

(1996), *Momozukuri kiban no kodoka to jinzai ikusei* (Upgrading of the Production Base and Raising Human Resources), Tokyo.

Rowthorn, R. and J. Wells (1987), *De-Industrialization and Foreign Trade*, Cambridge: Cambridge University Press.

Sabel, C. (1989), 'Flexible Specialization and the Re-emergence of Regional Societies' in P. Hirst and J. Zeitlin (eds.), *Reversing Industrial Decline? Industrial Policy in Britain and her Competitors*, Oxford: Berg.

Sabel, C. and J. Zeitlin (1985), 'Historical Alternatives to Mass Production: Politics, Markets and Technology in Nineteenth Century Industrialization' *Past and Present*, No.108, August.

Sakaiya, T. (1995), *'Taihen' na jidai: joshiki hakai to daikyoso* (Age of Upheavals: Fierce Competition and the Destruction of Common Sense), Tokyo: Kodansha.

Sakamoto, K. (1992), 'Shitauke kigyo ga abunai' (Subcontractors in Danger) in *Shizuoka shinbun*, 27 October.

Sako, M. (1992), *Prices, Quality and Trust*, Cambridge: Cambridge University Press.

(1996), 'Suppliers' Associations in the Japanese Automobile Industry' *Cambridge Journal of Economics*, forthcoming.

Sasaki, K. (1986), 'Ueda tsumugi' in T. Ichikawa and A. Takeuchi (eds.), *Nagano ken no jiba sangyo* (Localised Industry in Nagano Prefecture), Nagano: Shinnano kyoikukai shuppanbu.

Sato, Y. (ed.) (1981), *Kyodai toshi no reisai kogyo* (Micro Industry in Giant Cities), Tokyo: Nihon keizai hyoronsha.

(1990), 'Rekishi no naka de henyo suru chusho kigyo' (SMEs Changing Historically) in M. Tsuchiya and Y. Miwa (eds.), *Nihon no chusho kigyo* (Japanese SMEs), Tokyo: Tokyo daigaku shuppankai.

Sato, Y. *et al.* (1994), 'Ima, chusho kigyo no jidai' (Now is the Age of SMEs) in *Mita hyoron*, July.

Sayama, T. (1995), 'Nihon no chusho kigyo kin'yu' (SME Financing in Japan), in *Shoko kin'yu*, December.

Scase, R. and R. Goffee (1987), *The Real World of the Small Business Owner*, 2nd edition, London: Croom Helm.

Seki, M. (1994), *Beyond the Full Set Industrial Structure*, Tokyo: LTCB International Library Foundation.

Seki, M. and H. Kato (1990), *Gendai nihon no chusho kikai kogyo: nashionaru tekunoporisu no keisei* (Modern Japanese SME Machine Industry: Formation of a National Technopolis), Tokyo: Shinhyoron.

Sengenberger, W., G. Loveman, and M. Piore (1990), *The Re-emergence of Small Enterprises*, Geneva: International Institute for Labour Studies.

Sengenberger, W. and F. Pyke (1990), 'Industrial Districts and Local Economic Regeneration: Research and Policy Issues' in F. Pyke and W. Sengenberger (eds.), *Industrial Districts and Local Economic Regeneration*, Geneva: International Institute for Labour Studies.

Shakai seisaku gakkai (1918), *Shokogyo mondai* (The Small Scale Industry Problem), Tokyo: Dobunkan.

Sheard, P. (1983), 'Auto-production Systems in Japan: Organizational and Locational Features' *Australian Geographical Studies*, 21 April.

Shibata, K., K. Ishiro, and S. Ogihara (1992), 'Waga kuni kikai sangyo no tonan ajia ni okeru kokusai seisan bungyo no jittai (The International Division of Labour of Japan's Machine Industries in Southeast Asia) in Kikai shinko kyokai (ed.), *Kikai keizai kenkyu* (Machine Economy Research) No.23.

Shinagawa rosei jimusho (1988), *Kannai no kikai kinzoku seizogyo ni okeru rodo jokento jittai chosa* (Survey of Labour Conditions in the Metal/Machine Industries in Ota, Shinagawa and Minato Wards), Tokyo.

(1989), *Gaikokujin no koyo ni kansuru ishiki jittai chosa* (Survey on Conditions and Opinions of Employment of Foreign Workers), Tokyo.

Shizuoka shinbun (Shizuoka Newspaper) (27 October 1992).

Shoko chukin (ed.) (1983), *Shitauke chusho kigyo no shin kyokumen* (New Developments of SME Subcontractors), Tokyo.

Shoya, K. (1988), 'Nihon sangyo no shitauke torihiki ni okeru "fukosei torihiki"' (Unfair Trading in Subcontracting Relations in Japanese Industry) in Momoyama gakuin daigaku *Shakaigaku ronshu*, 21/2.

Small Business Research Centre (ed.) (1992), *The State of British Enterprise*, DAE, Cambridge University.

Smiles, S. (1859), *Self Help*, London: John Murray.

Smith, T. (1959), *The Agrarian Origins of Modern Japan*, Stanford: Stanford University Press.

(1987), *Native Sources of Japanese Industrialization*, Stanford: Stanford University Press.

Smitka, M. (1991), *Competitive Ties: Subcontracting in the Japanese Automotive Industry*, New York: Columbia University Press.

Somucho (ed.) (various years, followed by letter a), *Jigyosho tokei chosa hokoku* (Establishment Statistical Survey Report), Tokyo: Nihon tokei kyokai.

(various years, followed by letter b), *Rodoryoku chosa* (Labour Force Survey), Tokyo: Nihon tokei kyokai.

Sonoda, T. (1982), 'Kiryu yushutsu kinu orimono no tenbo' (Prospects for Export Silk Weaving in Kiryu' *Takachiho ronso*, (Takachiho Papers), No.2.

(1986), 'Ota shi seizogyo no genjo to kadai' (The Present State and Issues of Manufacturing Industry in Ota City), *Takachiho ronso* (Takachiho Papers), No.2.

(1991), 'Ota meriyasu kogyo no rekishi to genjo' (The History and Present State of the Knitted Goods Industry in Ota), *Takachiho ronso* (Takachiho Papers), 25/4.

Spencer, K, A. Taylor, B.Smith, J. Mawson, N. Flynn, and R. Batley (1986), *Crisis in the Industrial Heartland: A Study of the West Midlands*, Oxford: Oxford University Press.

Storey, D. (1994), *Understanding the Small Business Sector*, London: Routledge.

Suzuki, Y. (ed.) (1987), *The Japanese Financial System*, Oxford: Oxford University Press.

Takada, R. (1989), *Gendai chusho kigyo no kozo bunseki* (The Structure of Modern SMEs), Tokyo: Shin hyoron.

Takeuchi, A. (1978), *Kogyo chiiki kozoron* (Theory of Industrial District Structure), Tokyo: Taimeido.

(1983), *Gijutsu shudan to sangyo chiiki shakai* (Technology Groupings and Industrial District Society), Tokyo: Daimeido.

(1988), *Gijutsu kakushin to kogyo chiiki* (Technological Innovation and Industrial Districts), Tokyo: Daimeido.

Takeuchi, A. and H. Mori (1988), 'Noson chiiki ni okeru jimae no kikai kogyo gijutsu shudan' (Independently established machine industry technology centres in agricultural villages) in *Keizai chirigaku nenpo* (Economic Geography Annual), 34/1

Takeuchi, J. (1991), *The Role of Labour-Intensive Sectors in Japanese Economic Development,* Tokyo: United Nations University Press.

Takizawa, K.(1971), 'Rodo ryoku busokuka to reisai kogyo no zodai: Kiyonari Tadao shira no hihan ni kotaete' (The Labour Shortage and the Increase in Micro-industry: A Response to the Criticism of Kiyonari Tadao and others) in Shoko chukin (ed.), *Shoko kinyu*, 21/6.

(1985), 'Honshitsuron teki kenkyu' (Research on the Nature [of SMEs]) in Chusho kigyo kenkyujo (ed.), *Nihon no chusho kigyo kenkyu* (Japanese SME Research) Vol. I, Tokyo: Yuhikaku.

Tasugi, K. (1941, 1987), *Shitaukesei kogyo ron* (Theory of Subcontracting Industry), Tokyo: Yuhikaku.

Tatsuno, S. (1986), *The Technopolis Strategy,* New York: Prentice Hall.

Tilson, B. (ed.) (1989), *Made in Birmingham: Design and Industry 1889–1989*, Studley: Brewin Books.

Tokyo shoko kaigisho, Ota shibu (1992), *Ota ku ni okeru shokibo kogyo no jittai chosa hokokusho* (Survey Report on Small Scale Industry in Ota Ward), Tokyo.

Tokyoto (1991), *Kigyokan netowaku jittai chosa hokokusho* (Survey Report on Interfirm Networks), Tokyo.

Tokyoto (ed.) (1986), *Tonai chusho kigyo no kozo henka e no taio ni kansuru jittai chosa hokokusho* (Survey into SME Responses to Environmental Change in the Metropolitan Area), Tokyo.

(1989), *Tokyo to ni okeru kojo no kino henka oyobi kogyo seigen shoseido no eikyo ni kansuru chosa hokokusho* (Survey Report on Functional Changes in Factories and the Influence of Institutional Limitations on Industry in Tokyo), Tokyo.

(1990), *Keizai rodo tokei nenpo* (Economic and Labour Statistics Annual), Tokyo.

Tokyoto chusho kigyo shinko kosha (1993 and 1994), *Heisei 4/5nendo shitauke torihiki joken o jittai chosa hokokusho* (Survey Report on Subcontracting Conditions in 1992/93), Tokyo.

(1995), *Kosha no jigyo annai* (Guide to the Corporation's Activities), Tokyo.

Tokyo toritsu rodo kenkyujo (1983), *Chusho kigyo bunya ni okeru sangyo betsu rodo kumiai* (Industrial Labour Unions in the SME Sector), Tokyo.

(1984), *Chusho kigyo keieisha dantai no romu kankei kino* (Labour-Related Functions of SME Management Organisations), Tokyo.

(1989), *Chusho kigyo ni okeru noryoku shugi teki kanri to roshi kankei* (Industrial Relations and Ability-ist Management in SMEs), Tokyo.

(1990), *Chusho kigyo ni okeru jugyoin soshiki no yakuwari* (The Role of Employee Organisations in SMEs), Tokyo.

(1991), *Tokyoto ni okeru gaikokujin rodosha no shuro jittai* (Employment Situation of Foreign Workers in Tokyo), Tokyo.

(1992), *Jieigyosha no kyaria to shuro* (Work and Career of the Self Employed), Tokyo.

Tokyoto shoko shidojo (1986) *Ota ku nishi kojiya ni okeru kikai kinzoku kogyo no bunseki* (Analysis of Metal/Machine Industry in Nishi Kojiya, Ota Ward), Tokyo.

(1987), *Daitoshi juko konzai chiiki no seibi to senryakuteki kogyo shuseki no keisei* (Maintenance of Mixed Residential–Industrial Metropolitan Districts and the Formation of Strategic Industrial Concentrations), Tokyo.

(1989), *Chosa kenkyu: Chusho kigyo no yugoka katsudo to un'ei* (Survey Research: SME 'Fusion' Activities and Management), Tokyo.

(1990), *Chosa kenkyu: Tokyo no chusho kigyo to yugoka* (Survey Research: Tokyo SME's and 'Fusion'), Tokyo.

(1992), *Tokyoto chusho kigyo keiei hakusho* (White Paper on Management in Tokyo SMEs), Tokyo.

(1993), *Kisoteki jukakogyo no chiiki tenkai to ritchi kankyo henka* (Basic Heavy

Process Spatial Development and Changing Locational Environment), Tokyo.

Tsuchiya, M. and Y. Miwa (eds.) (1990), *Nihon no chusho kigyo* (Japanese SMEs), Tokyo: Tokyo daigaku shuppankai.

Tsujimoto, Y., Y. Kitamura and K. Ueno (eds.) (1989), *Kanto kigyo chiiki no kozo henka* (Structural Changes in Kanto's Textile Industry), Tokyo: Taimeido.

Tsusansho (ed.) (1995), *Tokutei kikai setsubi tokei chosa hokokusho* (Report on the 8th Census of Selected Machinery and Equipment), Tokyo: Tsusan tokei kyokai.

(various years), *Kogyo tokei hyo* (Census of Manufactures).

Ukai, S. (1990), 'Tokyo umetatechi kogyo danchi no chusho kikai kogyo' (SME Machine Industries in an Industrial Estate of Tokyo's Reclaimed Islands), Waseda Univ. Faculty of Commerce Occasional Paper No. 340.

(1992), 'Chusho kikai kogyo no gijutsu henka' (Technical Change in SME Machine Industries) in Kokumin kin'yu koko (ed.), *Chosa kiho* (PFC Survey Quarterly), Tokyo.

Veblin, T. (1914), *The Instinct of Workmanship*, New York: Macmillan.

Vestal, J. (1993), *Industrial Policy and Japanese Economic Development 1945–1990*, Oxford: Oxford University Press.

Vogel, E. (1963), *Japan's New Middle Class*, Berkeley: University of California Press.

(1967), 'Kinship Structure, Migration to the City and Modernization' in R. Dore (ed.), *Aspects of Social Change in Modern Japan*, New Jersey: Princeton University Press.

Watanabe, M. (1991), *Nihon chusho kigyo no riron to undo* (Japanese SMEs, Theory and Movement), Tokyo: Shin nihon shuppansha.

Watanabe, Y. (1983, 1984), 'Shitauke kigyo no kyoso to sonritsu keitai' (Subcontractor Competition and Typologies) in *Mitai gakkai zasshi*, 76/2; 76/5; 77/3.

(1985), 'Shitauke, keiretsu chusho kigyo' (Subcontractor and keiretsu SMEs) in Chusho kigyo kenkyujo (ed.), *Nihon no chusho kigyo kenkyu* (Japanese SME Research) Tokyo: Yuhikaku.

(1992), 'Kokusaika no shinten to kokunai chiikikan bungyo kozo no shintenkai' (New developments in Internationalization and the Domestic Inter-district Division of Labour) in *Shoko kin'yu*, July: 4–22.

(1994), *Sangyo kudoka* (Industrial Hollowing Out) in *Mita Hyoron*, no.960, July.

Weiss, L. (1988), *Creating Capitalism: The State and Small Business Since 1945*, Oxford: Oxford University Press.

West Midlands Enterprise Board (1992), *The West Midlands in the 1990's: A European Investment Region*, London: Economist Intelligence Unit.

Whittaker, D.H. (1990), *Managing Innovation: A Study of British and Japanese Factories,* Cambridge: Cambridge University Press.

(1994), 'SMEs, Entry Barriers and "Strategic Alliances"' in M. Aoki and R. Dore (eds.), *The Japanese Firm: Sources of Competitive Strength*, Oxford: Oxford University Press.

Wilkinson, F. and J. You (1992), 'Competition and Cooperation: Towards and Understanding of Industrial Districts' Cambridge University, SBRC Working Paper No.18.

Williamson, O. (1985), *The Economic Institutions of Capitalism*, New York: The Free Press.

Womack, J., D. Jones, and D. Roos (1990), *The Machine That Changed the World*, New York: Rawson Associates.

Yamamoto, S. (1981a), 'Keihin kogyo chitai no naritachi to Ota ku kindai kogyo no tanjo' (The Development of the Keihin Industrial Belt and the Birth of Modern Ota Ward Industry' in Ota ku (ed.), *Ota ku no shiwa* (Historical Talks of Ota Ward), Tokyo.

(1981b), 'Senso no Tsumeato' (The Scars of War) in Ota ku (ed.),*Ota ku no shiwa* (Historical Talks of Ota Ward), Tokyo.

Yamanaka, T. (ed.) (1944), *Nihon sangyo kozo no kenkyu* (Research on the Industrial Structure of Japan), Tokyo: Yuhikaku.

(1948), *Chusho kogyo no shomondai* (The Problems of Small and Medium-Scale Industry), Tokyo: Ito shoten.

(1950), *Chusho kogyo to keizai hendo* (Small and Medium-Scale Industry and Economic Change), Tokyo: Kunimoto shobo.

Yokokura, T. (1988), 'Small and Medium Enterprises' in R. Komiya, M. Okuno and K. Suzumura (eds.), *Industrial Policy in Japan*, Tokyo: Academic Press Japan, Inc.

You, J. (1992), 'Small Firms in Economic Theory: A Survey' Cambridge University, SBRC Working Papers No.17.

Zenkoku chusho kigyo dantai chuokai (1975), *Chusho kigyo kumiai seido shi* (History of the SME Association System), Tokyo.

(1991), *Chusho kigyo no henka to jigyo kyodo kumiai no jigyo katsudo no tenkai hoko ni kansuru chosa hokokusho* (Survey Report on Changes in SMEs and Developments in Cooperative Business Association Activities), Tokyo.

(1992), *Jigyo kyodo kumiai jittai chosa hokokusho* (Survey Report on Cooperative Business Associations), Tokyo.

(1993), *Shoko kumiai no soshiki oyobi jigyo katsudo no genjo to kongo no hoko ni kansuru chosa hokokusho* (Survey Report on the Current Situation and Future Directions of the Organization and Activities of Commerce and Industry Associations), Tokyo.

(1994a), *Dai 46 kai chusho kigyo dantai zenkoku taikai ketsugi* (Resolution of the 46th National SME Organization Convention), Tokyo.

(1994b), *Chishiki yugo kaihatsu jigyo no genjo oyobi kongo no tenaki ni kansuru chosa hokokusho* (Survey Report on the Current Situation and Future Developments of Knowledge-Fusing Development Activities), Tokyo.

(1995), *Dai 46 kai chusho kigyo dantai zenkoku taikai: ketsugi keika hokoku* (Report on the Progress of the Resolution of the 46th National SME Organisation Convention), Tokyo.

Zenkoku shoko dantai rengokai (1993), 'Shitauke seido no kaizen no tame ni' (Reforming the Subcontracting System), Tokyo.

Zukunftskommission Wirtschaft 2000 (1993), *Aufbruch aus der Krise*, Baden-Württemberg.

Index